D0445067

HILLSBORO PUBLIC LIBRARIES
Hillsboro, OR
Member of Washington County
COOPERATIVE LIBRARY SERVICES

The

Presidents

ALSO BY DENNIS GAFFNEY AND PETER GAFFNEY

The Seven-Day Scholar: The Civil War

The
Presidents

EXPLORING HISTORY
ONE WEEK AT A TIME

DENNIS GAFFNEY AND
PETER GAFFNEY

HYPERION
NEW YORK

HILLSBORO PUBLIC LIBRARIES
Hillsboro, OR
Member of Washington County
COOPERATIVE LIBRARY SERVICES

The majority of images in this book were reproduced from
the Prints & Photographs Division of the Library of Congress
(LOC). The others and their sources are listed below.
Pages 11 and 43: Manuscripts Division, LOC; Page 51: Geography & Maps Division,
LOC; Page 59: Rare Book & Special Collections, LOC; Page 275: Richard Nixon
Presidential Library & Museum; Page 291: Courtesy Ronald Reagan Library; Page 307:
Courtesy, William J. Clinton Presidential Library, Clinton Family Historical Collection;
Page 315: #P7365-23A, Courtesy George W. Bush Presidential Library; Page 357:
AP Photo/APTV with permission; Page 381: Charles Restifo, Veteran's History Project,
LOC; Page 389: The Carter Center/ Knudson Photos; Page 397: #P29416-36,
Courtesy George W. Bush Presidential Library

4822 4207 3/12

Copyright © 2012 Dennis Gaffney and Peter Gaffney
All rights reserved. No part of this book may be used or reproduced in any manner
whatsoever without the written permission of the Publisher.
Printed in the United States of America. For information address
Hyperion, 114 Fifth Avenue, New York, New York 10011.

Library of Congress Cataloging-in-Publication Data

Gaffney, Dennis.
The seven-day scholar : the presidents : exploring history one week at a time
/ Dennis Gaffney and Peter Gaffney. — 1st ed.
p. cm.
ISBN 978-1-4013-2375-2
1. Presidents—United States—Biography.   2. Presidents—United States—History.
3. United States—Politics and government.
I. Gaffney, Peter.   II. Title.   III. Title: Presidents.
E176.1.G16 2012
973.09'9—dc23
[B]
2011038246

Hyperion books are available for special promotions and premiums. For details contact
the HarperCollins Special Markets Department in the New York office at 212-207-7528,
fax 212-207-7222, or email spsales@harpercollins.com.

FIRST EDITION

10   9   8   7   6   5   4   3   2   1

THIS LABEL APPLIES TO TEXT STOCK

TO ALL THOSE LEADERS

WHO HAVE MADE THEIR COMMUNITIES

BETTER PLACES

CONTENTS

CIVIL WAR AND RECONSTRUCTION
(1849–1881)

ABRAHAM LINCOLN

REFORMERS
(1881–1897)

TAKING ON THE WORLD AND REFORM
(1897–1921)

BOOM AND BUST
(1921–1941)

WORLD WAR AND THEN COLD WAR
(1941–1960)

Part II. The Best, the Worst,
and the Most Interesting Presidents

ACKNOWLEDGMENTS

We wrote a book on the U.S. presidents, but in the process we received an education about American history and political leadership. Our guides on this journey were the numerous librarians, historians, and rangers at the presidential historical sites. Some who helped us work at privately owned sites, but most who pointed us to the best sources and through the historical debates were public servants at the National Historic Sites, part of the National Park Service. All were generous with their time, and this book couldn't have been written without their expertise. Many remain anonymous, but they know who they are. As we told them repeatedly, we couldn't imagine a better use of our public dollars.

Those we can mention are: Meg Kennedy, Montpelier's Research Project Coordinator; Marsha Mullin, Chief Curator of The Hermitage; Pam Sanfilippo, Site Historian, Ulysses S. Grant National Historic Site; Randy Sowell, Archivist, Harry S. Truman Library and Museum; Timothy P. Townsend, Historian, Lincoln Home National Historic Site; Franceska Macsali Urbin, Supervisory Park Ranger, Home of Franklin D. Roosevelt National Historic Site.

As ours isn't an academic book, footnotes were omitted. That said, we are indebted to hundreds of presidential scholars, and whenever we relied heavily on any one source, we said so in our endnotes.

Leslie Cohen and Dave Slaney did yeoman's work researching and writing many of the best entries in the book under tight deadlines. They took as much delight in learning about the presidents as we did, and our discussions made for some of the project's highlights. A special thanks again to Kate Cohen for her extraordinary editing skills and her steady encouragement. We also wanted to thank Steve Gillon, Resident Historian at History, Professor of History at the University of Oklahoma, and a true scholar, for reviewing the entries of some modern presidents.

Thanks also to Athena Angelos, our image researcher, who knows the Library of Congress prints and photo database like the back of her hand. And to Doe Coover, our agent, always smart and collected. Thanks as well to Leslie D. Wells and Elisabeth Dyssegaard, our editors at Hyperion, for believing in this series and for their skills in bringing the book to fruition.

Dennis also wanted to acknowledge that the book was largely written using library books in Albany's libraries—at Sage College, the University at Albany, and at the Albany Public Library, all wonderful, quiet spaces. Peter also wanted to thank Abbe Raven, President and CEO of A&E Television Networks, who taught him that history doesn't have to be dry and boring; Libby O'Connell, Chief Historian at History, for her guidance through this project; and Nancy Dubuc, President and General Manager at History, who encouraged him to pursue this project, introduced him to Hyperion, and who taught him that if you really want something, "just do it."

We also would like to thank each other; we've managed to maximize the pleasures of working together and avoid the pitfalls, and are better for the brotherly collaboration. Finally, we wanted to thank our friends and families—especially Kathy, Sophia, Julia, and Jason—for being there. Writing a book is engaging and educational, but it's often lonely work. Having family at the end of the day to share all the presidential history we absorbed made the process all the more fun.

INTRODUCTION

This series started with an idea. My brother, Peter, an executive at History, knows that people love history, but have little tolerance for textbooks, multi-volume tomes, or obscure academic books. In these hectic times, he was convinced what most people want to read is reliable history broken down into manageable bites. That led him to a history book idea: one organized like a calendar. Chapters would stretch out like weeks in the year, and each chapter would include seven related one-page entries, like the days in a week.

He even came up with a title: The Seven-Day Scholar. But my brother is neither a researcher nor a writer, and he had a full-time job. So he asked me, a writer and a history buff, if I wanted to pursue the book with him. I said no. It sounded like an encyclopedia, and I find them boring. Then I had my own "aha" moment: Why not write a book organized as Peter imagined, but full of historical stories?

We chose the Presidents as the subject of the second book in our series—the Civil War was the first—because they are fascinating both as individuals and as prisms through which to glimpse our country's rich history. In pursuing good real-life stories, well-known or obscure, we learned so much. That George Washington loved to dance. That Abraham Lincoln had to come quite far in his thinking to turn the Civil War into a war to end slavery. That Teddy Roosevelt took up boxing as a boy to strengthen his sickly body and boxed some rounds in the White House while President. That Dwight Eisenhower fought hard to corral military spending during his entire presidency.

We've collected what we've discovered as stories, mini-essays, historical debates, documents, and images. For those who want to learn more—budding scholars always do—we've recommended relevant books. Read this volume over a year or devour it in a week. It's your pace and your journey.

Best,
Dennis Gaffney

PART I

Presidents, Common *and* Uncommon

The FOUNDERS

(1778–1808)

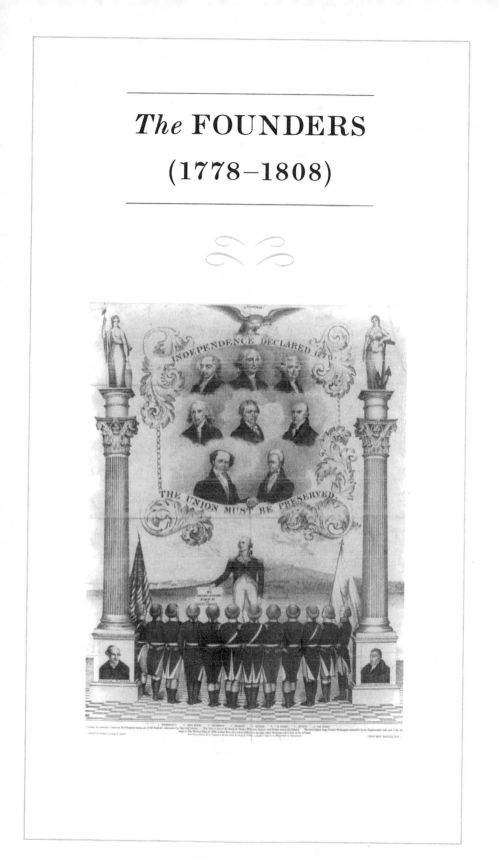

GEORGE WASHINGTON

More Than a Marble Hero

WEEK 1

DID GEORGE REALLY CONFESS
TO CHOPPING DOWN THE CHERRY TREE?

One of the old chestnuts about George Washington—a moral tale repeated in the *McGuffey Reader* over generations—depicts the young George cutting down one of his father's cherry trees. The account comes from a Pastor Mason Weems, who added it to the fifth edition (1806) of his book, *The Life and Memorable Actions of George Washington*. He said he heard it from Washington's nurse, and that it was "too valuable to be lost, too true to be doubted." Weems wrote that Washington was about six years old when he was given a hatchet and "was constantly going about chopping everything that came his way." One morning, George's father discovered one of his cherry trees gone.

Weems writes: " 'George,' said his father, 'do you know who killed that beautiful little cherry tree yonder in the garden?' This was a tough question; and George staggered under it for a moment; but quickly recovered himself: and looking at his father, with the sweet face of youth brightened with the inexpressible charm of all-conquering truth, he bravely cried out, 'I can't tell a lie, Pa; you know I can't tell a lie. I did cut it with my hatchet.' "

Weems wrote that the honest reply meant more to George's father "than a thousand trees, though blossomed with silver, and their fruits of purest gold." Weems said the stories he collected were important because "It *is* not, then in the glare of *public*, but in the shade of *private life*, that we are to look for the man. . . . [I]f he act greatly [in private], he must be great indeed."

Weems apparently did not act greatly privately or publicly, as historians, who have found next to nothing about young Washington's relationship to his father, have concluded his account was a fabrication. Weems apparently invented the morality tale for a higher *private* purpose: selling copies of his anecdotal biography. "I've something to whisper in your lug," Weems wrote his publisher Matthew Carey a month after Washington's death: "Washington, you know, is gone! Millions are gaping to read something about him. I am very nearly primed and cocked for 'em."

WASHINGTON—FOX HUNTER, GAMBLER, DANCER

Many Americans imagine George Washington as a wooden man, but he was actually someone who deeply enjoyed life's pleasures. Many of his favorite pastimes were typical of a Virginia planter of his day. Washington bred hounds, for example, and wrote in his diary that during one forty-nine-day stretch in 1768 he spent between two and five hours a day conducting foxhunts. After a hunt, the men often drank wine, usually Madeira, which Washington bought by the pipe (110 gallons) or by the butt (150 gallons). Washington, who drank in moderation, once joked that his Mount Vernon home was a "well-resorted" tavern, serving as a popular destination for many friends and neighbors.

Washington also enjoyed gambling and bet on horse races at Alexandria, Annapolis, and Williamsburg, and also bet on billiards, card games, and dice games.

But the pastime that Washington cherished most was dancing. At age fifteen, he paid three shillings nine pence to attend a dancing school, and he took what he learned to the dance floor, whether stepping to country reels, jigs, or minuets, his favorite. During their Mount Vernon days, George and Martha often danced at parties that went long into the night.

During his presidency, he danced at numerous balls held in his honor, and he noted that one in Portsmouth, New Hampshire, was attended by "about seventy-five well-dressed and many of them very handsome ladies." The ladies, too, found him an attractive partner. "The general danced every set," wrote the governor of Maryland after a ball held at Annapolis to honor Washington after the war, "that all the ladies might have the pleasure of dancing with him, or . . . get a touch of him."

RULES OF CIVILITY: THE BOOK THAT SHAPED
THE MAN—OR AN EXERCISE IN PENMANSHIP?

Washington's father died when he was eleven, the reason he was never sent to boarding school. Unlike many of the Virginia aristocracy, he didn't attend college or ever visit Europe, and he admitted to a "consciousness of a defective education." He later confessed that his poor education discouraged him from writing his memoirs.

"That Washington was not a scholar is certain," John Adams later observed. "That he was too illiterate, unlearned, unread for his station and reputation is equally past dispute."

Washington scholar Peter R. Henriques asserts that a book on etiquette and manners, written in 1595, *Rules of Civility and Decent Behaviour in Company and Conversation*, "most influenced his conduct." Washington copied rules from the book into a school notebook at about age sixteen. French Jesuits first wrote the 110 rules, some of which now seem amusing: "Spit not into the fire . . . especially if there be meat before it"; "Kill no vermin, or fleas, lice, ticks, etc. in the sight of others." When with others, "Do not Puff up the Cheeks, Do not Loll out the tongue, rub the Hands, or beard, thrust out the lips, or bite them or keep the Lips too open or too Close."

But some of the rules might have shaped the man Washington became. Rule #1 was: "Every action done in company ought to be done with some sign of respect to those that are present." Rule #45 urges restraint, which Washington needed to corral what one contemporary called his "tumultuous passions." Was this guide to the "virtues of humanity" Washington's handbook for how to behave? At least one scholar is skeptical: "It is quite possible," writes Joseph J. Ellis, "that he copied out the list as a mere exercise in penmanship."

RETREATING FROM THE JAWS OF DEFEAT—
WASHINGTON IN THE FRENCH AND INDIAN WAR

Washington was selected commander in chief by the Second Continental Congress in large part because he served as a colonel in the Virginia regiment during the French and Indian War. Washington had fired one of its first shots as a twenty-one-year-old leading a small force of men on the British side in Pennsylvania. He and his men bumped into French forces, and shooting broke out. "I heard the bullets whistle," Washington wrote his younger brother, "and, believe me, there is something charming in the sound."

But Washington earned his reputation the next year, in 1755, as a participant in a disastrous British defeat. Washington was serving as an aide to British General Edward Braddock with a force of about thirteen hundred troops on the march to Fort Duquesne (now Pittsburgh). Braddock and his army got caught in an open field by nine hundred of the Fort Duquesne men, two-thirds of them Indians. The British regulars, decimated, "broke & [ran] like sheep before Hounds," Washington remembered. After Braddock was shot down, Washington rallied the remnants of the forces. Two horses were shot from under him and four musket balls put holes in his coat, but somehow he remained unscathed while "death was leveling my companions on every side of me." The French and Indians counted twenty-three killed and sixteen wounded. The British and Americans suffered nine hundred casualties, nearly three in four men. Washington would forever remember the screams of the wounded being scalped. He gathered the survivors and retreated.

Braddock, dead, was blamed for the debacle. The public praised Washington as "the hero of the Monongahela." One newspaper commented that Washington had earned "a high Reputation for Military Skill, Integrity, and Valor; tho' Success has not always attended his Undertakings." Washington learned little about strategy, a prerequisite for even adequate generals. Yet he'd displayed bravery, and another trait that would prove useful many years later, when he would lead the revolutionary army against the British: an instinct for survival.

MARRYING UP—TO MARTHA CUSTIS

George Washington's marriage to Martha Dandridge Custis, widow of Daniel Custis, on January 6, 1759, is often portrayed as one of convenience. Washington, a colonel in the Virginia Regiment, needed a wife—better yet, the richest widow in Virginia—to make his Mount Vernon a home. Martha needed a manager of her estate and a father for her two children.

But clues suggest it was more than just a prudent pairing. Everyone spoke of Washington's magnetism, and despite the dowdy old portraits we associate with Martha, whom Washington called Patsy, her contemporaries described her as attractive (both were twenty-seven when they married). The fact that they didn't have any children of their own was likely because the "Father of the Country" was probably sterile, as Martha had had four children with Custis. Martha also had an attractive personality. Abigail Adams observed, "Mrs. Washington is one of those unassuming characters which create love and esteem."

Throughout their life together, hundreds of relatives, friends, and officials came for visits to Mount Vernon and none ever reported a discontented marriage—although posterity would know more if Martha hadn't destroyed their letters to each other upon George's death. In the handful of letters that remain, George addresses Martha as "My Dearest." Martha addresses George as "My dearest" and "My Love." In a letter George wrote in 1775, sixteen years into his marriage, he informed Martha that he'd accepted command of the Continental Army, writing, "I should enjoy more real happiness and felicity in one month with you, at home, than I have the most distant prospect of reaping abroad, if my stay was to be Seven times Seven years. . . . My dear Patsy . . . I retain an unalterable affection for you, which neither time or distance can change."

CURSED BY BAD TEETH

By all contemporary accounts, George Washington, six feet three inches tall, towered over most of his peers and was stronger and healthier as well. But the imposing leader had an Achilles heel—his mouth. From the age of twenty-one, when he lost his first tooth, until his death, the American leader was plagued by rotting teeth, ill-fitting dentures, and painful gums.

"His mouth is large and generally firmly closed, but which from time to time discloses some defective teeth," said George Mercer, a friend. Washington's copious records show he spent money nearly every year to extract teeth and purchase sponge toothbrushes. In 1788, his first year as president, his favorite dentist, John Greenwood, made a set of dentures with human teeth set into hippopotamus ivory, pinned in place to Washington's one remaining tooth, a lonely lower left premolar. Crackles in the ivory (cattle, elephant tusk, and human teeth were used in other dentures) stained by port wine or other drinks might have mimicked wood grain, the source of the still-pervasive myth that Washington had wooden teeth.

The various sets of dentures, with their wires, rough edges, and tightly wound gold springs that pressed the contraptions against the gums, often pained the president. In 1790, Washington ordered laudanum, an opiate mixed in alcohol that might have soothed his sore gums.

Dentures also distorted the geography of his face, and Washington complained that one pair "bulge my lips out in such a manner as to make them appear considerably swelled." You can see the lower thrust lip in the portrait done by Christian Gullager in 1789. In the famous Gilbert Stuart portrait of Washington, engraved on the one-dollar bill, the square-jawed president is also biting down on a full set of dentures. Historians wonder whether Washington's bad teeth might have led to another change that contemporaries noticed as he aged—a reluctance to smile.

When George Washington was about sixteen, he copied these *Rules of Civility and Decent Behaviour in Company and Conversation* into his school notebook. The question remains: Did Washington take these rules to heart, or were they just a lesson in penmanship?

GEORGE WASHINGTON

Learning Through Experience—
Washington the General

WEEK 2

DID WASHINGTON RESIST HIS APPOINTMENT
TO COMMANDER IN CHIEF?

In June 1775, at the Pennsylvania State House in Philadelphia, John Adams, worried about the fate of the colonies after fighting broke out with the British at Lexington and Concord, stood up and called upon "a gentleman from Virginia" to command the still-to-be-recruited Continental Army. Washington, seemingly embarrassed and surprised, fled the room. After discovering he'd been selected by the Congress, he directed his friend Edmund Pendleton to tell his peers he didn't seek the post and was unqualified to fill it.

"I have used every endeavour in my power to avoid it," he wrote Martha, "not only from my unwillingness to part with you and the Family, but from a consciousness of its being a trust too great for my Capacity. . . . But, as it has been a kind of destiny that has thrown me upon this Service, I shall hope that my undertaking of it, is designd to answer some good purpose."

But Washington was perhaps not as ill-disposed to the post as he claimed he was. He was the only congressional attendee who wore a military uniform hardly the outfit of a man looking to avoid command. On June 8, 1775, a week before he was appointed by Congress, Washington ordered five books on military tactics—which reveals an eagerness to lead and to learn, but perhaps an insecurity as well. Perhaps Washington was eager for responsibility, fame, and glory, but he also doubted his ability to lead a cause that appeared doomed.

AN AGGRESSIVE FIGHTER FAILS—WASHINGTON
LEARNS A LESSON IN NEW YORK CITY

Upon accepting the position of commander in chief from Congress, Washington told the gathered politicians that "I do not think myself equal to the command I am honored with." He was probably right: He'd never commanded more than a regiment and had never led an artillery or a cavalry. He knew little about constructing defensive positions or sieges. Compared to the British generals, he was a babe on the battlefield.

Before Washington figured out how to win the war, he nearly lost it. In June 1776, as Jefferson was drafting the Declaration of Independence, Washington was maneuvering his troops to repel British forces then arriving in Long Island and New York City. Washington planned to beat the British, but the plan showed more bravado than sense. Washington had only fifteen thousand poorly trained men, many suffering from smallpox, compared to roughly thirty thousand well-trained British and Hessian soldiers. Unlike Boston, where he'd prevailed, New York City was a Loyalist stronghold, made even less hospitable by the surrounding harbors and rivers that allowed the British to use their thirty warships.

Washington made matters worse by dividing his forces between Manhattan and Long Island. He lost Long Island in a day, August 27, 1776, and his men there suffered three hundred casualties, with a thousand more taken prisoner. Washington and his men managed to slip away to Manhattan under the cover of fog and rain. His generals voted 10 to 3 to abandon Manhattan, but Washington overruled them. Historian Joseph Ellis described Washington's stand on Manhattan this way: "It was as if a mouse, cornered by a bevy of cats, had declared itself a lion."

His men took a stand at Fort Washington in northern Manhattan, and three thousand of them were killed or captured. Washington had lost nearly five thousand men, one of the worst defeats in American history. He was forced to abandon his assumption that Britain's mercenary army could be defeated by sheer courage. Next he would try surprise.

CHRISTMAS, 1776—WASHINGTON RISKS HIS ARMY AND CROSSES THE DELAWARE

To escape the British army after the defeat in New York City, the Continental army retreated across the Delaware River on December 7, 1776. A more aggressive British general might have crossed the river to finish the American forces, but General William Howe dawdled. Having little respect for Washington, General Howe went back to New York City to rendezvous with his mistress.

Rather than having his troops wait out the winter, as was customary, Washington planned a daring middle-of-the-night crossing of the Delaware on Christmas to surprise the Hessian mercenaries. Beforehand, he wrote himself a note: "Victory or death."

Washington knew he was not an inspiring speaker, so instead of giving a speech to his men, he handed out copies of Tom Paine's *The American Crisis*, which officers read aloud as they began the crossing: "These are the times that try men's souls. The summer soldier and the sunshine patriot will, in this crisis, shrink from the service of their country; but he that stands it now, deserves the love and thanks of man and woman. . . ." The famous painting by Emanuel Leutze has Washington standing alone at the prow of a boat, but actually the soldiers stood with their general.

Two of his units couldn't make it across the icy Delaware, but Washington pressed ahead. When they met "a violent storm of snow and hail," Washington shouted from his horse, "Press on, boys, press on," knowing that they had to reach the Hessians before they awoke.

The Hessians hardly expected an attack in a snowstorm at dawn the day after Christmas. They fought hard, but were outgunned by the twenty-four artillery pieces that Henry Knox had transported across the river. Washington's twenty-four hundred troops caused about one hundred casualties among the Hessians; nine hundred were captured and a few hundred more slipped away. Only two Americans were injured (one a future president: Lieutenant James Monroe). After the victory, one English journalist wrote, "A few days ago, they had given up the cause for lost. Their late successes have turned the scale and now they are all liberty-mad again."

WINNING THE WAR WITH PATIENCE

George Washington had won the Battle of Trenton using surprise, but to win the Revolutionary War he had to learn another, less valued military virtue—patience. It was his reduced forces after the disastrous defeat in New York City in August 1776 that began to teach him patience and endurance.

"We should on all occasions avoid a general action, and never [be] drawn into a necessity to put anything to the risk," he wrote Congress in September 1776. "I am sensible a retreating army is incircled with difficulties . . . but when the fate of America may be at stake on the issue . . . we should protract the war. . . ." This strategy became more necessary as the defeated army limped across New Jersey, soldiers deserting until the rebel forces dwindled from nineteen thousand to about five thousand.

This defensive approach was sometimes called a Fabian strategy, after the Roman general Fabius Cunctator, who defeated the Carthaginians by retreating his army whenever it was threatened with destruction. By nature, Washington considered such retreats cowardly. But after New York he had to face the "melancholy truths" that "it is impossible . . . that any effectual opposition can be given to the British Army with the Troops we have." He had learned what all guerilla leaders learn: Victory came not by winning battles, but by surviving until the invader became exhausted and lost its political support at home.

Washington's Fabian strategy was tested in August 1777, when it became clear the British were going to attack Philadelphia. His instinct was to "take every measure in my power to defend it." When the British took Philadelphia, Washington had to overcome his desire to recapture it, as his generals reminded him that it was strategically more important to protect his army.

"The lion," biographer Joseph L. Ellis has written, "had to become the fox." His restraint, Ellis writes, "completed his transformation into a public figure whose personal convictions must be suppressed and rendered subordinate to his higher calling as an agent of history, which . . . meant that winning the war was more important than being himself."

THE SUFFERING AT VALLEY FORGE WAS NOT CAUSED BY THE WEATHER

Generations of Americans have heard the story of the heroic American soldiers battered by the winter of 1777–1778 at Valley Forge. One book says blizzards tested the fortitude of the men in "one of the cruelest winters in our country's history." The men persevered through this low point of the war, goes the story, finding "new courage, new resolve, new faith in their cause." This quiet determination was captured by the story— probably apocryphal—of George Washington kneeling in prayer asking God for help.

But the power Washington beseeched most often that winter was Congress. And he didn't complain about the winter—relatively balmy compared to the one that struck in 1779–1780, described by one historian as the "severest season in all American history." Instead, the general's ire was directed at the "total failure of Supplies." Washington said the army consisted of "Men without Cloathes to cover their nakedness, without blankets to lay on, without Shoes, by which their Marches might be traced by the Blood from their feet."

Incompetent and corrupt governmental commissaries had also failed to get food and clothing to the army that winter. This, exacerbated by a moist winter and poor sanitation, laid an inviting bed for disease— primarily typhus, pneumonia, and dysentery—that ravaged the Valley Forge camp, killing eighteen hundred men.

Before Christmas, Washington wrote to Congress, saying, "that unless some great and Capital change suddenly takes place in that [supply] line, this Army must inevitably be reduced to one or other of these three things: starve, dissolve or disperse . . ." In February 1778, Washington feared a general mutiny. He rode through the ranks and heard an ominous chant: "No pay, no clothes, no provisions, no rum." Close to two thousand men deserted over the winter.

After Valley Forge, provisioning of the army improved. Yet after the brutal winter of 1779–1780, two years after Valley Forge, Washington wrote to Congress that "there has never been a stage in the war in which the dissatisfaction has been so general or alarming."

KNOWING HOW TO EXIT—WASHINGTON RESIGNS
AS COMMANDER IN CHIEF

King George III of England asked painter Benjamin West what George Washington would do when he learned that a peace treaty had been signed with Great Britain. West said he thought Washington would retire to Mount Vernon. "If he does that," King George replied, "he will be the greatest man in the world."

On December 23, 1783, Washington went before Congress in Annapolis, Maryland, and pulled from his pocket a short speech, his hands visibly shaking. When he did speak, he was almost inaudible. He told the congressmen that he was surrendering a command he had taken in 1775 with "a diffidence in my abilities . . ." He concluded after about three minutes, his voice growing stronger: "Having now finished the work assigned me, I retire from the great theatre of action,—and bidding an affectionate farewell to this August body, under whose orders I have so long acted, I here offer my Commission, and take my leave of all the employments of public life."

His resignation led many to compare him with Cincinnatus. In the fifth century B.C.E., Roman senators gave Cincinnatus, a general turned farmer, the powers of a dictator to beat back the Aequi soldiers of central Italy. The general gathered an army, marched on the Aequi two weeks later, and defeated them in a day. He then resigned his dictatorship and returned to his farm.

After saying good-bye to each congressman, Washington rode back to Mount Vernon, as he'd promised Martha he'd be home for Christmas. On Christmas Eve, George Washington again laid his eyes on Mount Vernon, which had miraculously survived the British army, and entered his mansion, "an older man by near nine years, than when I left. . . ." He expected his "Official life" was now permanently behind him and that he would return to farming, managing Mount Vernon, and overseeing his business interests. But his nation would soon call on him again and demand a third act, as long as his service in the war, returning him to "the great theatre of action."

This engraving of George Washington is based on a John Trumbull painting that depicts General Washington on the battlefield in Trenton, New Jersey, where, on December 25, 1776, he led his army across the Delaware River to capture about nine hundred Hessian soldiers.

GEORGE WASHINGTON

America's Patriarch

WEEK 3

DID WASHINGTON OVERREACT TO THE WHISKEY REBELLION?

Washington's first political crisis was known as the Whiskey Rebellion. In 1791, the first year of his first term, Washington, guided by his Secretary of the Treasury Alexander Hamilton, had introduced an economic plan that included a tax on whiskey to help pay for a federal debt incurred during the Revolutionary War.

The whiskey tax fell hardest on poor frontier farmers in places such as western Pennsylvania, where one in five farmers distilled his own liquor. Resistance among farmers percolated until July 16, 1794, when a crowd of farmers in Pennsylvania surrounded federal revenue officers attempting to serve papers against distillers, and violence erupted.

Washington sent a commission to meet with the rebels as he organized a force of thirteen thousand militiamen from four nearby states— five times as large as the Continental Army at the Battle of Trenton. Washington led the federal troops westward—the only sitting president ever to lead troops in battle. The rebels dispersed back to their farms. Still, the troops rounded up 150 suspects; 20 were tried, 2 convicted of treason, but later pardoned by Washington.

Had Washington overreacted? Thomas Jefferson thought so, interpreting Washington's decision to send troops as an attack on the freedom of dissent and a betrayal of the revolution. "An insurrection was proclaimed," Jefferson declared, "but could never be found."

But Washington thought the betrayers had been the protesters. His generation had rebelled because they were taxed without representation by the British. But the whiskey resisters were resisting laws passed by their own *representative* government. "If the laws are to be so trampled upon with impunity [and] a minority . . . is to dictate to the majority, there is an end put at one stroke to republican government," Washington wrote in a letter. "For some other man or society may dislike another law and oppose it with equal propriety until all laws are prostrate, and everyone will carve for himself." Washington and Congress left the whiskey tax on the books, as did John Adams. Jefferson, elected in 1800, had the tax repealed.

WASHINGTON STANDS FIRM ON THE UNPOPULAR JAY TREATY

Washington went into his first term a demigod, but he was dragged back down to earth in his second by a controversy that erupted over whom to support in the war between France and England. Should Americans support the British, the country's top trading partner, or the French, who helped America win the Revolutionary War and whose own revolution in 1789 was sweeping monarchies from power?

Washington feared that war with either would destroy the country economically and perhaps snuff out the infant nation (for more on Washington's desire for peace, see page 367). He issued a proclamation declaring the United States neutral, but it was unpopular with French sympathizers in America, who formed societies promoting the "spirit of freedom and equality." These societies celebrated pro-French politicians such as Thomas Jefferson, and believed Washington's proclamation of neutrality to be "pusillanimous truckling to Britain, despotically conceived and unconstitutionally promulgated."

Even harsher criticism followed when Washington sent Chief Justice John Jay in April 1794 to negotiate lingering disputes with England—such as their seizure of neutral American ships—and avoid war. When Jay came back, having settled less-than-favorable terms, protests exploded. Adams later recalled that Washington's house in Philadelphia was "surrounded by an innumerable multitude, from day to day buzzing, demanding war against England, cursing Washington, and crying success to the French patriots." Washington thought the treaty the best the country could get, and maintained peace, yet admitted that "at present the cry against the Treaty is like that against a mad dog; and everyone, in a manner, seems engaged in running it down."

Washington pushed the treaty through the Senate, believing that it put off war with the British "for about twenty years." (The War of 1812 proved Washington nearly clairvoyant.) Republicans continued to toss editorial spears at Washington, who suffered them silently. "I think he feels those things more than any other person I ever met with," Jefferson said.

WASHINGTON BETRAYS JEFFERSON—OR DID JEFFERSON BETRAY WASHINGTON?

As Thomas Jefferson saw it, George Washington made the American Revolution a success. "The moderation and virtue of a single character . . ." wrote Jefferson, "probably prevented this revolution from being closed . . . by a subversion of that liberty it was intended to establish."

But after Washington was elected president, the relationship became strained by diverging politics. When farmers resisted a federal excise tax on whiskey, Washington crushed it, fearing the tyranny of the minority against a representative government of laws. Jefferson sided with the overtaxed farmer. Washington saw the virtue of a national bank promoted by Alexander Hamilton; Jefferson thought it concentrated power in the hands of northeastern bankers. Washington believed the Jay Treaty would provide peace; Jefferson saw it as a sop to the British monarchy and a betrayal of the Revolution.

For Jefferson, political enemies often became personal ones. He began a whispering campaign in private and in the press that Washington had become soft-minded, even semisenile. Jefferson believed that his enemy Hamilton pulled the strings now. Despite the rumors, Washington chose not to believe that Jefferson was disparaging him. But then a letter Jefferson wrote his Italian friend Philip Mazzei in May 1797 became public. "Our politics has . . . changed since you left us," Jefferson wrote Mazzei. "In place of that noble love of liberty and republican government, . . . a . . . monarchical . . . party has sprung up. . . . It would give you a fever were I to name to you the apostates who have gone over to these heresies, men who were Samsons in the field and Solomons in the council. . . ."

The "monarchical party" was the Federalists, and it was clear that Jefferson's "apostate" was Washington. The two never met or wrote again. Martha Washington later called Jefferson "one of the most detestable of mankind." The worst day of her life, she said, was the day her husband died. The second worst? The day President Jefferson came to pay his respects.

THE FAREWELL ADDRESS

By 1796, George Washington knew it was time to leave public office for the "vine and fig tree" of Mount Vernon. Washington asked James Madison, a Republican, to write a final address to the nation when he considered retiring in 1792, and Madison had suggested printing it in newspapers as "a direct address to the people who are your only constituents." Now, four years later, he asked Alexander Hamilton, a Federalist and an enemy of Madison's, to take Madison's draft and update it.

Yet the ideas were all Washington's, and he carefully checked all the changes. "[M]y wish is that the whole may appear in a plain style," he told Hamilton.

On September 19, 1796, Washington's address appeared in the *American Daily Advertiser*, a Philadelphia newspaper, addressed to "the PEOPLE of the United States." It was signed, "G. Washington, United States." The address was reprinted in newspapers across the country and would become known as "Washington's Farewell Address." But it was more like a letter of advice delivered by a wise elder to his maturing children, "sentiments . . . which appear to me all important to the permanency of your felicity as a People."

He made two major points. First, he urged Americans to overcome their regional and political differences at home. He decried political parties, urging all to act as Americans. "With slight shades of difference, you have the same Religion, Manners, Habits, and Political Principles."

Second, he urged the country to remain neutral in foreign affairs, and avoid taking sides in the tangled politics of Europe, the behemoths on the political landscape as the new century approached. (The phrase "entangling alliances" is often attributed to Washington, although Jefferson coined the term in his inaugural address.) Unity at home and independence abroad—the advice was simple, but hard to follow and often dismissed.

WHY WAS THE CAPITAL MOVED TO WASHINGTON?

How was a swampy bank of the Potomac River chosen as the capital of the United States? Politics landed it there. Thomas Jefferson, then secretary of state, recalled walking near the president's house in the spring of 1790 when he ran into Secretary of the Treasury Alexander Hamilton, who was distraught because Congress was deadlocked on his funding bill. The bill would have moved state debt from the Revolutionary War to the federal government and established a national bank, part of Hamilton's vision of a strong central government that could tax, borrow, and lend, thereby encouraging business interests. Failure to pass the bill, he told Jefferson, could destroy the nation's credit and lead to collapse.

Jefferson and James Madison, the leading congressman opposed to Hamilton's bill, preferred a weak national government that couldn't impose its will on Virginia and other states. Still, Jefferson suggested that he, Hamilton, and Madison might dine together and find a compromise. In June 1790, the three men struck what is termed "the candlelight bargain."

Madison agreed to end his opposition to the bill and release the votes needed to pass it. In return, Congress would bypass New York and Philadelphia for the choice of the nation's capital, instead creating one somewhere on the Potomac River in Virginia ten years hence. The concession pleased Jefferson and Madison, both Virginians. Washington (also a Virginian) selected the exact location, which turned out to be a natural lowland that held heat and bred mosquitoes. Washington also selected French architect Pierre L'Enfant to create a grand plan for ten square miles.

Jefferson later claimed he'd been "duped" by Hamilton in the deal and "made a tool for forwarding his schemes, not then sufficiently understood by me; and of all the errors of my political life, this has occasioned me the deepest regret." The city's first name was District of Columbia, after Columbus, but it soon became Federal City, and then Congress named it Washington.

WASHINGTON FREES HIS SLAVES

George Washington inherited his first ten slaves when his father died in 1743. He was eleven years old. By 1799, the year he died, Washington owned 123 slaves, with 153 more at Mt. Vernon owned by the estate of Martha's first husband.

Washington's early views on slavery were typical of a pre–Revolutionary War slave owner in Virginia. In correspondences, Washington described slaves in language that could have been used for horses, saying he wanted all of his slaves "to be . . . in every respect strong and healthy. . . ." He once ordered his field manager to give a slave "a good whipping," and he sent slave catchers after runaways. Still, his refusal to break up slave families by selling them revealed him to be less cruel than many slave owners. He also never spoke of African-Americans as congenitally inferior, as Thomas Jefferson did.

The Revolutionary War changed his views, as he passed through farms that were worked with freed African-Americans. Free African-Americans and slaves promised freedom also fought in his army. In 1786, Washington wrote of his wish to "see a plan adopted for the abolition of [slavery]."

Why, then, didn't Washington act politically against the institution? Most historians agree that if Washington had put slavery on the table, the infant nation might never have been born or would have split in two. Washington finally resolved the question personally in his will, written during the last summer of his life, freeing his slaves upon the death of his wife Martha, making him the only member of Virginia's founding fathers to act on the famous words written by Jefferson in the Declaration of Independence.

Washington's will also required slaves under the age of twenty-five to be taught to read and write, and "brought up to some useful occupation." Washington asked that the old and infirm slaves "shall be comfortably cloathed and fed by my heirs while they live." After her husband's death, a few suspicious fires at Mount Vernon convinced Martha to free George's slaves immediately, aware that it was in their interest to get rid of her.

This idealized scene depicts George Washington mingling with slaves while they harvest grain on his plantation in Mount Vernon, Virginia. Washington was considered less cruel than many slave owners, and the will he wrote at the end of his life called for the freeing of all of his slaves upon the death of his wife, Martha.

John Adams—A Volatile, Principled President

JOHN ADAMS—IRASCIBLE AND INTELLECTUAL

John Adams was brilliant. Founding Father Benjamin Rush said that the consensus among his peers was that Adams contained "more learning probably, both ancient and modern, than any man who subscribed the Declaration of Independence."

Yet Adams was awkward around people, and preferred books to social pleasures like cards and dancing. He read Cicero and Tacitus in Latin, and Plato and Thucydides in Greek, the first among all languages in his view.

To understand what he called the "labyrinth" of human nature, he was drawn to Shakespeare and Swift, and often carried poetry in his pocket. "You will never be alone in the world," he once told his son Johnny, "with a poet in your pocket."

Adams's intellectual curiosity was matched by his passion. Historian Bernard Bailyn wrote that Adams "felt the world, directly and sensitively, before he thought about it." He lived passionately—for friendship, for his wife, for politics, and for his country.

But his emotions were unpredictable, and often destructive. His cabinet irritated him; party politics irritated him; even the office of the presidency irritated him. "A peck of troubles in a large bundle of papers often in a handwriting almost illegible comes every day . . . ," he wrote while in office, "thousands of sea letters . . . commissions and patents to sign. No company. No society. Idle, unmeaning ceremony."

His entire life he tried to bridle his explosive anger, but he often failed. Historian James M. Banner described him as "insecure, volatile, impulsive, irritable, suspicious, self-pitying, self-righteous, and filled with often combustible rage."

His saving grace might have been his self-awareness. When a correspondent asked him later in life to describe his temperament, Adams replied that he was by nature "tranquil, except when any instance of madness, deceit, hypocrisy, ingratitude, treachery or perfidy, has suddenly struck me. Then I have always been irascible enough."

JOHN ADAMS SHOWS HIS PATRIOTISM—
BY DEFENDING THE BRITISH

John Adams is often identified as a Federalist arguing against Republicans, but he prided himself on his independence, a trait that never was clearer than his stand defending British soldiers involved in the Boston Massacre.

On a moonlit evening on March 5, 1770, a crowd of Bostonians began taunting a British soldier outside the custom house. Soon the crowd grew to a few hundred, and the soldier was reinforced with eight more redcoats, brandishing muskets. The crowd attacked, the soldiers fired, and five colonists were killed.

John's cousin Samuel Adams called the killing "bloody butchery" and circulars went around portraying it as a slaughter of innocents. When the soldiers couldn't get an attorney to represent them, they asked John Adams. He immediately agreed, arguing that no man in a free country should be denied a fair trial. The stand was unpopular; he feared not only for his safety, but for that of his pregnant wife, Abigail.

In the first trial, the British captain was acquitted of ordering the men to shoot. In the second trial of the remaining soldiers, Adams gave a closing statement that was described as "electrical." Never afraid to provoke, he called the American mob in the melee a "motley rabble of saucy boys, Negroes and mulattoes, Irish teagues and outlandish jacktars."

He explained that the shrieking "rabble" had pelted the soldiers with ice, rocks, oyster shells, sticks, and "every species of rubbish," and had called out, "Kill them! Kill them!" Adams argued that it was worth having many guilty people let free to ensure one innocent person wasn't jailed. "Facts are stubborn things," he told the jurors, "and whatever may be our wishes . . . they cannot alter the state of facts and evidence."

Six of the British soldiers were acquitted. Two were convicted of manslaughter, receiving a branding on their thumb. Editors pilloried Adams, who said later he lost close to half of his practice afterward. But his reputation was lifted.

As an old man, he would say it was the most exhausting case of his career, but also "one of the most gallant, generous, manly and disinterested actions of my whole life, and one of the best pieces of service I ever rendered my country."

JOHN ADAMS—THE "ATLAS" OF THE AMERICAN REVOLUTION

July 1, 1776, began as a muggy day in Philadelphia, and John Adams, the delegate from Massachusetts, knew it would be a momentous day for the Continental Congress. "This morning is assigned the greatest debate of all," he wrote to a former delegate. "A declaration, that these colonies are free and independent states. . . ."

Only seven of the thirteen states were committed to independence, hardly a resounding majority. The men debated whether to stay with Britain or to sever its ties. John Dickinson of Pennsylvania cautioned against a "premature" break, voicing the fears of many.

The room was quiet except for the rain that began pelting against the windows until Adams stood up. Earlier in his career, he had tried to write down his speeches, but the technique never worked for him. He also avoided ostentatious oratory, calling "affectation . . . disagreeable."

He organized his comments in his head and spoke with what he called "rapid reason." His voice was sonorous, and to emphasize a point, he'd sometimes smack his walking stick on the floor. He was already the most respected revolutionary—his credentials included selecting Thomas Jefferson to write the Declaration of Independence, nominating George Washington as commander in chief of the Continental army, and pushing a government divided into three branches—a structure of checks and balances that would be cemented in the Constitution.

He had long pushed and prodded his compatriots to rebel, and would do so again this day. The speech was not recorded, but Adams would say he'd been " 'carried out in spirit,' as enthusiastic preachers sometimes express themselves." "He it was who sustained the debate, and by the force of his reasoning," wrote Richard Stockton, a New Jersey delegate, "demonstrated not only the justice but the expediency of the measure. I call him the Atlas of American independence." The debate went nine hours, and the next day twelve colonies unanimously decided to declare independence (New York abstained).

Adams wrote to Abigail afterward, "The second day of July 1776 will be the most memorable epocha in the history of America. I am apt to believe that it will be celebrated by succeeding generations as the great anniversary festival. . . . It ought to be solemnized with pomp and parade, with shows, games, sports, guns, bells, bonfires, and illuminations from one end of this continent to the other from this time forward forever more."

ADAMS WANTS TO CALL THE PRESIDENT "HIS MAJESTY THE PRESIDENT"

On Thursday, April 30, 1793, on his inauguration day, George Washington rode to Federal Hall in New York City in a carriage pulled by six white horses. Among the New Yorkers gathered to hear Washington's address, many "were heard to say they should now die contented— nothing being wanted to complete their happiness . . . but the sight of the savior of his country."

Washington swore to "preserve, protect, and defend the Constitution of the United States," and then improvising (and setting a precedent), added, "So help me God."

"It is done," said New York's Chancellor Robert R. Livingston. Washington took office, but politicians were uncertain what to call the country's first leader. The House immediately voted to address him as "George Washington, President of the United States."

But the Senate debate became heated. One senator argued that titles were used all over the world, another moved that Washington be called "Excellency," and a third observed that "President" was too ordinary a term.

John Adams agreed, arguing that the word *president* was appropriate for leaders of fire companies and cricket clubs. He believed that the federal government should have more power than state governments, and that the title of the chief executive should reflect that. While Adams said he did not personally care what title was chosen, he suggested "His Majesty the President."

But Adams, always pugnacious, was out of step with his country and his fellow senators. Most agreed with Senator William Maclay, who said, "Let us read the Constitution," and referred to a line from Section 9 of Article 1: "*No title of nobility shall be granted by the United States.*" Finally, after a month of debate, senators, sick of the matter, voted, like the House, to call Washington "the President of the United States."

In the meantime, even Adams's allies turned against him. Senator Ralph Izard suggested an alternative title for Adams—"His Rotundity." That one never made it to the Senate floor, but proved as popular as any in the debate.

ADAMS MOVES INTO THE EXECUTIVE MANSION—
AND THEN MUST LEAVE

A few months before his term as president ended—November 1, 1800—
John Adams moved into the White House, the largest private residence
in America, half as big as the Capitol. The mansion still smelled of wet
paint and plaster. Closet doors hadn't yet been added; bells used to ring
servants hadn't been hung. Only one painting decorated the walls—a
full-length portrait by Gilbert Stuart of George Washington in a black
velvet suit.

The next morning Adams took a plain sheet of paper, and under the
heading "President's House, Washington City, Nov. 2, 1800," he wrote
to his wife a letter that was as much prayer as prose: "I pray heaven to
bestow the best of blessings on this house and all that shall hereafter
inhabit. May none but honest and wise men ever rule under this roof."

Abigail arrived two weeks later and observed that it was necessary to
keep thirteen fireplaces lit daily "or sleep in wet and damp places." She
called it the "great castle," and was depressed by the presence of slaves
who were working on the grounds.

On December 3, 1800, electors convened to choose the next president. Adams expected to lose (for more on the election of 1800, see
page 343), but the election was closer than predicted considering the
unpopular Alien and Sedition Acts; a raising of taxes; dissension in his
cabinet; the backstabbing by Alexander Hamilton and the split in the
Federalist Party; and Adams's refusal to go to war with France. (For
more on Adams's presidency, see pages 359 and 368.)

Inauguration day for Thomas Jefferson was Wednesday, March 4.
Adams could have stayed for the noon inauguration, but embittered by
the ugly campaign and the betrayal he felt from Jefferson, he departed
the mansion in the wee hours of the morning, his way lit by a quarter
moon.

But the patriot was proud to have left his successor a country "with
its coffers full," as he wrote later, and "fair prospects of peace with all
the world smiling in its face, its commerce flourishing, its navy glorious,
its agriculture uncommonly productive and lucrative."

ADAMS AND JEFFERSON REKINDLE A LOST FRIENDSHIP

Starting in 1805, ex-President John Adams and Founding Father Benjamin Rush wrote to each other about their dreams. In 1809, Rush reported a remarkable one: that Adams and Thomas Jefferson had begun a correspondence and rekindled their friendship.

That friendship had died an anguished death during the bitter presidential election in 1800. Now Rush imagined them discussing their shared personal and national histories until each "sunk into the grave nearly at the same time, full of years and rich in the gratitude and praises of their country."

Adams told Rush, "I always loved Jefferson, and still love him." When Jefferson heard this, he wrote Rush: "This is enough for me. I only needed this knowledge to revive towards him all of the affections of the most cordial moments of our lives." On July 15, 1813, Adams wrote the first of what would be 158 letters between them, spanning fourteen years.

"You and I ought not to die," Adams wrote in an early letter, "before We have explained ourselves to each other." Their conversation was as broad as their minds, covering the French Revolution, books they'd read, old friends, American Indians, education, and the British. Jefferson's were restrained and organized; Adams's were mercurial, opinionated, and humorous. Again and again they circled back to the Revolution. "Who shall write the history of the American Revolution?" Adams asked. ". . . . Who will ever be able to write it?" Jefferson responded. "Nobody, except perhaps its external facts."

The two men also discussed their philosophies of life: "You ask if I would agree to live my 70, or rather 73, years over again?" Jefferson wrote Adams. "To which I say Yea. I think with you that it is a good world on the whole, that it has been framed on a principle of benevolence. . . . I steer my bark with Hope in the head, leaving Fear astern."

As Rush had dreamed, the two men would die within hours of each other on July 4, 1826, the fiftieth anniversary of the signing of the Declaration of Independence. Adams's last words were "Jefferson still survives."

This watercolor by William Birch shows the White House as John Adams would have seen it when he moved into it in 1800, one month before he was voted out of office. While buildings can be seen in the distance, Washington, D.C. was hardly a bustling city at the time.

THOMAS JEFFERSON

The Early Jefferson—
a Builder, a Thinker, a Writer

WEEK 5

THOMAS JEFFERSON TAKES TO A LIFE OF THE MIND

In 1760, after learning Latin and Greek from a local schoolmaster, Thomas Jefferson left his home in Shadwell, Virginia, in the foothills of the Blue Ridge Mountains, to study at the College of William and Mary in Williamsburg. The first of his father's family to attend college, Jefferson was an obsessive student.

At William and Mary, much of his education came outside the classroom from the professor William Small. Small introduced him to Francis Fauquier, who would become Virginia's governor, and to George Wythe, with whom Jefferson later studied law. Jefferson often joined the other men for dinner at Fauquier's, where, he later said, he "heard more good sense, more rational and philosophical conversations, than in all my life besides."

Jefferson learned French and Italian, and claimed to have taught himself Spanish by reading *Don Quixote* with a Spanish grammar book at hand. John Quincy Adams recorded the story, adding, "But Mr. Jefferson tells large stories." Adams was hardly a neutral source regarding Jefferson, but there might be some truth in his observation. After five years in France as a diplomat under George Washington, Jefferson never felt comfortable conversing in French, and in formal correspondences he always employed a translator to write for him. Biographer Joseph Ellis writes: "Jefferson was adept at learning how to read foreign languages, but not to speak or write them."

Throughout his life, Jefferson read continuously in a broad range of fields, including astronomy, architecture, horticulture, and political theory. "I cannot live without books," he wrote Adams. One of his practices, which he called "commonplacing," consisted of copying over phrases and passages from books, sometimes interjecting his words into the original text. He dismissed most novels as a "mass of trash" and read fewer newspapers as he aged, writing to James Monroe, "Indeed my skepticism as to every thing I see in a newspaper makes me indifferent whether I ever see one."

IDEAS BECOME A HOME—MONTICELLO

In 1768, at age twenty-six, Jefferson decided to build a house on a hill on the 1,053 acres he'd inherited from his father. He called it Monticello, meaning "little mountain" in Italian. For the rest of his life, it would be his home, overlooking Charlottesville and the University of Virginia, which he founded (for more on the University of Virginia, see page 384).

From 1770 to 1779, he built a boxy house with fourteen rooms. In 1793, after he resigned as secretary of state under George Washington, he began building the home that exists today; it was finished in 1809. This house served as a laboratory for architectural ideas he had developed during his time in Paris as an ambassador. It also allowed him to double the house's size, making it large enough for his children and grandchildren.

For the first three years, the property was largely a construction site. He told one visitor to Monticello that "architecture is my delight, and putting up and pulling down, one of my favorite amusements." It became a low, red-brick structure with a white dome and a Doric portico, initiating the Roman Revival style in the United States. Among other Jeffersonian inventions, the home contained a writing device that connected two pens, one you wrote with and another that produced a duplicate. It also included another innovation he saw in France—indoor bathrooms.

JEFFERSON WAS NOT THE NATURAL CHOICE TO WRITE THE DECLARATION OF INDEPENDENCE

Thomas Jefferson was not the obvious choice to write the Declaration of Independence. His disqualifications were many: He was one of the youngest members of the Continental Congress and a poor public speaker who was more comfortable in his study than in public, where reputations were made. He was even considered one of the weaker members of the Virginia delegation to the Continental Congress in 1776—which included George Washington and Patrick Henry. Why, then, was he chosen to write the document?

John Adams and Jefferson had differing memories of Jefferson's selection. Writing in his autobiography, Adams remembered that Jefferson suggested that Adams write the declaration, but that he declined.

"Why?" Jefferson asked, according to Adams's recounting.

"Reasons enough," Adams answered.

"What can be your reasons?" asked Jefferson.

"Reason first: You are a Virginian and a Virginian ought to appear at the head of this business. Reason second: I am obnoxious, suspected, and unpopular. You are very much otherwise. Reason third: You can write ten times better than I can."

Jefferson only remembered that the committee selected him. "I consented: I drew it [up]." He also might have been given the task because others were too busy—Adams was serving on twenty-three committees at the time—and thought it a comparatively unimportant task.

Jefferson wrote the document over a few days on a portable writing desk that he'd designed himself (for more on Jefferson's writing, see page 335) One romantic notion holds that the declaration was the product of a great mind of a great man, but Jefferson denied that interpretation his entire life. "Neither aiming at originality of principle or sentiment, nor yet copied from any particular and previous writing," he explained in a letter a half century later, "it was intended to be an expression of the American mind, and to give to that expression of the proper tone and spirit called for by the occasion."

JEFFERSON'S DECLARATION OF INDEPENDENCE— HOW ORIGINAL WAS IT?

Ninety local "declarations" of independence were written in the months leading up to the Second Continental Congress. One was Virginia's Declaration of Rights, written in the spring of 1776 by George Mason, adopted less than two weeks before Thomas Jefferson wrote the Declaration of Independence. Did Jefferson use Mason's document as a starting point for his document? Judge for yourself:

GEORGE MASON'S VIRGINIA DECLARATION OF RIGHTS	THOMAS JEFFERSON'S DECLARATION OF INDEPENDENCE
SECTION 1. All men are created equally free and independent and have certain inherent and natural rights . . . among which are the enjoyment of life and liberty, with the means of acquiring and possessing property, and pursuing and obtaining happiness and safety.	We hold these truths to be self-evident, that all men are created equal, that they are endowed by their Creator with certain unalienable rights, that among these are Life, Liberty and the pursuit of Happiness.
SEC. 2. That all power is vested in, and consequently derived from, the people; that magistrates are their trustees and servants and at all times amenable to them.	That to secure these rights, governments are instituted among men, deriving their just powers from the consent of the governed,
SEC. 3. That government is, or ought to be, instituted for the common benefit, protection, and security of the people. . . . [and provides the] greatest degree of happiness and safety . . . ; and that, when any government shall be found inadequate . . . the community hath an . . . inalienable, . . . right to reform, alter, or abolish it. . . .	That whenever any Form of Government becomes destructive to these ends, it is the Right of the People to alter or to abolish it, and to institute new Government, laying its foundation on such principles and organizing its powers in such form, as to them shall seem most likely to effect their Safety and Happiness.

Jefferson admitted his thoughts were not original. "What made Jefferson's work surpassing was the grace and eloquence of expression," writes historian David McCullough. "Jefferson had done superbly and in minimum time."

IN WITH A WHISPER—JEFFERSON'S DECLARATION OF INDEPENDENCE CLIMBS TO FAME SLOWLY

Thomas Jefferson's Declaration of Independence was born largely un-noticed. Because the proceedings of the Second Continental Congress were secret, the public wasn't at first aware who had written the declaration. States that drafted their own declarations after Jefferson's didn't borrow phrasing from his. Instead, four of them—Pennsylvania, Massachusetts, New Hampshire, and Vermont—borrowed wording from Virginia's Declaration of Rights, including the phrase "all men are born equally free and independent." And during the eight-year Revolutionary War, Jefferson's declaration wasn't read at Fourth of July celebrations as would become tradition later.

When it came time to draft the Constitution, the declaration was referred to only a few times. When Patrick Henry addressed the Virginia Convention during the debate to ratify the Constitution, he asked, "What, sir, is the genius of democracy?" As his answer, he read Mason's Declaration of Rights, not Jefferson's Declaration of Independence.

It was the polarized politics of the 1790s that lifted the declaration and its author into fame. Conservative Federalists such as John Adams distrusted Jefferson and his declaration, with its references to "liberty" and "equality," which sounded much like the rhetoric of the bloody French Revolution. Republicans, who were anti-Federalist, celebrated Jefferson and the Declaration of Independence at their own Fourth of July parties. The elevation of the declaration continued during the early nineteenth century, after Jefferson was elected president and Republicans came to dominate national politics.

John Adams complained that Jefferson was not the sole author—it had been revised by the committee and the Continental Congress—and that he had steered the document through the Congress. "The Declaration of Independence I always considered as a theatrical show," Adams wrote. "Jefferson ran away with all the stage effect of that . . . and all the glory of it."

MARTHA JEFFERSON EXTRACTS A DEATHBED
PROMISE FROM THOMAS

At the age of twenty-seven, Jefferson met Martha Wayles Skelton, a wealthy twenty-three-year-old Virginia widow. The story, perhaps apocryphal, is that other suitors stepped back when the two engaged in a duet—Jefferson on his cherished violin, Martha on her harpsichord.

By most accounts, the marriage pleased both partners. Perhaps the strongest evidence of their bond is what happened after Martha fell ill after the birth of her sixth child in May 1782. Years later, the couple's daughter Patsy recalled her mother's death on September 6, 1782, when Patsy was nine. She said Jefferson's sister took Thomas "in a state of insensibility" to the library where "he fainted, and remained so long insensible that they feared he never would revive." For six weeks, Jefferson was heard sobbing in the night, and he often broke down when he had to speak. Some friends feared he might lose his mind from grief. In the weeks afterward, he wandered Monticello on horseback and on foot, which Patsy referred to as "those melancholy rambles . . . beyond the power of time to obliterate." It was mid-October before Jefferson found himself "emerging from that stupor of mind which had rendered me as dead to the world as she was whose loss occasioned it."

Martha also extracted a promise from Jefferson that he would never remarry, as she wanted to spare her three surviving daughters from being raised by a stepmother, as she had been. The promise was described by Edmund Bacon, Jefferson's overseer, and by the descendants of a slave girl who nursed Martha on her deathbed. The slave was Martha's half sister, as they shared the same father, who had fathered Martha in his marriage and fathered the slave girl in a relationship with Betty Hemings, one of his slaves. The girl's name was Sally Hemings and she would later become Jefferson's lover, mother to a second set of children, and a source of generations of scandal.

This is a rough draft of the Declaration of Independence as Thomas Jefferson wrote it. It reveals some important edits made by John Adams, Benjamin Franklin, and the Continental Congress, before the document was adopted on July 4, 1776.

THOMAS JEFFERSON

A Charmed First Term

WEEK 6

JEFFERSON'S FIRST INAUGURAL— A CONCILIATORY MESSAGE

John Adams left the White House at 4:00 A.M. on March 4, 1801, to escape watching Thomas Jefferson's inaugural procession. Just before noon, Jefferson, tall and lanky, approaching his fifty-eighth birthday, walked rather than take a ceremonial carriage from his boardinghouse to the Capitol. Observers gathered in the only finished room in the Capitol, the Senate Chamber, and struggled to hear what would one day be considered one of the most eloquent presidential inaugurals. Jefferson began by speaking generally about his political beliefs, stressing the "sacred principle that, though the will of the majority is in all cases to prevail, that will, to be rightful, must be reasonable." He attacked the Alien and Sedition Act passed under Adams by arguing that "the minority possess their equal rights, which equal laws must protect, and to violate would be oppression." Later in the speech he would repeat an election promise to protect "equal and exact justice to all men of whatever state or persuasion, religious or political."

People wondered whether Jefferson would undermine the centralized government and the powerful presidency. But his words were conciliatory: "We have called by different names brethren of the same principle. We are all republicans: we are all federalists." He emphasized his trust in the people, a sentiment he doubted most Federalists shared. "Sometimes it is said that man cannot be trusted with the government of himself. Can he then be trusted with the government of others? Or have we found angels in the form of kings to govern him? Let history answer this question."

He also listed practical goals: to put the military under civilian control and dismantle the standing army and navy; pay the national debt; and promote agriculture. He would sum up his foreign policy plan with a single sentence: "Peace, commerce and honest friendship with all nations, entangling alliances with none."

A REPUDIATION OF POMP—THE STYLE OF A
PEOPLE'S PRESIDENT

Jefferson called his election "the revolution of 1800," and one of the ways he wanted to express the overturning of the old order was to dispense with "the rags of royalty" that George Washington and John Adams had enjoyed. Jefferson believed such pomp tipped the presidency toward monarchy, which he despised. The first piece of pageantry Jefferson cut was the annual address that Washington and Adams had delivered to Congress. Jefferson delivered his in writing to avoid the British monarchy's practice of a speech and a formal response.

Jefferson expressed his more populist style in other ways. He sometimes answered the front door of the president's home. He rode his horse unaccompanied by aides. Jefferson made clear his desire for modesty and simplicity in a memorandum he sent to the men in his administration: "When brought together in society, all are equal, whether foreign or domestic, titled or untitled, in or out of office." He gave up formal receptions, abandoning the strict code of etiquette that foreign diplomats expected in the courts of Europe. From his first day in office, Jefferson wrote, his administration "buried levees, birthdays, royal parades, processions with white wands, and the arrogance of precedence in society. . . ." He used a round table rather than a square one, in part to reject hierarchical seatings.

Instead of coming to social events dressed formally, he wore his riding clothes, including corduroy pants and riding boots. In 1803, this change in etiquette peeved Anthony Merry, the British minister to the United States, who showed up at the White House dressed in a coat decorated with black velvet and gold braid. When Jefferson greeted him in his "usual morning attire," Merry found his "pantaloons, coat, and underclothes indicative of utter slovenliness and indifference to appearances. . . ." After Jefferson escorted Dolley Madison rather than Mrs. Merry to a dinner table, the Merrys rejected invitations to the White House altogether. Jefferson, well aware of what he was up to, probably relished the snub.

LETTING THE ALIEN AND SEDITION ACTS EXPIRE

Of all the policies enacted under John Adams, Thomas Jefferson most despised the Alien and Sedition Acts. The Alien Act gave the president the power to deport aliens considered "dangerous" to the United States. The Sedition Act gave the president the power to suppress "False, scandalous, and malicious" speech or writings critical of the government. Federalists defended the acts as measures to protect the country if war broke out with France, but Jefferson believed both unconstitutional. The Sedition Act clearly violated the freedom of speech guaranteed by the Bill of Rights.

Jefferson and other Republicans felt certain the Sedition Act was directed at stifling Republicans and their views, especially given that it was meant to expire on March 3, 1801, the last day of Adams's term. Given that Republican editors were the only ones arrested or convicted under the law, they were probably right.

After it passed, Jefferson worked to repeal it. "A little patience," he wrote the pamphleteer and planter John Taylor, "and we shall see the reign of witches pass over, their spells dissolve, and the people recovering their true sight, restore their government to its true principles." Jefferson quietly authored a document that would become the Kentucky Resolutions, adopted in 1798 and 1799, which declared that states could nullify unconstitutional federal laws within their boundaries. The resolutions were a harbinger of states' rights, and Jefferson hoped that they would inspire other states to follow suit, but only Virginia did so.

Jefferson was so angered by the political state of affairs that he surreptitiously hired James Callender, a propagandist, to blacken the Federalists' reputation, particularly Adams's. Callender charged that Adams was a monarchist who wanted to go to war with France and was a "repulsive pedant." Callender paid by going to jail under the Sedition Act.

After Jefferson was elected, he would let both acts expire and pardon Callender. But the journalist, thinking his pieces sullying Adams got Jefferson elected, wanted a plum appointment in the Jefferson administration. When the president declined, Callender turned his pen against Jefferson, writing that Jefferson had fathered children through his slave Sally Hemings, accusations that have stuck to Jefferson for over two hundred years. (For more on this scandal, see page 351.)

PRAGMATISM OVER PRINCIPLES—
JEFFERSON MAKES THE LOUISIANA PURCHASE

In his first year in office, President Thomas Jefferson was faced with one of the most momentous decisions in presidential history: Stick with his political principles and adhere to the Constitution, or betray both to take advantage of one of the greatest opportunities in U.S. history.

Jefferson and his Republicans believed in both reducing the national debt and deferring to Congress, the primary branch of government. These beliefs were challenged just weeks into Jefferson's presidency, when Secretary of State James Madison learned that Spain, in decline, had secretly signed a treaty to turn over to France its North American colonies, a swath of land that stretched from the Mississippi River to the Rocky Mountains. Rumor had it that Napoleon planned to reestablish the French empire, including New Orleans, the port through which all midwestern American commerce passed.

Jefferson warned the French that if they took over the territory they would face the same fate as the English had during the Revolutionary War. Then he pulled back: "You know how much I value peace," he wrote, "and how unwillingly I should see any event take place that would render war a necessary recourse." Jefferson suggested France sell New Orleans to the Americans, as well as the area from the Gulf Coast to Pensacola, for $6 million.

Another twist followed. Napoleon had invaded the island of Santo Domingo, but a half million former slaves overcame the assault of sixty thousand French soldiers, forcing Napoleon to abort plans to capture New Orleans. "I renounce Louisiana," Napoleon declared, opting to trade the territory for cash he needed to fight a war with England and Russia.

Jefferson sought a constitutional amendment to authorize the sale, as he thought was required, but abandoned that approach when he received word that Napoleon was equivocating. The president authorized the purchase, and for $15 million, or three cents an acre, the United States doubled its size. The land added would become the country's breadbasket. Jefferson put the nation in debt and had made the kind of imperial decision he had often criticized in others. But many consider the Louisiana Purchase his greatest achievement as president.

JEFFERSON'S LIMITED VISION OF
THE LOUISIANA PURCHASE

Critics of the Louisiana Purchase feared that the huge expansion of territory would make the country too vast to govern. Jefferson thought the opposite. "The larger our association," he maintained, "the less will it be shaken by local passions; and in any view, is it not better that the opposite bank of the Mississippi should be settled by our own brethren and children, than by strangers from another family?"

Jefferson envisioned the land as an "empire of liberty," populated by farmers, Jefferson's ideal citizens. However, Jefferson's empire was limited. Thomas Paine, a friend of Jefferson's, urged him to keep slavery from these territories. In 1804, Senator James Hillhouse of Connecticut offered an amendment to a bill organizing the Louisiana territory that banned slavery in the territory. But Jefferson didn't support it, remaining publicly silent on the issue of slavery, as he would during and after his presidency, and the amendment didn't pass. Over the next half century, territories within the Louisiana Purchase, such as Missouri and Kansas, would become battlegrounds over slavery.

The new territory also provided Jefferson with a place to imagine a vast reservation where Indians from the Ohio Valley and Southeast could be relocated. Even before the purchase was finished, Jefferson called upon governors and military men in the Ohio Valley to drive Indian groups into debt, "thereby speeding their extinction or removal," writes Joseph Ellis in his book, *American Creation.*

As eastern tribes were moved westward, the United States could sell their vacated land to white settlers to pay off the $15 million debt to the French incurred in making the Louisiana Purchase. To Jefferson, the new land could become an "empire of liberty"—but for whites only.

JEFFERSON REDUCES THE NATIONAL DEBT

In his first inaugural address in 1801, Thomas Jefferson described his vision of "a wise and frugal Government, which shall . . . leave them otherwise free to regulate their own pursuits of industry and improvement, and shall not take from the mouth of labor the bread it has earned. This is the sum of good government . . ."

For Jefferson, a "frugal government" included eliminating the federal debt, which he believed encouraged political corruption and even war. When Jefferson took office in 1801, the national debt was at $80 million. The federal government took in $9 million in revenues from customs duties and the sale of public lands each year. Albert Gallatin, his treasury secretary, came up with a plan that allocated $7 million a year to reducing the deficit and left just $2 million for the government. This was fine by Jefferson, who distrusted the federal government and found it wasteful. "We are hunting out and abolishing multitudes of useless offices," he wrote to his son-in-law.

Attacking the debt also gave Jefferson a reason to limit the military. "Sound principles will not justify our taxing the industry of our fellow citizens to accumulate treasure for wars to happen we know not when," Jefferson wrote in his first inaugural address, "and which might not perhaps happen but from the temptations offered by that treasure." Jefferson reduced the size of the U.S. Army and Navy.

Gallatin would continue as James Madison's treasury secretary, and in fifteen years of service he reduced the public debt from $80 million to $45 million—not bad when you factor in the $15 million the government paid out in the Louisiana Purchase. Even more impressive, Jefferson and his treasury secretary cut the debt while cutting taxes, including ending the hated whiskey tax imposed by George Washington. After his first term, Jefferson wrote rhetorically, "What farmer, what mechanic, what laborer ever sees a tax-gatherer of the United States?" It was a question few presidents would be able to ask.

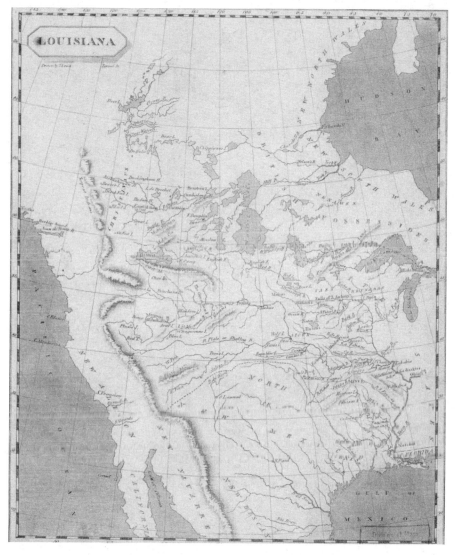

London publisher Aaron Arrowsmith prepared this map in 1804, the first published of the Louisiana Purchase. Depicting how Jefferson's contemporaries envisioned the territory, one can see less-than-daunting Rocky Mountains and a river system that allowed for easy passage to the West.

THOMAS JEFFERSON

Stumbling Through a Second Term

WEEK 7

JEFFERSON'S ATTITUDE—AND ACTIONS—ON SLAVERY

How did Jefferson's ownership of slaves and his actions on slavery compare to his soaring rhetoric on liberty and freedom?

Jefferson's most principled action on slavery came in 1784, when he proposed a measure to the Continental Congress that banned slavery in all the territories west of the Appalachian Mountains, north and south, by 1800. If it had passed, the firestorm over the future of slavery in the territories, which ignited the Civil War, might have been doused while still an ember. The bill lost by a single vote. But it did inspire the Northwest Ordinance of 1787, which prohibited the importation of new slaves into the region, bordered by the Great Lakes and the Ohio and Mississippi rivers.

But Jefferson's later actions more closely resembled those of a Virginia slaveholder than those of the author of the Declaration of Independence. During the Haitian Revolution, which overthrew the French in a bloody decade-long insurrection that ended in 1803, Jefferson held back recognition for the first slave revolt and the Western Hemisphere's second republic.

After Jefferson brokered the Louisiana Purchase, Thomas Paine urged him to keep slavery from that territory. In 1804, Senator James Hillhouse of Connecticut offered an amendment to ban slavery in the Louisiana territory as part of a bill to organize the territory. Jefferson didn't support the measure, or any more moderate ones that might have brought gradual emancipation there (the course chosen in states such as Pennsylvania). But one of the last major acts of his presidency was perhaps his most powerful assault against slavery.

The Constitution forbade any prohibitions against the importation of slaves before 1808, Jefferson's last year in office. When that ban expired, Jefferson presented Congress with a bill that would permanently ban the importation of slaves, and it passed. But Jefferson would move no further. In his postpresidency, he stopped criticizing slavery publicly. He was immobilized by the assumption that if slaves were emancipated, the lingering animosity between freedmen and whites would lead to war that would annihilate one side or the other.

JEFFERSON'S INDIAN POLICY—ASSIMILATE OR SUFFER EVICTION

In his *Notes on Virginia*, Thomas Jefferson's only book, he celebrates America's first inhabitants, praising their "eloquence in council, bravery and address in war." He spent many hours studying Native American languages and their origins. At times, he seemed to recognize the tragedy that had befallen them. "Endowed with the faculties and rights of men," he wrote, "breathing an ardent love of liberty and independence, and occupying a country which left them no desire but to be undisturbed . . . they have been overwhelmed by the current, or driven before it."

But Jefferson increased the speed of that current. He believed that for the Native American, progress consisted of giving up their traditional ways, which usually included nomadic hunting and gathering on communal property. In his second inaugural address in March 1805, Jefferson chastised traditionalist Native Americans for "a sanctimonious reverence for the customs of their ancestors." The proper Native American, in Jefferson's view, would speak English, farm, wear American clothes, and adopt Christianity. If they assimilated, they'd be tolerated.

Many Native Americans didn't accept this path. For these resisters, Jefferson had an alternative: Move them west of the Mississippi. "Should any tribe be foolhardy enough to take up the hatchet," Jefferson wrote, such actions should be used as justification "to seize the whole country of the tribe, driving them across the Mississippi as an example to others, and a furtherance of our final consolidation." The United States could then sell the vacated land in parcels to white settlers, Jefferson argued, to pay for the debt incurred during the Louisiana Purchase. One scholar argued that that strategy planted the "seeds of extinction" of Native Americans in the century ahead.

THE EMBARGO ACT—JEFFERSON'S MISERABLE DECISION

War was good to the United States in Thomas Jefferson's first term—
Napoleon Bonaparte's need for cash to fund France's conquests led directly to the sale of the Louisiana territory. The war also fed American
prosperity, as American merchants, neutral in the conflict between Great
Britain and France, brought in huge profits trading with both countries. Import duties on the trade helped pay down the national debt.

But that same European conflagration would singe America—and
Jefferson's reputation—during his second term. As the war on the continent heated, both Great Britain and France tried to stop trade between
the United States and their enemy. The British, with their superior
navy, were far more successful in their efforts, lurking off the coast to
confiscate any goods they believed were destined for France. They also
began searching American ships for British seamen who had deserted the
Royal Navy.

Jefferson was desperate to avoid war with England. He considered
returning all British seamen on American ships before he learned that
half of the eighteen thousand sailors on American trading ships were
British. The conflict escalated on June 22, 1807, when the HMS *Leopard*,
a British frigate, confronted the USS *Chesapeake* off Norfolk, Virginia.
The British charged the American ship with harboring deserters from
the Royal Navy. The American captain claimed he had no deserters and
refused to allow the British to board. The *Leopard* then fired four broad-
sides into the *Chesapeake*, killing three and wounding eighteen, including
the captain. Then the British boarded, taking four sailors they claimed
were British.

Many considered the attack an act of war. Jefferson ordered all British
ships to leave American waters and called for the raising of a hundred
thousand militiamen to enforce the proclamation.

Still, British and French ships bore down on American traders, who
lost an estimated $10 million worth of goods to French theft in a single
year, with losses many times that to the English. To avoid war, Jefferson
decided to withdraw rather than attack, but his decision would devas-
tate both the economy and his own popularity.

THE EMBARGO ACT FAILS—AND JEFFERSON
WITHDRAWS FROM THE PRESIDENCY

On December 18, 1807, Thomas Jefferson asked Congress to pass a bill to bar any ship from trading with or carrying goods for any European power, and within days, both the House and the Senate obliged.

The bill was called the Embargo Act. In a letter to a friend, Jefferson explained that the "embargo keeping at home our vessels, cargoes & seamen, saves us the necessity of making their capture the cause of immediate war: for if going to England, France had determined to take them; if to any other place, England was to take them. Till they return to some sense of moral duty therefore, we keep within ourselves." Jefferson expected that the embargo would hurt France and England enough financially that by spring they'd agree to respect American rights of neutrality. But the Embargo Act hurt American shippers far more than the economies of France or England. Napoleon's French Empire was largely self-sufficient. And three-quarters of American trade was with Great Britain, but only 10 percent of British trade was with the United States. Before the embargo, foreign trade totaled roughly $108 million a year. In the fifteen months of the embargo, it fell three-fourths, to $22 million.

The embargo injured New England shippers most, and many smuggled goods across the Atlantic to circumvent Jefferson's law. Huge rallies, especially in Massachusetts, called for secession if the embargo wasn't lifted. Instead of backing down under pressure, Jefferson squeezed tighter, sending naval warships into key harbors, allowing them to search ships on mere suspicion that they were breaking the embargo. In February 1808, Congress repealed the law in an act that went into effect the day after Jefferson left office.

The British began to attack American shipping again until they defeated Napoleon at the Battle of Waterloo, and finally settled their differences with the United States. Jefferson, tired, welcomed a retreat to Monticello: "Never did a prisoner released from his chains feel such relief as I shall on shaking off the shackles of power."

JEFFERSON'S LAST LETTER—AND TIMELY DEATH

Thomas Jefferson, known for his letters, wrote his last one on June 24, 1826. In response to an invitation by the committee organized to celebrate the fiftieth anniversary of the Declaration of Independence, Jefferson, eighty-three, explained that deteriorating health prevented him from making a final journey from his home in Monticello to Washington. He used the occasion to sum up his political ideas:

> . . . . May [the Declaration] be to the world, what I believe it will be . . . the signal of arousing men to burst the chains under which monkish ignorance and superstition had persuaded them to bind themselves, and to assume the blessings and security of self-government. That form which we have substituted, restores the free right to the unbounded exercise of reason and freedom of opinion. All eyes are opened, or opening, to the rights of man. . . . These are grounds of hope for others. For ourselves, let the annual return of this day forever refresh our recollections of these rights, and an undiminished devotion to them.

The political ideas that he championed for half a century were there—his passion for self-government and "the rights of man"; his belief that these rights were universal and exportable; his preference for the "light of science" over opinions and beliefs. His final words would come nearly two weeks later: "Is it the Fourth?" he asked, feverish. "It soon will be," he was told. He drifted off. Less than an hour Into the day he had waited for as a young man, and now waited for as an old one, he died.

At sunrise that same day, Jefferson's great friend and rival, John Adams, in Quincy, Massachusetts, was bedridden. Finding it difficult to breathe and thinking Jefferson was still alive, he uttered his last words some time before he died at midday: "Thomas Jefferson survives."

JEFFERSON'S DISAPPEARING LEGACY

In *American Sphinx*, Joseph Ellis compares many of Jefferson's legacies to sand castles that the waves of history have dissolved. The first wave was the Civil War, which disproved Jefferson's assumption that America's political salvation lay in the migration of settlers to the West. White migration into the territories only increased pressure on the fault line of slavery. Abraham Lincoln's strong federal government and a juggernaut Union war machine also eroded the Jeffersonian principle that supreme sovereignty belonged with the states. Jefferson's ideal of an America built on the virtues of farmers also faded by the end of the nineteenth century, as huge waves of Europeans and Asians packed American cities.

The New Deal crushed Jefferson's dream of a small government. If Lincoln had launched a powerful federal government, Franklin Roosevelt captained it, believing only that a strong government could counter the powers of business and ameliorate the vicissitudes of capitalism. The cry against government and debt often rings out, but it's hard to imagine any modern president repeating Jefferson's spartan budget. The civil rights movement washed away the assumptions that blacks were inferior to whites and that racial oppression could not be battled politically without devastating consequences. And if Jefferson was right that a standing army wasted taxpayer money and tempted the powerful into war, few today are willing to say so.

The castle that still stands contains his ideals of equality and individual liberty, expressed in his soaring words. His Declaration of Independence is America's creed, flexible and durable enough to be borrowed by groups as diverse as American feminists, who used it as a model in their Seneca Falls Declaration and Resolves of 1848; civil rights leaders, who repeated his affirmation that "all men are created equal"; and even by Ho Chi Minh's Communists, who used it for their Declaration of Independence of the Republic of Vietnam. Jefferson's life was flawed, and much of his legacy has gone out with the tides, but his finest writings still inspire people all over the world.

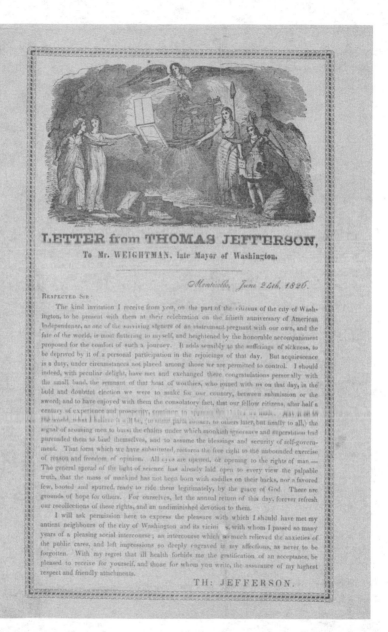

This is a printed version of the letter that Thomas Jefferson wrote to Roger C. Weightman, the mayor of Washington, explaining why he would not attend the celebration of the fiftieth anniversary of the Declaration of Independence. Written in June 1826, it was the last letter that Jefferson, eighty-three and in declining health, would ever pen. He died ten days later on the Fourth of July—as would John Adams.

Thomas Jefferson's Followers— James Madison, James Monroe, and John Quincy Adams

WEEK 8

JAMES MADISON—THE (QUIET) FATHER
OF THE CONSTITUTION

James Madison is often portrayed as Thomas Jefferson's loyal and younger lieutenant—Jefferson "lite." Some of this perception probably arose from his looks—"little Jemmy Madison" was just five feet six inches tall and weighed 140 pounds, and was once described as "no bigger than a half piece of soap." Historian Joseph J. Ellis says Madison "had the frail and discernibly fragile appearance of a career librarian or school-master, forever lingering on the edge of some fatal ailment. . . ." But inside this unimpressive exterior was probably the most superb and well-prepared mind of his generation.

Politicians from all over the country came together at the Constitutional Convention of 1787 in Philadelphia to revise the Articles of Confederation, a document which was woefully inadequate to run the country. It didn't give the nation the authority to stabilize currency, regulate commerce, levy taxes, pay war debts, make capital improvements, or protect individual rights. When General George Washington rode into the city on his horse, forty thousand people came out to cheer him. But Washington would remain mute during the convention; Jefferson and John Adams were absent. Madison, just thirty-six years old, was the primary thinker and leader—speaking his opinion, crafting compromises, and writing many of the *Federalist Papers*, which defended the new Constitution.

Should states or the federal government reign supreme? Madison won a compromise that balanced state and federal interests. Madison, wary of concentrated power, also thought it best to divide the national government into three parts—legislative, executive, and judicial—to check a president or an oppressive majority.

When it was decided that the Constitution should protect the rights of individuals and the minority, Madison wrote the first ten amendments that became the Bill of Rights, including freedom of religion, speech, the press, assembly, and protest. While his contemporaries referred to him as the "father of the Constitution," he always defused credit, protesting that it was "the work of many heads and many hands."

MADISON'S FAILED ADVENTURE—THE WAR OF 1812

James Madison's war—the War of 1812—shouldn't have been fought. Some say he drifted into it, pushed by the so-called war hawks who chafed under Britain's insults; others say he welcomed the war. Either way, Madison was foolish to believe that American forces could occupy Canada and hold it as ransom, or that Americans could inflict damage on the mightiest nation on earth with a nonexistent navy. Even depleted from conflicts with Napoleon, Britain was able to control the Atlantic and raid at will up and down the East Coast, burning Washington— including the Capitol and the president's mansion.

What did the war achieve? Very little. It lasted for nearly three years, and cost the lives of twenty thousand Americans, most from disease in the army camps. Killed in battle were 2,260 men, including 205 soldiers executed for desertion. Another 4,400 men were wounded. Money was squandered as well as blood. When the war started, the national debt was $45 million; when it ended, it was $127 million. Taxation, something that Madison and his mentor Jefferson deplored, reached levels that wouldn't be replicated until the Civil War. The British had successfully blockaded the eastern seaboard, and the economy was wrecked. By November 1814, the federal government was as good as bankrupt. (For more on how Madison protected civil liberties during the war, see page 361.)

The Treaty of Ghent, which negotiated the end of the war, resolved none of the issues that had spurred the Americans to declare war. The British kept boarding American ships and kidnapping American sailors. America did not gain access to the Canadian fisheries or the right to remain neutral. The only capitulation made by the English was to evacuate their forts in the west and to give up the land they had taken during the war. Two war-weary countries simply laid down their arms and exchanged prisoners.

Perhaps the only achievement of the standoff was to boost America's pride. Madison congratulated the country for its "success," the "natural result of the wisdom of the legislative councils, of the patriotism of the people, of the public spirit of the militia, and of the valor of the military and [navy]."

DID MONROE SHIRK HIS RESPONSIBILITY
ON THE MISSOURI COMPROMISE?

In the early nineteenth century, the country confronted a fundamental question: Should slavery be extended into the newly acquired western territories?

While James Monroe was president, the question had concentrated itself in the Missouri territory, which would apply for statehood in 1819. Southerners wanted Missouri to come into the Union as a slave state, which would give them a one-vote majority in the Senate. Northerners opposed it for just that reason. They hoped that the institution would lose its grip on the nation if more people—and their representatives— came in as free states. The fate of Missouri, abolitionists and slaveholders believed, would determine the future of slavery.

"I have never known a question so menacing to the tranquility and even the continuance of our Union," Monroe wrote his friend Thomas Jefferson of the fate of Missouri.

What was Monroe's position on Missouri? He stayed out of the debate, and ordered his cabinet members to stay out of it as well. Was this negligence—or wise management?

Some historians argue that Monroe shirked his duty in avoiding the burning issue of his day. Others say that by staying above the fray, he put off a crisis that could have torn the country apart. In the end, he signed the Missouri Compromise of 1820, which drew a line westward from Missouri's southern border, at 36° 30'. States above the line came in as free states, and those below became slave states. Maine then joined the Union as free, and Missouri as a slave state.

Jefferson understood that the agreement merely postponed the conflict between the American slaveholder and abolitionist. "[T]his momentous question," wrote Jefferson to a friend in 1820, "like a firebell in the night, awakened and filled me with terror. I considered it at once as the knell of the Union. It is hushed indeed for the moment. But this is a reprieve only, not a final sentence. A geographical line, coinciding with a marked principle, moral and political, once conceived and held up to the angry passions of men, will never be obliterated; and every new irritation will mark it deeper and deeper. . . ."

THE MONROE DOCTRINE—USED AND MISUSED
THROUGH THE YEARS

On December 2, 1823, James Monroe strode into Congress to deliver one of his last annual addresses. He was dressed in what was by then old-fashioned attire: knee breeches, silk hose, and buckle-top shoes. Much of his two-hour speech was dreary, but his voice rose when he came to a three-paragraph passage buried in the message that would change America's relation to the world and resound through American foreign policy for the next two centuries.

Monroe told the European monarchies to stop colonizing Central or South America, adding that any attempts to do so would be considered a threat to the United States. Men at the time called these the Principles of 1823. But history knows them as the Monroe Doctrine.

The United States had been buffeted by the winds of European power politics for half a century. But the landscape had shifted. By 1822, nearly all of Central and South America had broken from Spain and Portugal, and other European countries were looking to fill the vacuum.

Previous presidents had striven to stay disentangled from the politics and wars of Europe. Now Monroe was telling Europeans, whose armies and armadas still dwarfed America's, to disentangle from the politics of the Americas. While keeping European powers from colonizing in the Americas had a democratic ring to it, the doctrine would be used to justify many aggressive and militaristic escapades by American presidents.

Since Monroe declared his doctrine, America has engaged in over seventy military engagements in Central and South America. James Polk cited it when he went to war against Mexico in 1846. William McKinley used it to justify war against Spain in 1898. Woodrow Wilson referred to it when he sent American forces to Cuba, the Dominican Republic, Haiti, Mexico, and Panama; and John F. Kennedy cited it as a warning to the Soviet Union during the Cuban Missile Crisis.

"I conclude that the Monroe Doctrine is not a doctrine but a dogma," Salvador de Madariaga, the Spanish historian and diplomat, said, "of the infallibility of the American President and . . . the immaculate conception of American foreign policy."

JOHN QUINCY ADAMS—A PRECOCIOUS BOY
IS PUSHED HARD TO SUCCEED

John Adams, the second U.S. president, said that his firstborn son, John Quincy, seemed "so far beyond his years" that "the world says they should take him for my younger brother."

Adams was proud of his son, and ambitious for him too. In 1776, while busy with the Revolution, he wrote to his wife Abigail to educate the children well. "Cultivate their Minds, inspire their little Hearts, raise their Wishes. Fix their Attention upon great and glorious Objects, root out every little Thing, weed out every Meanness, make them great and manly." Later, he harangued a young John Quincy by saying, "You come into life with advantages which will disgrace you if your success is mediocre. And if you do not rise to the head not only of your profession, but of your country, it will be owing to your own *lasiness, slovenliness* and *obstinacy*."

"Many parents tell their floundering children to pull themselves together and work," writes Richard Brookhiser in *America's First Dynasty.* "Few tell them to pull themselves together and become president."

His father would take him along on his diplomatic missions to Europe. While there, John Quincy hobnobbed with Benjamin Franklin and other American diplomats. "Spent the evening with Mr. Jefferson . . . ," he wrote one day in March 1785, "whom I love to be with because he is a man of very extensive learning, and pleasing manners."

Like Jefferson, John Quincy had a voracious and restless mind, dabbling as a poet, historian, diarist, scientist, Harvard professor, and politician. As a diplomat, he created a vigorous routine for his body and mind. He rose as early as four, never after six, and would start the day reading chapters from the Bible, sometimes in Greek, French, or German, often comparing translations.

The law bored him—he preferred the interplay of politics. George Washington would appoint him minister to Holland, and later praised him as "the most valuable public character we have abroad." He would serve as minister to Prussia, Russia, and England, and secretary of state in James Monroe's administration. In 1811, he turned down James Madison's offer to sit on the U.S. Supreme Court. He had higher ambitions.

THE AMBITIOUS—BUT FAILED—
PRESIDENCY OF JOHN QUINCY ADAMS

The presidency of John Quincy Adams was poisoned before he reached the White House. The election of 1824 was a four-way race, and Adams received only a third of the popular vote. Because no one candidate received the majority of the electoral votes, the election was thrown into the House of Representatives, where the powerful Henry Clay threw his votes to Adams, giving him the presidency over Andrew Jackson, the runner-up. Adams immediately made Clay secretary of state. Everyone assumed the men had made a deal, and Jackson called it a "corrupt bargain." (For more on the election of 1824, see page 344.)

Adams recognized the perception, confessing in his inaugural address that he was "less possessed of [public] confidence in advance than any of my predecessors." Yet, he moved boldly, the first president to lead Congress on an aggressive agenda. He proposed selling land and putting up a tariff to provide the government money to build roads and canals, which he hoped would unite the country politically and commercially. He also wanted to use the money to spur the sciences and encourage nationalism with a naval academy, a national university, scientific expeditions, and even an astronomical observatory. "Of the cost of these undertakings . . . ," Adams said, "it would be unworthy of a great and generous nation to take a second thought."

The nation did take second thoughts—unpleasant ones—for Adams's rather cerebral national program. People mocked the observatories, and even Clay called the president's program "entirely hopeless." Adams, stubborn as his father, also took unpopular positions, such as refusing to sign a fraudulent Indian treaty that removed Creeks from Georgia—which irritated Southerners. Seeing himself above party politics, he neglected to fill patronage positions with Democratic-Republicans, which might have won him more support. In the midterm elections of 1826, Jackson's men gobbled the majority of offices in both houses, and the hostile Congress thwarted almost anything Adams proposed.

THE BRITISH TORCH WASHINGTON, D.C., IN THE WAR OF 1812

This 1815 engraving depicts the attack of Washington, D.C., by the British during the War of 1812. The U.S. capital is in flames as the British army gathers in the foreground.

PRESIDENTIAL MUSCLE: ANDREW JACKSON *and* THOSE WHO FOLLOWED

(1829–1849)

ANDREW JACKSON

Wild, Headstrong, Ambitious

WEEK 9

A YOUNG JACKSON FIGHTS THE BRITISH
IN THE EVOLUTIONARY WAR

Andrew Jackson and his two brothers were raised by their mother, Elizabeth. Their father died just before Andrew was born in 1767. In 1778, during the Revolutionary War, the Jackson family sided with the American revolutionaries. Andrew's mother often recounted stories of her own father's suffering at the siege of Carrickfergus, and urged her sons "to expend their lives, if it should become necessary, in defending and supporting the natural rights of man."

In 1779, in that defense, Andrew's older brother, Hugh, sixteen, died after one battle. In April 1781, Andrew and his brother Robert were trapped by redcoats in a relative's house. A haughty English soldier ordered Jackson to polish his boots. Jackson refused. "Sir," said the fourteen-year-old, "I am a prisoner of war, and claim to be treated as such." The officer swung his sword, and Jackson raised his arm to protect himself. The sword cut his hand and head, scarring him for life. Andrew's brother Robert also refused to shine the boots, and he, too, was hit with the sword and would die later after being imprisoned. After Jackson's mother nursed Andrew back to health from the smallpox he also caught in the British prison, she went to care for two nephews, and then she died suddenly of cholera. Jackson was now without family, an orphan left to fend for himself in the western frontier.

"Sometime in his early life," writes Jackson historian H. W. Brands, "perhaps when the blood from that British saber wound streaked his face, perhaps when his mother and brothers died and he found himself alone, perhaps when he crossed the mountains to the frontier West—he became peculiarly attached to the cause of his country. Lacking a family, he identified with the American people. . . . Whatever endangered them—the designs of the British, the weakness of the Spanish, the resistance of the Indians, . . . the machinations of the nullifiers, the corruption of the Whigs—elicited an immediate response, and sometimes an intemperate one. . . ."

A WILD YOUTH

At age seventeen, Jackson was a teacher, but soon found that the profession did not provide the adventure, advancement, or financial rewards he needed to support the pleasures of horse racing and cockfighting. He decided to study the law instead, and in 1784 he traveled seventy-five miles to Salisbury, North Carolina, to join a law office. But after hours, he "was the most roaring, rollicking, game-cocking, horse-racing, card-playing, mischievous fellow, that ever lived in Salisbury," according to one fellow rabble-rouser. An acquaintance of Jackson's later said that few in Salisbury expected much of him. "None of them believed he would ever settle down. Most of them thought he would get himself killed before long."

He attended a dance school, and managed to dust up trouble there while organizing a Christmas ball. Jackson sent invitations to Molly Wood and her daughter, Rachel, two of the town's finest ladies of the evening. When they walked in the door, the more respectable ladies stopped dancing until mother and daughter were escorted from the room. Jackson was reprimanded, and gave the excuse that he meant it only as a joke and never expected the pair to attend.

Another night, Jackson and his friends had a glorious evening drinking at the Rowan House, the town tavern. Thinking the glasses they used sacred and believing they never should be desecrated, they smashed them in the fire. They then smashed their table, the chairs, and a bed. They then torched a pile of clothes and curtains.

When Jackson gained national prominence years later, those who knew him in Salisbury were stunned. "What!" cried an elderly matron in the village. "Jackson up for the President? *Jackson? Andrew Jackson?* . . . Why, when he was here, he was such a rake that my husband would not bring him into the house! It's true, he *might* have taken him out to the stable to weigh horses for a race, and might drink a glass of whiskey with him *there*. Well, if Andrew Jackson can be President, anybody can!"

JACKSON'S REJECTION OF WASHINGTON AND JEFFERSON

Many politicians of the early American Republic followed the political star of George Washington or Thomas Jefferson, choosing sides in the political divide between Federalists and Republicans. But Andrew Jackson was one of the few politicians who rebuked *both* political giants, yet somehow managed to get elected president.

Jackson had arrived at the end of Washington's second term. Albert Gallatin, Washington's financial minister, described Jackson as "a tall, lank, uncouth-looking personage, with long locks of hair hanging over his face, . . . tied in an eel skin; his dress singular, his manners and deportment those of a rough backwoodsman." On the third day of the congressional session, Jackson was present to hear Washington's Farewell Address. A largely ceremonial vote was held for its adoption, but Jackson was one of the few congressmen to vote against it. He had disapproved of the controversial Jay Treaty with Great Britain pushed by Washington, believing it belittled and dishonored the infant nation. He also disapproved of Washington's relatively enlightened Native American policy, which respected the signed treaties between the new American nation and Native American ones, which Jackson would one day undermine.

Jackson's dispute with Jefferson was more related to personal politics than policy. Jackson lobbied Jefferson hard for the governorship of the Orleans Territory, one of the territories carved out of the Louisiana Purchase. Jackson convinced the entire Tennessee congressional delegation to sign a petition for his appointment, but Jefferson selected someone else for the post. For many politicians, it would have been a disappointment, but all politics was personal for Jackson, and he was forever after bitter toward Jefferson. In 1808, he took his revenge by supporting James Monroe to succeed Jefferson rather than James Madison, Jefferson's handpicked successor.

Still, it was voting against the tribute to Washington that became an issue when Jackson himself ran for president. How could a man who so disrespected Washington, Jackson's detractors asked, consider himself deserving of the presidency?

A DESIRE TO DUEL

Much of Andrew Jackson's personality—his love of gambling, his explosive temper, his fierce love of his wife, his steely will—was evident in a duel he fought in 1806 with Charles Dickinson, a Tennessee dandy. The dispute started over the question of how much Dickinson owed Jackson for a horse race. Dickinson had apparently also bad-mouthed what Jackson called the "sacred name" of his wife, Rachel, most likely alluding to the oft-repeated charge that she had taken up with the young Jackson while she was still married.

Jackson demanded a duel, and Dickinson, reputedly the best shot in Tennessee, agreed. Dickinson was said to be in good spirits on the morning of their duel. They stood eight paces from each other when Jackson's "second" in the duel, Thomas Overton, asked, "Are you ready?" Both responded that they were.

"Fire!" Duels depended as much on strategy as they did on aim. The dueler could aim quickly and fire first, killing or disabling his opponent. Or he could let his opponent shoot first, betting on a miss or a nonlethal wound that would give him time for a more leisurely return shot. Dickinson decided to fire quickly. A puff rose from the breast of Jackson's coat. Jackson's reaction was so restrained that Dickinson cried, "Great God! Have I missed him?" Finally Jackson raised his gun and fired, hitting Dickinson in the gut. Dickinson dropped to the ground. In a few hours, he was dead.

Jackson mounted his horse and rode to a nearby tavern, the extent of his wound unclear until his boot filled with blood. The shot had fractured one of his ribs and clipped his breastbone. It had lodged about an inch from his heart, complicating his health for the rest of his life. The woman who nursed Jackson back to health was the woman whose honor he had fought to protect—Rachel. "If he had shot me through the brain, sir," Jackson told a friend afterward, "I should still have killed him."

JACKSON WINS THE BATTLE OF NEW ORLEANS

The winter of 1814–1815 was the bleakest America had faced since Valley Forge thirty-seven years earlier. The British had torched Washington in the summer of 1814, and planned to take New Orleans and sever the Louisiana Purchase from the United States, which would have diminished the country by half. Tennessee's Andrew Jackson had gained fame fighting Indians, but few expected he could stop the British army and fleet, the mightiest in the world.

The eighty-gun British warship, the *Tonnant*, led fifty-nine warships to New Orleans, carrying fourteen thousand redcoats. They were led by Major General Sir Edward Michael Pakenham, who had fought with the Duke of Wellington against Napoleon's best-trained troops—and had beaten them.

Jackson, arriving in New Orleans first, assembled one of the oddest assortment of men ever to fight together in the U.S. Army, including Indians, frontiersmen, Creoles, blacks, Spaniards, and even patriotic pirates.

Panic struck New Orleans when the British landed. Swearing that "[t]he enemy shall never reach the city," Jackson attacked the invaders at night. Then the general had his men dig earthworks along a mile-wide front extending from the Mississippi.

On January 8, 1815, Pakenham attacked. But the British didn't have enough ladders to scale the American breastworks. The American sharpshooters and batteries killed three hundred redcoats, including Pakenham, wounding another twelve hundred and capturing hundreds more. Only thirteen Americans died.

Jackson, forty-eight years old, had secured the most thorough American victory against the British ever. "Glory be to God that the barbarians have been defeated," wrote the *Niles' Weekly Register*, ". . . . Glory to Jackson . . . Glory to the militia . . . Sons of freedom—saviors of Orleans—benefactors of your country and avengers of its wrongs, all hail!" For the rest of his life, Jackson would be the most popular man in America.

FIGHTING SEMINOLES—AND TAKING FLORIDA

As white settlers moved southward into the Gulf Coast, they sparred with Seminole Indians along the border of Florida, still controlled by the Spanish. In late 1817, American soldiers burned an Indian village, killing Seminole soldiers and women, and the Seminole retaliated, ambushing a boat, killing forty U.S. soldiers, seven wives, and four children. The day after Christmas 1817, President James Monroe called on General Andrew Jackson to lead U.S. soldiers and quell the Seminoles (for Jackson's later anti-Indian policies, see page 362).

The Seminoles fled to Florida. Either exceeding orders or acting on the hidden agenda of President James Monroe, Jackson followed, invading the Spanish territory. Jackson hunted down what Seminoles he could find, and then captured the "hated dons" in the territory in May 1818, taking Pensacola. The Spanish governor demanded that Jackson retreat from Florida, but the general, thinking he had the president's support, sailed the Spanish governor, soldiers, and officials to Havana.

With the Seminoles subdued and the Spanish removed, Jackson returned to Nashville, where he was showered with adulation. But politicians in Washington were more circumspect, given that Jackson had invaded Spanish territory and banished its government, roiling international political waters. The Spanish minister wanted Florida returned and Jackson punished.

Some ambitious Washington politicians, including Henry Clay and John Calhoun, feared Jackson's popularity, and thought he had trampled on the Constitution by starting a war without congressional approval. Monroe denied involvement, explaining to the Spanish that Jackson had only invaded Florida to get the Seminoles, and he returned the Florida forts. But Spain, having lost territory in South America and reminded of its vulnerability to American conquest in Florida, decided to cut its losses. Under the Adams-Onís Treaty, signed on February 22, 1819, Americans purchased Florida from Spain for $5 million.

Jackson's popularity exploded again, as it had after the Battle of New Orleans, and crowds hailed him at parades and honorary dinners. Jackson didn't realize it yet, but his military days were now mostly behind him. He soon developed a habit of tipping his hat, a gesture not of the general, but of the humble politician.

THE BATTLE OF NEW ORLEANS

The Battle Of New Orleans, January 8, 1815, was the final major battle of the War of 1812, and a great American victory. In this 1910 painting, Major General Andrew Jackson stands on an embankment as his troops fight off the British army, preventing them from taking the city—and becoming famous as he did so.

ANDREW JACKSON

Jackson Grabs the Reins of Power

WEEK 10

JACKSON LOSES THE 1824 ELECTION
TO A "CORRUPT BARGAIN"

By 1824, Andrew Jackson, self-made man, Indian fighter, hero at New Orleans, was well positioned for a presidential run. "His strength lay with the masses," wrote one observer, "and he knew it." Jackson dominated the popular vote, winning 152,901 votes; John Quincy Adams, son of John Adams, finished second with 114,023. Jackson also won the most electoral votes—99 to Adams's 84—but he needed a majority of 131 to claim the presidency.

As required by the Twelfth Amendment to the Constitution, the House of Representatives would select the winner among the top three candidates. Congressman Henry Clay, who finished fourth, had enough clout in the House to "end the presidential election within the hour" if Jackson would dismiss Adams as secretary of state and appoint Clay. Jackson refused, telling a supporter that his election "must be the free choice of the people. . . ."

Clay was naturally inclined toward Adams, and dismissed Jackson as a "military chieftain." As he wrote of Jackson's actions in the War of 1812: "I cannot believe that killing 2500 Englishmen at New Orleans qualifies for the various, difficult and complicated duties of the Chief Magistrate." Clay also liked Adams's experience and approved his promise to invest in infrastructure and a national university.

Privately, Adams apparently offered Clay the position of secretary of state, often the stepping-stone to the presidency. In return, Clay publicly supported Adams, which gave him the presidency. At a reception given by James Monroe the night of Adams's victory, the defeated Jackson walked up to the president-elect and offered his hand.

"How do you do, Mr. Adams?" he said. "I hope you are well, sir."

"Very well, sir," replied Adams. "I hope General Jackson is well."

Jackson was seething. When Adams announced his appointment of Clay a few days later, Jackson exploded. "So you see," he roared, "the Judas of the West has closed the contract and will receive the thirty pieces of silver." He spoke of a "corrupt bargain" between the two men, and the charge, levied just days after one election ended, became the rallying cry for the next.

JACKSON'S BITTERSWEET ELECTION OF 1828

Andrew Jackson suffered many slanders during the presidential campaign of 1828, one of the most malicious in American history (for more on the election of 1828, see page 344). But the one that hurt most was made by supporters of John Quincy Adams against Jackson's beloved wife, Rachel. They said that Jackson had cavorted with Rachel while she was still married—which was probably true. Newspapers called her an adulteress and smeared her as a "dirty, black wench!"

Jackson confessed to his advisor William Lewis of "such feelings of indignation that I can scarcely control." He vowed that "[t]he day of retribution and vengeance must come when the guilty will meet with their just reward." That day was the election, when Jackson won 647,000 votes to Adams's 508,000, and prevailed in the electoral college, 178 to 83. The general of the people had crushed the aristocratic Adams, winning every state south of the Potomac and west of the Alleghenies. Rachel was happy for her husband's success, but she wasn't looking forward to life as the president's wife. "Hitherto my Savior has been my guide and support through all my afflictions (which I must confess for the last four years have been many and unprovoked), and now I have no doubt but he will still aid and instruct me in my duties which I fear will be many and arduous."

On December 18, just two weeks after Jackson was officially elected, Rachel suffered a heart attack. For three days she lingered, but on the fourth day she deteriorated, and died. A friend noted that Jackson clutched her so tightly that she had to be pried from him. Another witness said he looked "twenty years older in a night." Jackson blamed her attackers for her death. He dragged himself to his inaugural at the last minute. "O, how fluctuating are all earthly things," he wrote a friend the following summer. "At the time I least expected it, and could least spare her, she was snatched from me, and I left here a solitary monument of grief, without the least hope of happiness here below. . . ."

AN INAUGURATION UNLIKE ANY OTHER

March 4, 1828, came springlike, with Andrew Jackson's supporters shooting a cannon to herald his inauguration, one of the most enduring memories in American presidential history. The people mobbed the Capitol grounds in anticipation of the ceremonies and a ship's cable was pulled across the steps of the portico to keep them at bay. "It is beautiful," Francis Scott Key said of the attendance of high and low, "it is sublime."

When the crowds spotted the general through the columns of the portico they erupted in shouting that seemed "to shake the very ground . . . ten thousand upturned and exultant human faces, radiant with sudden joy." Jackson bowed low before "the majesty of the people." The oath was given, Jackson kissed the Bible—eliciting more cheers—and then the president quietly read his speech, which lasted ten minutes. Then Jackson struggled to get to his white stallion, which slowly walked to the White House, followed by "[c]ountry men, farmers, gentlemen, mounted and dismounted, boys, women and children, black and white."

Jackson began the White House festivities by shaking hands, but the press of the crowd proved so great he fled out a side entrance to his lodging at Gadsby's Hotel. The crowd then turned to the food and drink, spilling liquor on White House carpets, muddying sofas when they climbed upon them to get a look around, and shattering china and glassware. Vats of orange punch and liquor were carried to the White House garden to entice the mob outside, and some climbed out windows to get to it. One congressman called it a "regular Saturnalia," and labeled the people gathered as "one uninterrupted stream of mud and filth . . . many subjects for the penitentiary. . . ." An associate justice of the Supreme Court concluded: "The reign of King 'Mob' seemed triumphant."

Others saw the unprecedented swarming of the White House as the common man celebrating one of their own elected to the presidency. "It was the People's day," said one longtime Washington observer, "and the People's President, and the People would rule."

"ROTATION IN OFFICE"—OR JACKSON'S SPOILS SYSTEM

The victory of Andrew Jackson over John Quincy Adams was a hostile takeover. Congressman Henry Clay spoke of "the greatest . . . apprehension" among the Washington elite. John Quincy Adams explained, "A large portion of the population of Washington are dependent for bread upon these offices. . . . Every one is in breathless expectation, trembling at heart, afraid to speak." These men saw the replacement of the governmental class as more than personal misfortune; they saw it as the ruin of professional government, and the ruin of the country.

Experience had led many to believe that their appointments were nearly permanent. According to a count made by James Parton, an early Jackson biographer, George Washington and John Adams had removed just nine people from office between them; James Madison, five; James Monroe, nine; and John Quincy Adams, just two. Thomas Jefferson replaced thirty-nine, partly as an effort to replace the Federalist appointees of Washington and Adams with Republicans.

Jackson saw the removal of former bureaucrats as a moral as well as a political necessity. He compared himself to Hercules whose job it was to "cleanse the Augean stables." He believed that too cozy a seat in government bred corruption. "[Office holders] are apt to acquire a habit of looking with indifference upon the public interests and of tolerating conduct from which an unpracticed man would revolt," Jackson said.

Best estimates say that Jackson replaced between one or two in ten officeholders, about the same rate as Jefferson's housecleaning. Jackson tried to portray the replacement of the governmental appointees as good government, a "rotation in office." But Governor William Marcy of New York, a Jackson ally, said that politicians in his state saw "nothing wrong in the rule that to the victor belong the spoils." Marcy's phrase has stayed with us; today we call the replacement of bureaucrats by a new administration the "spoils system."

FROM PRESIDENTIAL CABINET TO KITCHEN CABINET

Andrew Jackson pronounced his new cabinet "one of the strongest . . . that ever have been in the United States. . . ." But in truth it was weak, with only Martin Van Buren meriting the praise. Even Jackson didn't respect them enough to keep them around, leading to turnover hard to match in presidential cabinet history. In eight years he had five treasury secretaries, four secretaries of state, three attorneys general, three navy secretaries, three postmasters general, and two secretaries of war.

The rule was simple: Follow Jackson's wishes, or be fired. In 1831, as a result of political sniping about the virtue of the wife of one cabinet member, Jackson forced his entire cabinet to resign.

For advice, Jackson turned to an informal and unofficial group of advisors called the Kitchen Cabinet—who didn't have to be approved by the Senate. (The term connoted men sneaking into the White House via the back, or "kitchen," stairs.) Many of these advisors were men who had helped him get elected, old Tennessee men such as John H. Eaton, William B. Lewis, and Andrew J. Donelson. Others included newspaper editors, including Amos Kendall and Isaac Hill, who had both previously wrestled up support for the general, or Francis Blair, of the Washington Globe.

Others in the group included Roger B. Taney, whom Jackson would later appoint to the Supreme Court. Also part of the inner circle was Martin Van Buren, who would become Jackson's second-term vice president and handpicked successor. Jackson sought the advice of the Kitchen Cabinet more often than his regular cabinet, but they were not the power behind the throne. They simply helped Jackson pursue his agenda. Through it all, it was never one advisor, or a group of advisors, who made the final decision. It was President Jackson.

THE PETTICOAT AFFAIR

Margaret "Peggy" Eaton had married John Henry Eaton just before Jackson appointed him secretary of war. Peggy had worked at her family's tavern, the Franklin House in Washington, and had gained a scandalous reputation as a teen. Rumored indiscretions included one suitor who swallowed poison when she turned him down; a brief affair with the son of President Thomas Jefferson's treasury secretary; and a planned elopement with an aide to General Winfield Scott that went awry when her father caught her exiting a bedroom window. Her reputation was further muddied when her first husband, John Timberlake, a navy officer, died in Europe; rumor had it that he had killed himself over Margaret's infidelities.

One of Jackson's advisors recommended he not appoint Eaton secretary of war because many of the cabinet officer wives disapproved of Peggy. When Jackson defiantly appointed Eaton, his administration was immediately afflicted by what Secretary of State Martin Van Buren called "Eaton malaria."

Wives of cabinet members snubbed Peggy. Some of the attacks were probably provoked by jealousy—Peggy was beautiful, well educated, a French speaker, and a fine piano player. Jackson took up her cause, as the pillorying she received echoed the slanders directed earlier at his wife, Rachel. He personally investigated Peggy's reputation and devoted entire cabinet meetings to her defense. The controversy dragged on for two years.

The president soon suspected that ambition was involved in the attacks on Peggy. He believed John Calhoun, his vice president and a Jackson rival, was encouraging Margaret's detractors—cabinet members as well as their wives—to hurt his presidency.

Finally, Jackson realized he needed to take action. Van Buren came up with a solution. He and Eaton offered their resignations. Jackson accepted them, then asked the rest of the cabinet to offer theirs. He appointed an entirely new cabinet. "If other revolutions partake of the sublime," John Quincy Adams said, "this one entirely and exclusively belongs to the next step." He was referring to the ridiculous.

ANDREW JACKSON DEMANDS
THAT HIS ENTIRE CABINET RESIGN

Andrew Jackson's cabinet was often in turmoil. This political cartoon, titled "The Rats Leaving a Falling House," depicts how Jackson forced cabinet members out in the spring of 1831 in the wake of the Peggy Eaton, or Petticoat, affair.

ANDREW JACKSON

Jackson Creates a Powerful Presidency

WEEK 11

JACKSON EXPANDS THE PRESIDENCY
THROUGH THE VETO POWER

After Andrew Jackson's first string of presidential vetoes, John Quincy Adams said: "These are remarkable events. . . . The Presidential veto has hitherto been exercised in great reserve. No more than four or five Acts of Congress have been thus arrested by six Presidents, and in forty years. He has rejected four in three days. The overseer ascendancy is complete."

The early presidents used the veto only to block legislation that they found blatantly unconstitutional. Using it to block other legislation would undermine the power of Congress, which they believed was the dominant branch of government. For Jackson, the veto became a political tool that the president—a national figure, as opposed to the parochial figures in Congress—could wield to protect what he perceived as the interests of the American people. Or just to kill legislation he didn't like. The threat of a presidential veto forced legislators to negotiate their bills with the executive office before putting them up for a vote, a new wrinkle in the American political process.

The first six presidents used the veto nine times, three times for important legislation. Jackson vetoed twelve bills during his two terms. His vetoes were accompanied with strong political statements as to why the measures were unwise, unjust, or simply foolish. His example would be followed by some of America's strongest presidents, including Theodore Roosevelt, Woodrow Wilson, and Franklin Roosevelt, who all used the veto to shape or kill legislation.

"Those who . . . insisted on characterizing him as an arrogant, militaristic hothead, slamming around the White House and shooting from the hip and lip at the slightest provocation, will never admit to his statesmanship or understand his contribution to the presidency," writes Jackson biographer Robert Remini. "But those who will gauge his skills and insights into the political process, and measure the distance he stretched the executive powers, will discover some of the factors that constitute his greatness as an American President."

THE TRAGEDY OF THE INDIAN REMOVAL ACT

Should Americans coexist with the Indians, or should they defeat them militarily and move them westward to land where whites hadn't yet settled? Few Indians still resided in the Northeast during the 1820s, but it was still a pressing question in the South. Plantation owners wanted rich soil to grow cotton in what is now Georgia, Florida, Alabama, and Mississippi, land that was then occupied by Creek, Cherokee, Chickasaw, Choctaw, and Seminole tribes.

The conflict flared in late 1827, when officials in Georgia and Alabama claimed that despite treaties, they, not the tribes, had sovereignty over the land. President Andrew Jackson, who had fought the Creeks in Georgia and Alabama and the Seminoles in Florida in his military days, sided forcefully with the states. He wrote to the Creeks: "Where you now are, you and my white children are too near to each other to live in harmony and peace. . . . Beyond the great river Mississippi, where a part of your nation has gone, your father has provided a country large enough for all of you. . . . It will be yours forever."

Jackson's pronouncement contained an implied threat: Leave voluntarily, or we will run you off the land. "Those tribes cannot exist surrounded by our settlements," he would say later. "They have neither the intelligence nor the moral habits. Established in the midst of a superior race, they must disappear." Besides, in Jackson's view, Indians threatened to "Butcher our Citizens."

Jackson's belief that the rights of Indians were secondary was common, but many of Jackson's contemporaries found his determination to drive southern Indians from their lands excessive. When Jackson pushed through the Indian Removal Act midway into his first term, one congressman called the law "inconsistent with the plainest principles of moral honesty." Under the law, Jackson forcibly moved tens of thousands of Indians west of the Mississippi, opening twenty-five million acres to white settlement, cotton, farming—and to slavery.

THE NULLIFICATION CRISIS—
THE UNION VS. STATES' RIGHTS

Of all the political battles Andrew Jackson fought, the battle he waged with South Carolina and his vice president, John C. Calhoun, was one of the toughest. It had an innocuous name—the Nullification Crisis of 1832—but it was a classic case of federal vs. state power that would lead Jackson and his opponents to the brink of civil war.

The conflict was sparked in 1828 when Congress established steep tariffs on goods—as high as 60 percent—to protect northern manufacturers. Southern agricultural states bitterly opposed these tariffs, and argued the Union was merely a compact between states that had the right to "nullify" any federal act they felt violated their sovereignty or rights. The congressional "Nullifiers," as they were called, planned to make twenty-four toasts to support the doctrine of nullification on April 13, 1830, the annual celebration of Thomas Jefferson's birthday.

Jackson got word of the planned political theater the day before the event, and wrote his own toast. "Our Union," he said in an even voice. "It *must* be preserved." Those six words were the most famous Jackson would ever utter. The issue simmered until 1832, when South Carolinians passed a law forbidding the collection of tariffs in the state and said that if Congress authorized force for their collection, the state would secede. Jackson responded by publishing his own Nullification Proclamation that said if a state had "a right to secede and destroy this union . . . then indeed is our constitution a rope of sand; under which I would not live."

Jackson said that the federal government must be prepared to "crush the monster in its cradle." He sent word to South Carolinians that fifty thousand soldiers could be sent to the state in forty days, and fifty thousand more in another forty. Many, including Jackson, expected civil war to break out, but Henry Clay brokered a compromise. A week later, South Carolina's agitators backed down and Congress passed a bill that would gradually lower tariff rates over ten years until none was higher than 20 percent. The bill would cause economic havoc down the road, but it gave a chance for everyone to declare victory—Calhoun, the South Carolinians, the tariff supporters—and Jackson.

BATTLING THE BANKS ON BEHALF OF THE PEOPLE

Andrew Jackson didn't know or care much about economics, which makes it rather odd that the greatest battle he would wage as president was over the Second Bank of the United States, established by Congress in 1816 as a central bank to regulate credit and stabilize the currency.

The bank branched out into twenty-nine cities. It handled one in five loans in the country and one-third of all bank deposits and specie, but was largely unregulated by government or law. Congress easily passed a bill to recharter it in the early summer of 1832; even some of Jackson's Democrats went along with the bill, fearing that without it "the country will be ruined . . . & no sound currency extant."

Martin Van Buren, Jackson's close aide, returned to Washington in July and found the president lying on a sofa in the White House, looking old, tired, and ill. Some had talked of changing the bank's charter to allow government oversight of the largely unregulated bank. But Jackson didn't want to compromise; he saw the bill as a personal battle, and one where the winner would take all. There were rumors that the bank had used its vast power against him in the election of 1828 and would do so again.

"The bank, Mr. Van Buren, is trying to kill me," he said, "*but I will kill it.*"

Jackson vetoed the rechartering, pointing out that $8 million of the bank's stock was held by foreigners, "and why should the few enjoy the special favor of this country?" Worse yet, he said, "the rich and powerful too often bend the acts of government to their selfish purposes" and could "destroy our republican institutions." Indeed, it had extended loans to important politicians, including Daniel Webster and Henry Clay.

Jackson called on support from "the humble members of society . . . who have neither the time nor the means of securing like favors to themselves. . . ." Jackson was reaching to his people—the masses—willing to gamble that he and antibank sentiment would prevail in the 1832 election.

CRUSHING THE FEDERAL BANK

The bank became the issue of the 1832 election. Henry Clay, Andrew Jackson's presidential rival, argued the bank provided a stable currency and an orderly financial climate. Jackson's supporters maintained that the bank was shifting wealth and power to the country's aristocracy.

Jackson won by a landslide, defeating Henry Clay by a 219 to 49 vote in the electoral college and winning 687,502 votes cast to 566,297 for his two rivals.

Jackson took the vote as a mandate and determined to transfer money from the federal bank to state banks. Under the 1816 law that established the bank, only the secretary of the treasury could withdraw its money. When Treasury Secretary Louis McLane indicated he wouldn't do it, Jackson asked Congress for authority to withdraw the funds. When they refused, he went back to McLane, who refused again. Jackson replaced McLane with William J. Duane. When Duane refused, Jackson fired him as well, moving Roger B. Taney from his post as attorney general. Taney finally agreed, but the Senate would censure both Taney and Jackson for the act.

To get Jackson to back down, Nicholas Biddle, the bank's chief, called in the bank's loans, and a general financial panic followed. Many called for compromise, but not Jackson. "I have it chained," he fumed, "*the monster must perish.*"

Jackson killed the bank, and an economic crisis did follow after he left office. "On balance, it seems most reasonable to say that the nation's interests would have been best served had the Bank been reformed rather than altogether crushed," writes John Meacham in his Jackson biography, *American Lion.* "The more important point . . . is that the president of the United States made a bold bid to place himself at the absolute center of the country's life and governance, eliminating a rival by building an emotional case, repeating his point over and over again . . . then seeking and winning vindication at the polls." It was a political game plan that powerful presidents would often repeat.

JACKSONIAN DEMOCRACY

Andrew Jackson, biographer Robert Remini says, is "the man whose name is forever linked to the magnificent egalitarian surge that occurred in the middle period of American history." He is the only president who has an entire age named after him—the Jacksonian Era, during which Jacksonian Democracy flourished. His presidency was an answer to that of John Adams, who doubted the ability of ordinary Americans to rule themselves. Adams saw the election of Jackson as one more example of the decline of the Republic and the poor judgment of the masses. Jackson believed in the people.

Jackson instigated two fundamental upheavals in American politics. First, he launched the modern party system, with its reliance on rallies and parades, buttons and barbecues, and even the beginning of public appearances by candidates. More fundamentally, he made the president the advocate of the people. In his written protest to his congressional censure during the bank fight, Jackson perhaps best expressed the role of the president and government, as he saw it. All he had meant to do, he wrote, was

to return to the people unimpaired the sacred trust they have confided to my charge; to heal the wounds of the Constitution and preserve it from further violation; to persuade my countrymen, as far as I may, that it is not in a splendid government supported by powerful monopolies and aristocratical establishments that they will find happiness or their liberties protection, but in a plain system, void of pomp, protecting all and granting favors to none. . . .

This daguerreotype of Andrew Jackson was taken in April 1845, months before Andrew Jackson's death on June 8 at the age of seventy-eight. Contributing to his death were chronic tuberculosis, dropsy, and heart failure.

Struggling in Jackson's Shadow—
Martin Van Buren, William H. Harrison,
John Tyler, and James K. Polk

WEEK 12

MARTIN VAN BUREN ENDS
THE PRESIDENTIAL SILENCE ON SLAVERY

Until Martin Van Buren came into office in 1837, presidents remained silent on the contentious slavery issue in public. But in the 1830s, as Van Buren approached the office, the issue slipped from the shadows. By the time of his election, 274 abolition societies had formed in New York State. In 1837, a man named John Brown committed his life to ending slavery; in 1838, Frederick Douglass escaped from bondage.

In the South, the institution many expected would fade expanded dramatically with the invention of the cotton gin in the early 1800s, making the ownership of humans more profitable than ever. Abolitionists and slaveholders were on a collision course.

Van Buren, a New Yorker, tried to prevent the northern and southern wings of the Democratic Party from tearing apart over the issue. John Quincy Adams, the former president, described him as a "northern man with southern feelings." He'd grown up in a home with domestic slaves and had owned a slave who'd run away. To court southern Democratic support in his presidential run, Van Buren had his supporters disrupt abolitionist meetings and mailings in New York. Nationally, he supported the so called gag rule, requiring all abolitionist petitions to be tabled in Congress.

He was the first president to mention slavery in his inaugural address, announcing unequivocally that he was "the inflexible and uncompromising opponent of every attempt on the part of Congress to abolish slavery in the District of Columbia." He also assured Southerners that he would not present "the slightest interference with [slavery] in the States where it exists," a refrain that presidents would repeat over the next quarter century. He acted on this conviction to stay neutral when he ordered mutinied slaves on the slave ship *Amistad* returned to Spanish owners.

But Van Buren would take one principled stand against slavery. That was his refusal to annex Texas, rightfully fearing that the question about whether to allow slavery in new territories could tear the nation apart. That caution sealed his inability to get a follow-up presidential nomination in 1844. Van Buren would live until 1862, just long enough to see the fight over slavery nearly destroy the nation.

MARTIN VAN BUREN—
UNDERMINED BY THE PANIC OF 1837

Throughout his entire political career, Martin Van Buren had been acknowledged as a deft politician. He served as a key advisor to Andrew Jackson, the most dominant figure of his era, who chose him as his heir apparent in 1836. Van Buren promised he would "follow in the footsteps of his illustrious predecessor," and to prove his sincerity, he kept on Jackson's entire cabinet.

But within weeks of his inauguration, Van Buren and the country were hit with what insurance brokers call an "act of God"—the Panic of 1837. The word *panic* exaggerates some economic calamities; in this case, it didn't do it justice. It was the worst economic collapse up to its time, and the worst until the Great Depression nearly a century later. Of the 850 banks around the country, 343 went bankrupt and another 62 partially failed. In six months, unemployment spiked above 25 percent; wages fell more than that. The decentralized banking system that Jackson had willed on the country and his other fiscal policies probably contributed to the collapse. Van Buren had ridden Andrew Jackson's monetary policies into power; now he was dragged down by the association.

A fiscal conservative, the president slashed public expenditures by 20 percent, opposing public works projects that might have eased unemployment. It was the worst thing he could have done. Then Van Buren redecorated the White House. He spent moderate sums, but the painters and upholsterers who paraded through the White House gave ammunition to political enemies and editorial writers. The man who'd been given many flattering nicknames during his political rise—the Red Fox, the Great Manager, the Master Spirit—was now tagged as Martin Van Ruin.

In the election of 1840, Whigs sang, "Van, Van's a used-up man," and politically, he was. The election of 1840 is considered the first modern one, with two well-organized parties that whipped up the electorate with torchlight parades, speeches, and mass rallies. Eighty percent of the eligible electorate voted, the third highest turnout on record. Unfortunately for Van Buren, most came out for Whig William Henry Harrison, who won in a landslide, even taking Van Buren's home state of New York.

WILLIAM HENRY HARRISON—
DIED FROM TRYING TOO HARD

What William Henry Harrison wanted to do at his inauguration in 1841 was to dispel the notion that he was a drunken backwoodsman—a stereotype conjured up during the country's first full-fledged presidential campaign that brought him into the presidency. His Whig Party men had claimed that Harrison was born in a log cabin, a claim made to win Harrison western votes, although the truth was that he was raised on a Virginia plantation. That led Democrats to mock his pretensions by suggesting that with "a barrel of hard cider and . . . a pension of $2,000," old Tippecanoe could "sit the remainder of his days in his log cabin."

Harrison hadn't liked the branding and planned to adopt a more presidential profile by giving a scholarly inaugural address. He intended to show off his classical learning to prove he was on a par with other well-schooled Virginian presidents such as Thomas Jefferson and James Madison. Harrison's colleague, Daniel Webster, edited the speech, and showed up late for one preinaugural dinner party, explaining, "I've just killed seventeen Roman proconsuls." The joke was a reference to all the classical references he'd deleted from Harrison's speech.

Even with Webster's editing, Harrison managed to give the longest inaugural address in American history on March 4, 1841, speaking for an hour and forty minutes. To show his vigor, the former general decided to make the speech without an overcoat or a hat as an icy rain fell. Afterward, he attended receptions in his soggy, cold clothes. Exposure to the weather hadn't hurt him as a young farmer, soldier, or outdoorsman; but this time he caught a cold, which turned into pneumonia. Doctors made efforts, using heated suction cups to draw out the disease and bleeding him, but exactly one month later, on April 4, Harrison became the first president to die in office. His would also be the most fleeting presidency in American history.

JOHN TYLER—DEFIANT FROM BEGINNING TO END

Throughout his presidency, John Tyler battled his cabinet, his Congress, and his party. Tyler, who had held Virginia offices such as governor and senator, was added to the presidential ticket of Ohio politician William Henry Harrison to provide a southern balance to the Whig ticket. When Harrison died, Tyler was in a confusing constitutional position.

The Constitution specified that on the removal or death of a president, the "powers and duties . . . shall devolve on the Vice-President." But what the Constitution writers left unclear was whether that meant the vice president *became* president or just took on the role until a new presidential election could be held. The Whigs who had elected the Tippecanoe and Tyler ticket, not enamored with Tyler's politics, thought an election was called for, and addressed him as "Vice President, Acting as President." But Tyler insisted on being called President Tyler and told all he planned to serve Harrison's four-year term.

The next confrontation was with his Whig cabinet members, who wanted Tyler to obtain a consensus on all important decisions, a practice followed by such presidents as James Madison, James Monroe, and John Quincy Adams. "I am the President," Tyler responded. "When you think otherwise, your resignations will be accepted."

Tyler next wrestled with the Whig Congress, which passed a law to resurrect the national bank that Andrew Jackson had condemned and killed. Tyler vetoed it, instigating the resignation of his entire cabinet except his secretary of state. Whig congressmen issued a statement disowning the president and called for his resignation. Tyler was now a man without a party. Tyler chose Democrats for his cabinet, and the Whigs tried to impeach the president but failed. "He looked somewhat worn and anxious," said Charles Dickens when he visited Tyler in the White House, "and well he might, being at war with everybody."

The Whigs refused to put Tyler up for a second term. He began a third-party run, but quickly withdrew to make way for the election of Democrat James K. Polk, who would replace him in the White House. Tyler's last political office? Another contentious position: Virginia representative in the Confederate House during the Civil War.

JAMES POLK SETS FOUR "MEASURES"
FOR HIS ONE TERM

A little over a century after James Polk served as president, Harry Truman listed his top eight presidents, and in the chronological list behind Washington, Jefferson, and Jackson, he listed Polk. "A great president," Truman said of the eleventh president. "He said exactly what he was going to do, and he did it."

Truman was referring to an exchange that was remembered by George Bancroft, a historian who was also Polk's secretary of the navy. As Bancroft told it, one day early in the administration, Polk "raised his hand high in the air and bringing it down with force on his thigh" confided that he had "four great measures" of his administration, two domestic and two in foreign affairs.

He would begin by lowering the tariff, thereby sending a message that he served farmers, who detested tariffs, more than eastern industrialists. He also would establish an independent treasury. These two measures would be ready when Congress came into session in the fall of 1845.

He would also act on his belief that the nation had a manifest destiny to expand its territory from one coast to the other. Polk did this by buying Oregon from the British, his third measure. His fourth was to take California from the Mexicans. And since he promised to stay in office for just one term, he'd do it in four years, driving himself every day of the year.

"He was an obsessed workaholic, a perfectionist, a micromanager," writes biographer John Seigenthaler, "whose commitment to what he saw as his responsibility led him to virtually incarcerate himself in the White House for the full tenure of his presidency." He prodded recalcitrant congressmen; met often with his cabinet; and ceaselessly attacked paperwork, only leaving the house to attend church with his wife, Sarah, or to take an occasional horseback ride. He avoided social functions, and took vacations only when Sarah insisted his health demanded it.

In the first year and a half in office, Polk's diligence had enabled him to achieve three of his goals. But the fourth, control over California, would take more than hard work; it would take war.

POLK LAUNCHES THE CONTROVERSIAL MEXICAN WAR

President James Polk believed in "manifest destiny," the phrase editor John O'Sullivan coined in 1845 that held it was the destiny of white Americans to "overspread the continent allotted by Providence for the free development of our yearly multiplying millions." Polk achieved part of what he wanted when he'd convinced England to give up Oregon. But he also wanted disputed lands along the Texas-Mexico border and the territories of New Mexico and California. He wanted them so badly, in fact, that many at the time, including the freshman congressman Abraham Lincoln, accused him of provoking war with Mexico to get them.

Polk began by trying to negotiate a purchase of the Southwest Territories, but the Mexican government, angered by the U.S. annexation of Texas at the end of 1845, rebuffed two envoys. The envoys reported to Polk that the Mexicans were eager for war. The president ordered American troops south of the Nueces River, land that had traditionally been Mexican. The Mexican army responded to the provocation by ambushing sixteen Americans on a cavalry patrol—the incident Polk used to declare war. He disingenuously claimed, "War exists, notwithstanding all our efforts to avoid it. . . ." Then he sent the American army into Mexico to "conquer a peace."

Many rallied round the flag, but many also opposed the war, including Lincoln, who called it one "of conquest brought into existence to catch votes" and charged that Polk had exceeded his presidential authority by provoking war. Abolitionist Frederick Douglass saw the push for western lands as a sign of the nation's "cupidity and love of dominion." Many accused Southerners of instigating the war to bring in one more slave state to the Union, tipping the balance of power in Washington to slaveholders.

Polk thought the war would last a few weeks, but it lasted nearly two years. The Treaty of Guadalupe Hidalgo granted the United States a third of Mexico. In less than four years, Polk added 1,200,000 square miles to the country. But the war would cost $97 million (plus the payment of $15 million for the land) and thirteen thousand American lives, most lost to disease.

"Peace, plenty, and contentment," said a self-satisfied Polk afterward, "reign throughout our borders."

This photograph was taken of Martin Van Buren after he served his term as president from 1837 to 1841. Van Buren would live twenty-one years after he left office, long enough to witness the beginning of the Civil War.

CIVIL WAR *and* RECONSTRUCTION

(1849–1881)

Stumbling into Crisis—Zachary Taylor, Millard Fillmore, Franklin Pierce, and James Buchanan

ZACHARY TAYLOR: A SLAVEHOLDER STANDS
UP TO THE SOUTH

The acquisition of vast territory from Mexico in 1848 put an increasingly divisive question at the center of the nation's political agenda: Should the federal government allow slavery to expand beyond the borders of the existing slave states? When Zachary Taylor took office on March 5, 1849, he had no political record to suggest how he would answer that question. A career soldier and a Mexican War hero nicknamed "Rough and Ready," he had never held office, belonged to no political party, and never even voted before he ran for president.

Those who wanted slavery to expand into the Southwest Territories, however, had good reason to hope that Taylor would side with them, for Taylor was himself a slave owner, buying his first plantation, along with "18 prime hands," in 1823.

Not only did Taylor own slaves, he also was personally close to Jefferson Davis, a proslavery firebrand and the future president of the Confederacy. Davis had married Taylor's daughter Sarah without Taylor's approval, but ten years after her untimely death on their honeymoon, Taylor forgave Davis and thereafter embraced him as a son-in-law.

Taylor's ownership of slaves and his bond with Davis proved poor predictors to his actions in office. Four months after taking office, he proclaimed that the "people of the North need have no further apprehension of the extension of slavery." A year later, he vigorously opposed the efforts of Davis and other expansionists to deny California statehood unless the government opened the Southwest to slavery. And when Texas, a slave state, mobilized a militia to seize large parts of the Southwest and bring slavery to it at gunpoint, Taylor not only ordered U.S. troops to resist any attack, but threatened to "be there" in person to lead the troops into battle.

Taylor died suddenly on July 9, 1850. He had bequeathed 131 slaves to his children, asking that they "be only moderately worked." At Taylor's funeral, Jefferson Davis sat with the members of the family, but he was now far removed from his father-in-law on the issue of slavery.

MILLARD FILLMORE: PROFILE IN PREJUDICE

Millard Fillmore, the thirteenth president, never missed an opportunity to be on the wrong side of a moral issue. He was first elected to public office in 1828 as a candidate of the Anti-Masonic Party, which pandered to popular fears of a vast freemason conspiracy. In the 1844 New York gubernatorial race, he openly courted anti-Catholic and anti-immigrant voters, and then blamed his subsequent defeat on "foreign catholics."

Upon the death of Zachary Taylor in 1850, Fillmore inherited the presidency, and with it a prolonged and acrimonious congressional debate over the most politically divisive issue of the day: whether the federal government should allow slavery to expand beyond the existing slave states. Fillmore supported the expansion of slavery and successfully lobbied for the bills that, as a group, became known as the Compromise of 1850. One of these bills, in the words of Georgia's jubilant Senator Toombs, reestablished "the right of the people of any state to hold slaves in the common territory."

Denied renomination by the Whig Party in 1852, Fillmore gravitated to the nativist Know-Nothing Party, for which he was the 1856 presidential candidate. He ran on a platform to bar Catholics from holding public office or teaching in public schools, to establish a twenty-one-year residency requirement for naturalization, and to severely restrict immigration, especially from Catholic countries. Abraham Lincoln observed that if "the Know Nothings get control, [the Declaration of Independence] will read 'all men are created equal except negroes, *and foreigners, and Catholics.*'"

They didn't. Returning home to Buffalo after his defeat in 1856, Fillmore managed to put himself on the wrong side of history one last time. Although he initially supported the North during the Civil War, in 1864 Fillmore accused Lincoln of "desolating the fairest portion of our nation." He urged Lincoln to extend to "the deluded multitude [of Southerners] who have been seduced or coerced into . . . rebellion . . . every act of kindness" and to restore "them to all their rights under the Constitution"—including the right to own slaves.

MILLARD FILLMORE, SLAVE CATCHER

When Millard Fillmore assumed the presidency after the sudden death of Zachary Taylor, one of his first acts was to sign into law the Fugitive Slave Act of 1850. Passed by Congress to appease Southern extremists who were threatening secession, the law was virtually unprecedented in the scope of its assault upon civil liberties. It inflamed abolitionist sentiment in the North and provoked Harriet Beecher Stowe to write the influential antislavery novel *Uncle Tom's Cabin.*

The Fugitive Slave Act denied accused runaways the protection of habeas corpus, trial by jury, or the right to testify in court. Under it, judges who ruled for runaways would earn five dollars; those who found for slave owners would get ten. It required federal marshals to assist slave catchers, and, in the statute's words, "commanded all good citizens to aid and assist in the prompt and efficient execution of this law." Any citizen who aided escaped slaves—or even refused an order to join a federal posse to pursue them—could be fined and imprisoned.

Fillmore argued that if "experience should show [that the Act] was unnecessarily harsh, or . . . endangered the liberty of the free, . . . Congress will remedy the evil." In the meantime, he devoted himself zealously to executing it in the face of Northern resistance.

In September 1851, a Maryland slave owner, accompanied by a U.S. marshal, attempted to seize a fugitive slave in Lancaster, Pennsylvania. As a crowd sympathetic to the escaped slave gathered, the marshal tried unsuccessfully to enlist white onlookers to capture the runaway. In the ensuing melée, the slave shot and killed his master. Enraged, Fillmore had forty-one of the bystanders arrested and charged with treason. In the largest treason trial in U.S. history, the presiding judge dismissed the charges.

"God knows that I detest slavery," Fillmore wrote to Daniel Webster as he enforced the infamous law. Historian Paul Finkelman ventured, "Perhaps the Almighty did know that Fillmore secretly detested slavery but no human being would have seen this in his policies, his speeches, or the acts of his administration."

FRANKLIN PIERCE: A TRAGIC LIFE,
A TRAGIC PRESIDENCY

Tragedy marred both the life and the presidency of Franklin Pierce. Although there is no evidence that drinking impaired his work as president, he struggled with alcoholism throughout his life. He resigned from the Senate in 1842 at least in part to distance himself from the heavy-drinking culture of Washington, D.C., and eventually drank himself to death in the solitude of his New Hampshire seaside retreat. His political opponents derided him as "the hero of many a bottle."

In 1834, Pierce married Jane Appleton. Of their three children, the first died in infancy, the second succumbed to typhus at age four, and the youngest, Benjamin, perished before their eyes in a train wreck two months before Pierce's inauguration. Jane, already a semi-invalid with psychological problems, never recovered. For the first two years of her husband's presidency, she sequestered herself in her room, often writing letters to the dead "Bennie." Pierce apparently loved his wife, but one visitor to the Pierce White House observed that "[e]verything in that mansion seems cold and cheerless."

Pierce inflicted infinitely greater calamities on the nation with his decision to support the expansion of slavery. Although the Missouri Compromise of 1820 prohibited slavery in the territory of Kansas, by 1854 Southern extremists were demanding that Congress lift the prohibition. Although Pierce had campaigned on the promise that he would "resist all attempts at renewing, in Congress or out of it, the agitation of the slavery question," Southern senators persuaded Pierce to back the repeal of the Missouri Compromise, called the Kansas-Nebraska Act.

With Pierce's vigorous support, Congress voted to let residents in the Kansas and Nebraska territories decide themselves whether they would join the Union as a free or a slave state. Thus began the "bleeding [of] Kansas," as pro- and antislavery forces battled violently to determine whether the territories would become free or slave states, tipping the balance of power in Washington one way or the other. The brutal conflict inflamed sectional passions that burst into civil war soon afterward. Pierce's decision would prove to be among the most tragic a president ever made.

BUCHANAN SUPPRESSES REBELLION—IN UTAH

"This is the first rebellion which has existed in our territories, and humanity itself requires that we should put it down in such a manner that it shall be the last. To trifle with it would be to encourage it and render it formidable." Thus did President James Buchanan justify the use of military force to quell an insurrection. But it was against the Mormons of Utah in 1857, not the secessionists of South Carolina in 1860, that Buchanan aggressively defended the territorial integrity of the United States.

The Mormons had trekked to the Salt Lake Valley in 1847 to escape religious persecution. There, in what became the Utah Territory one year later, they established a theocracy, whose leader, Brigham Young, was a law unto himself. The Mormons drove out a succession of federal officials and repeatedly defied federal laws.

Two months after taking office, Buchanan ordered twenty-five hundred troops to Utah to install and protect a new governor. Brigham Young defiantly declared that Mormons "constituted henceforth a free and independent state, to be known no longer as Utah, but by their own Mormon name of Deseret." Young mobilized a two-thousand-man army, recruited Native American allies, and prepared to repel the federal troops. Fearful and paranoid, a mixed party of Mormons and Paiute tribesmen set upon and slaughtered a party of 120 pioneers in what came to be known as the Massacre at Mountain Meadows. Buchanan ordered up four more regiments. However, bureaucratic delays and bad weather prevented federal troops from reaching Utah until the spring of 1858, by which time Young had backed down and submitted to federal authority.

In the light of Buchanan's later decision to acquiesce to South Carolina's secession, it is unclear why he forcefully acted to suppress the Mormon insurrection. But whatever his reasons, Buchanan could proudly tell Congress a year later, "The Territory of Utah is [now] a subject for congratulation."

BUCHANAN—FLIRTING WITH TREASON?

Abraham Lincoln precipitated an immediate secession crisis by winning the presidency on November 6, 1860. But until Lincoln's inauguration on March 4, 1861, the Union's fate would depend upon the actions of his predecessor, James Buchanan.

Soon after the election, Buchanan almost signaled the South to secede. On December 3, 1860, when not a single state had yet left the Union, he told Congress that "the incessant and violent agitation of the slavery question throughout the North has at last produced its vulgar influence on the slaves and inspired them with vague ideas of freedom." He granted that secession was unconstitutional, but stated that neither the president nor Congress "has the power to coerce a State into submission which is attempting to withdraw or has actually withdrawn from the [Union]."

Seventeen days after Buchanan's extraordinary speech, South Carolina seceded, seizing all federal property in that state except for two small forts in Charleston Harbor. Buchanan thereupon negotiated a truce with South Carolina, thus treating it as a sovereign entity. When South Carolina subsequently demanded the removal of federal troops from Fort Sumter, Buchanan drafted a letter of acquiescence. However, his cabinet divided bitterly over the issue, and two Northerners, Secretary of State Stanton and Attorney General Black, eventually persuaded Buchanan that surrendering the fort "would be treason."

To maintain the troops at Fort Sumner, however, Buchanan had to resupply them. He dispatched an unarmed troop transport to Charleston Harbor. South Carolina shore batteries fired upon and hit the ship, which then retreated. Just as when South Carolina had seceded and secessionists seized federal property, Buchanan did nothing.

Emboldened by the federal government's passivity, six other Southern states seceded before Lincoln could take office. In his last three months in office, Buchanan had given the Confederacy the time and perhaps even the tacit approval to organize and arm a seditious conspiracy to destroy the Union. In the judgment of one of his biographers, "Buchanan came closer to committing treason than any other president in American history."

FRANKLIN PIERCE SUPPORTS
THE KANSAS-NEBRASKA ACT

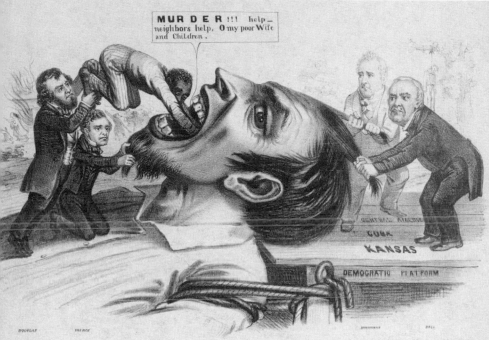

FORCING SLAVERY DOWN THE THROAT OF A FREESOILER

This cartoon depicts how the passage of the Kansas-Nebraska Act of 1854 was like "forcing slavery down the throat" of Kansas Free-Soilers, who opposed the extension of slavery into the state. On the left, President Franklin Pierce and Democratic Senator Stephen A. Douglas force a black man into the mouth of the Free-Soiler, while presidential nominee James Buchanan and Democratic Senator Lewis Cass restrain him from the right.

ABRAHAM LINCOLN

Farm Boy, to Lawyer, to President

WEEK 14

RAISED AS A FARM BOY—A LIFE HE REJECTED

In May 1860, at the Illinois state Republican convention, Abraham Lincoln's political supporters were searching for an image to sell their favorite son candidate. He was already known as "Old Abe" or "Honest Abe," but they thought those nicknames were so milquetoast they'd damage his political prospects. The men were looking for a name that evoked a man of the people, as "Log Cabin and Hard Cider" did for William Henry Harrison in 1840. That's how Lincoln, the skillful law-yer and politician, became "The Rail-Splitter" for the work he'd done splitting logs into fence rails for neighbors as a young man.

Lincoln had split rails as part of his rural upbringing, but the name "Rail-Splitter" was really a misnomer because he never had a passion for physical labor. The neighbors Lincoln worked for called him "awful lazy," and, as one remarked, "he was no hand to pitch in at work like kill-ing snakes." "He was always reading," said Dennis Hanks, who lived with the Lincoln family when Abe was a boy, "scribbling—writing—ciphering—writing Poetry."

The young Lincoln's passion was learning. He received some instruc-tion from itinerant schoolmasters but was largely self-taught. Sarah Bush Lincoln, his stepmother, brought some books with her from Ken-tucky that Abraham devoured, including *The Pilgrim's Progress*. He read and reread *Aesop's Fables* until he knew the stories by heart, including the one about the lion and the four bulls, which ended with the moral "A Kingdom divided against itself cannot stand." His stepmother also owned *Lessons in Elocution*, where Lincoln would first discover excerpts from Shakespeare, his favorite writer.

One of his favorite books was Parson Mason Weems's *Life of George Washington*. In 1861, traveling to the Capitol for his inauguration, he told the New Jersey Senate that Weems's account of Washington's struggles at Trenton—"crossing the river; the contest with the Hessians; the great hardships endured at that time"—had impressed him deeply. "I recol-lect thinking then, boy even though I was," he said, "that there must have been something more than common that those men struggled for."

WAS LINCOLN A POLITICAL FAILURE
BEFORE HE BECAME PRESIDENT?

Lincoln failed at almost everything—and then was elected president. That's the basic story line one "Dear Abby" column followed as well as the plotline summarized on one billboard—"Failed, failed, failed. And then . . ." (The punch line is a photo of Lincoln as president.) One popular poster rattles off his political failures: "Defeated for state legislator in 1832 . . . Defeated for Speaker in 1838 . . . Defeated for nomination to Congress in 1843 . . . Lost renomination [to Congress] in 1848 . . . Defeated for U.S. Senate in 1854 . . . Again defeated for U.S. Senate in 1858."

The story line is appealing: If a faltering Lincoln could become president, maybe all of us could rise to the top.

But the list leaves out Lincoln's many successes, political and otherwise. While he lost the race for state legislator in 1832, for example, his fellow soldiers in his New Salem militia at the time elected him captain. After Lincoln was nominated for President of the United States, he said he had "not since had any success in life which gave him so much satisfaction."

He might have failed to become Speaker of the Illinois House in 1838, but he was reelected to four consecutive terms. He wasn't renominated by the Whigs to run for Congress in 1843 because he'd agreed to turn over the nomination to another Whig candidate. And in the years preceding he started a successful law practice and married one of the most sought-after young women in Springfield, Mary Todd.

As for his failure to be renominated to Congress in 1848, he didn't get the nomination because he didn't run; he'd agreed to rotate his position with two other prominent Whigs and he was keeping his word. He probably would have lost if he had run because of his opposition to the Mexican War, which he saw as a land grab by President James Polk to create new territory for slavery. Would that have been a failure—or a principled stand by a politician willing to risk his position by opposing a popular war?

Finally, his stand against slavery might have lost him his Illinois Senate race against Stephen Douglas in 1858, but it propelled him to the Republican Party nomination for president in 1860. Was that failure—or success?

LINCOLN MAKES HIS NAME IN THE DEBATES WITH STEPHEN DOUGLAS

In mid-1858, Abraham Lincoln, a Republican and the underdog in the race for senator from Illinois, did what underdog politicians have done for generations: He challenged the formidable Democrat Stephen Douglas—the "Little Giant"—to a series of debates. Douglas grudgingly agreed. Seven times, the men—the stout, dapper Douglas and the lean, plain-dressed Lincoln—debated in front of crowds as large as fifteen thousand, who jostled for a spot to stand for the three-hour confrontations. Newspapers from all over the country recorded their words. The men debated only one topic: slavery and its future.

Douglas's first principle was that people had a right to choose or reject slavery in the western territories that were becoming states, a principle established in the Kansas-Nebraska Act of 1854, which Douglas had brokered. "I care more for the great principle of self-government, the right of the people to rule," Douglas said, "than I do for all the negroes in Christendom."

Lincoln's first principle was the eventual emancipation of slaves. Lincoln argued that the question was between "one class that looks upon the institution of slavery *as a wrong*, and of another class that *does not* look at it as a wrong. . . . That is the issue that will continue in this country when these poor tongues of Judge Douglas and myself shall be silent. . . ."

In Lincoln's "house divided" speech, which kicked off this senatorial campaign, he argued that the country could not continue as half-slave and half-free (for more on Lincoln's writing and speaking, see page 336). But if the division could not persist, Douglas reasoned, that meant "warfare between the North and the South, to be carried on with ruthless vengeance, until the one section or the other shall be driven to the wall. . . ."

Lincoln would lose the election, but the debates propelled him to national fame as an articulate, yet moderate antislavery leader. He wrote of the Senate race: "It gave me a hearing on the great and durable question of the age. . . . I believe I have made some marks which will tell for the cause of civil liberty long after I am gone."

WAS LINCOLN A RACIST?

Was Lincoln the Great Emancipator—or was he a racist?

After Lincoln's assassination, he was seen as the Great Emancipator, and he was often depicted in images as signing the Emancipation Proclamation. By the time the Lincoln Memorial was completed in 1922, many Americans had turned their eyes away from the race issue and emphasized instead that Lincoln had saved the Union. The early civil rights movement lionized Lincoln; Martin Luther King Jr. gave his historic "I have a dream" speech at the Lincoln Memorial and called Lincoln a "great and shining beacon light of hope." Later civil rights activists, who measured Lincoln against the higher standards of the 1960s, emphasized Lincoln's prejudices.

Lerone Bennett drew international attention when he published an article in *Ebony* magazine in 1968 with the title "Was Lincoln a White Supremacist?" Bennett emphasized Lincoln's jokes about blacks and spoke of Lincoln's support for a "colonization" policy that advocated resettling freed blacks to Africa or Central America. Bennett quoted from the 1858 senatorial debate with Stephen Douglas, in which Lincoln admitted that he thought "there's a physical difference" between blacks and whites, "which will probably forever forbid their living together upon the footing of perfect equality."

But Lincoln adds that blacks are entitled "to all the natural rights enumerated in the Declaration of Independence, the right to life, liberty and the pursuit of happiness. I hold that he is as much entitled to these as the white man. I agree with Judge [Stephen] Douglas [that the black man] is not my equal in many respects—certainly not in color, perhaps not in moral or intellectual endowment. But in the right to eat bread, without leave of anybody else, which his own hand earns, he is my equal and the equal of Judge Douglas, and the equal of every living man."

So was he the Great Emancipator? Lincoln's steadfastness in prosecuting the war was critical in the emancipation of slaves, and by the end of the war he was pushing to give African Americans the vote—the reason given by John Wilkes Booth for assassinating him.

WAS LINCOLN MELANCHOLIC?

Did Abraham Lincoln suffer from depression—or a "melancholic" disposition, as it was then called? In his book *Lincoln's Melancholy—How Depression Challenged a President and Fueled His Greatness*, Joshua Wolf Shenk says he did. Shenk's research began in 1998 after he stumbled across a sociologist's account of Lincoln's suicidal writings. He discovered that historians favoring documentary evidence had dismissed as gossip the contemporary accounts of Lincoln's depression. But those accounts were clear on the point. Lincoln's colleague Henry Whitney said, "No element of Mr. Lincoln's character was so marked, obvious and ingrained as his mysterious and profound melancholy." William Herndon, his law partner of many years, wrote: "His melancholy dripped from him as he walked."

Twice, Shenk writes, at age twenty-six and thirty-two, Lincoln was nearly broken by emotional collapses. After Anne Rutledge, believed to be Lincoln's first love, died of typhoid, Lincoln spoke of suicide, and his friends watched over him, fearing he might act on his words. The second depression, when Lincoln was thirty-two, may have been triggered by the departure of his best friend, Joshua Speed, or by his severe doubts about marrying Mary Todd, or even by Illinois's bleak midwinter.

"Lincoln went Crazy," Speed wrote. "—had to remove razors from his room—take away all Knives and other such dangerous things—&—it was terrible." "If what I feel," Lincoln said, "were equally distributed to the whole human family, there would not be one cheerful face on the Earth. . . . I must die or be better, it appears to me."

Shenk argues that Lincoln's depression largely made him who he was. It developed his humor; Lincoln noted that jokes "are the vents of my moods & gloom." He was also consoled by poetry, literature, and the Bible, which fueled his great writing. His bouts of despair also taught him perseverance. Shenk writes that Lincoln's suffering also made him more compassionate: "With malice toward none; with charity for all . . ." as he wrote in his second inaugural. A melancholy disposition, Shenk writes, creates "both an awful burden and what Byron called 'a fearful gift.' The burden was a sadness and despair. . . . The gift was a capacity for depth, wisdom—even genius."

LINCOLN WINS THE REPUBLICAN NOMINATION—
AND THE PRESIDENCY

"The city is thronged with Republicans," wrote the *Chicago Evening Journal* of the convention held in May of 1860. "Republicans from the woods of Maine and the green valleys of New England; Republicans from the Golden Gate and the old plantation, Republicans from everywhere. What seems a brilliant festival is but a rallying for a battle. It is an army with banners!"

Excitement was high along with Republican hopes. Six years earlier, the party had formed as an angry response by Northerners who didn't want slavery extended into the territories, and this year they believed they had a chance to win the presidency. Many at the convention knew Lincoln from his debates with Stephen Douglas over slavery during the 1858 Illinois senatorial race. But the front-runners were Salmon P. Chase of Ohio, Edward Bates of Missouri, Simon Cameron of Pennsylvania, and the favorite, William Seward of New York.

A roll call of delegates at the end of the second day was expected to give Seward the nomination, but the papers to tally the votes were not ready. That night Horace Greeley, the editor for the *New York Tribune* and a longtime Seward enemy, told one delegation after another that Seward would need "the entire North . . . if we hope to win . . . [but] cannot carry New Jersey, Pennsylvania, Indiana, or Iowa." In other words, Seward would lose the election and would take the party with him.

Lincoln's well-organized supporters followed in Greeley's wake, hoping to leave delegates "in a mood to come to us, if they shall be compelled to give up their first love." Seward failed on the first ballot. Lincoln became a favorite second choice, and he won on the third ballot.

Lincoln would win the general election by taking every free state except New Jersey. He received virtually no support in the South. In Virginia, he won only 1,929 votes—just over 1 percent—and received only 1,364 votes of the 146,216 cast in his home state of Kentucky. Lincoln's name didn't even appear on a ballot in ten Deep South states. The debate over slavery in the territories had cracked the bonds between North and South. The election of Lincoln broke them.

ABRAHAM LINCOLN—WITHOUT A BEARD

This 1860 Presidential campaign button depicts a beardless Abraham Lincoln. On the (unseen) opposite side of the button is Hannibal Hamlin, Lincoln's vice presidential candidate.

ABRAHAM LINCOLN

Into the Presidency—and into War

WEEK 15

THE TOUCHING SCENE OF LINCOLN'S FAREWELL
TO HIS FRIENDS IN SPRINGFIELD

A crowd stood gripping umbrellas as a cold rain fell in the early morning on February 11, 1861, waiting at the train station in Springfield to see Abraham Lincoln off to Washington, D.C., where he would be sworn in as the sixteenth president of the United States. He had come to Springfield as a twenty-eight-year-old "on a borrowed horse, with no earthly property save a pair of saddle-bags containing a few clothes," his friend Joshua Speed had said. At the train station, the president-elect shook hands with hundreds of friends and well-wishers, his face pale. Just before 8:00 A.M., he stepped onto the platform of his private car, took off his hat, and spoke. "My friends," he began,

no one, not in my situation, can appreciate my feeling of sadness at this parting. To this place, and the kindness of these people I owe every thing. Here I have lived for a quarter of a century, and have passed from a young to an old man. Here my children have been born, and one is buried. I now leave, not knowing when, or whether ever, I may return, with a task before me greater than that which rested upon Washington. Without the assistance of that Divine Being, who ever attended him, I cannot succeed. With that assistance I cannot fail. Trusting in Him, who can go with me, and remain with you and be every where for good, let us confidently hope that all will yet be well. To His care commending you, as I hope in your prayers you will commend, me, I bid you an affectionate farewell.

Less than two weeks earlier, Lincoln had visited his elderly stepmother Sarah Bush Lincoln, who had encouraged him to read and whom he called "Mother." She worried about her son's safety, and feared he would be killed in Washington. "No, no Mama," he assured her, "they will not do that. Trust in the Lord and all will be well."

AN INEXPERIENCED LINCOLN
WON'T PUT OFF OFFICE SEEKERS

From almost the day Abraham Lincoln moved into the White House, office seekers crawled through the White House from nine in the morning until well into the evening. When Lincoln broke to take lunch—usually a quick meal of bread, fruit, and milk—he would inevitably bump into men eager for a job in a Washington office, a post office back home, or perhaps the military.

Maine Senator William Fessenden called them an "ill-bred, ravenous crowd," and Lincoln's secretary John Nicolay wrote that with the constant pecking of job seekers "we have scarcely had time to eat sleep or even breathe." A more seasoned politician might have kept most of them away, but Lincoln was no seasoned politician. "You will wear yourself out," warned Massachusetts Senator Henry Wilson.

"They don't want much," was Lincoln's feeble response, "they get but little, and I must see them." Lincoln's inability to put off petty office seekers—and even ordinary people with their problems—during the country's worst crisis was seen by many as infuriating at best and as incompetent at worst. "He has no conception of his situation," Massachusetts Senator Charles Sumner complained to Representative Charles Francis Adams. Adams looked to Secretary of State William Seward to keep the ship of state from crashing. Seward griped in a letter home that the inexperienced president attempted to "do all his work," taking "that business up, first, which is pressed upon him most."

Yet Lincoln's willingness to meet the ordinary as well as the noteworthy did send a message: that the president's door was open to all. Word spread that the man advertised as the humble, honest man from Illinois might just be that after all. Common people sent common gifts, including one man from Johnsburgh, New York, who sent the president a live eagle, "the bird of our land," which had lost a foot in a trap. "But," the New Yorker wrote, "his is yet an Eagle and perhaps no more cripled [sic] than the Nation whose banner he represented."

LINCOLN CHOOSES HIS RIVALS FOR HIS CABINET

"I began at once to feel that I needed support," Lincoln said after his election as president, "others to share with me the burden." As the crowds ended their election night celebrations, Lincoln pulled out a blank piece of paper and made a list of seven men he wanted to guide him from different parts of the country and different political factions. "[B]efore the sun went down," Lincoln said, "I had made up my Cabinet. It was almost the same as I finally selected."

He chose his three main rivals for the Republican nomination for top posts—Missouri's elder statesman Edward Bates as attorney general, New York Senator William Seward as secretary of state, and Ohio's Salmon Chase as treasury secretary. "No President ever had a Cabinet," said New York politician Chauncey Depew, "of which the members were so independent, had so large individual followings, and were so inharmonious."

All the men thought themselves far more qualified for the presidency than the relatively inexperienced Illinois lawyer. This was perhaps most true of Seward, who had served nearly twelve years as a senator and four as governor of New York. After Lincoln's inauguration, Seward told Lincoln that Fort Sumter in South Carolina should be given up to the Confederates as a gesture of good will that would reassure the Upper South and win over Union supporters in the Deep South. Then he suggested that the United States should consider provoking a war with Spain and France for their meddling in Santo Domingo and Mexico, a move that might unite the North and the South.

Lincoln ignored Seward's suggestion to provoke a war, and told him that whatever policy was pursued, "*I* must do it." Seward would soon emerge as one of Lincoln's most important advisers—and a good friend.

Later in his administration, Joseph Medill, editor of the *Chicago Tribune* and loyal to Lincoln, asked the president why he had appointed political opponents. "We needed the strongest men of the Party in the cabinet," Lincoln replied. "We needed to hold our own people together. I had . . . concluded that these were the very strongest men. Then I had no right to deprive the country of their services."

LINCOLN MANEUVERS THROUGH
THE CRISIS AT FORT SUMTER

On the morning after Abraham Lincoln's inauguration, a dispatch from Major Robert Anderson, commander of the Union garrison in Charleston Harbor, informed him that the garrison's supplies would run out in a few weeks. What should Lincoln do?

He could send ships that could shoot their way into the bay to reinforce Anderson, but this would probably cause secession of the border states and trigger a civil war. Union General Winfield Scott recommended that they surrender the fort because it was too hard to defend, and most of Lincoln's cabinet agreed.

But to yield the fort would be to renege on Lincoln's pledge to "hold, occupy and possess" U.S. property. A surrender would alienate the Republicans who elected him and divide Northerners. It also would be an implicit recognition of the Confederacy that might entice England and France to recognize the secessionists and even support them if war broke out.

For six weeks, Lincoln agonized over what to do. He had many sleepless nights. He finally settled on a third option: to supply Fort Sumter with provisions but not with weapons. By keeping gunships out of the reprovisioning, he was letting the Confederates take responsibility for the war.

The Confederate leadership decided to preempt the provisioning and attack the fort, which was quickly surrendered. In their history of Lincoln, his private secretaries John G. Nicolay and John Hay wrote that he "was master of the situation . . . master if the rebels hesitated or repented, because they would thereby forfeit their prestige with the South; master if they persisted, for he would then command a united North." When Fort Sumter was attacked, the North rallied around the Union flag. On the day of the attack, Lincoln issued a proclamation calling for seventy-five thousand volunteers to put down the insurrection. Virginia, Arkansas, North Carolina, and Tennessee soon joined the Confederate nation.

"Both parties deprecated war," Lincoln would say in his second inaugural address just weeks before his death, "but one of them would make war rather than let the nation survive; and the other would accept war rather than let it perish. And the war came."

LINCOLN IGNORES DEATH THREATS, EXPOSING HIMSELF TO THE PEOPLE

When Lincoln received death threats in the White House mail, he placed them in a large envelope in his desk drawer. He wrote one word on the envelope: ASSASSINATION. In one letter a Lincoln hater wrote, "May the hand of the devil strike you down before long—You are destroying the country." Another wrote, "Your days are numbered. . . . You shall be a dead man in six months."

Ward Hill Lamon, his friend and unofficial bodyguard, sometimes slept outside Lincoln's bedroom armed with pistols and knives. But Lincoln was not always guarded. He would sometimes walk alone from the White House to get a morning newspaper, or to hospitals to visit wounded and he would speak with strangers. He would also take carriage rides with Mary around the city. A friend of Mary's remembered that she sensed "danger in every rustling leaf, in every whisper of the wind."

When an admirer sent Lincoln a clublike oak walking stick, Mary implored him to carry it with him for protection when he went out in the evening. "Mother [Mary] has got a notion in her head that I shall be assassinated," he explained to a newspaper reporter. "And to please her I take a cane when I go over to the War Department at night." Then Lincoln grinned, and delivered his punch line—"When I don't forget it."

Lincoln recognized that to protect himself completely would cut him off from the people. "I see hundreds of strangers every day, and if anybody has the disposition to kill me he will find opportunity," Lincoln said. "To be absolutely safe I should lock myself up in a box."

IN LINCOLN'S EYES, A WAR OF UNION

Slaves called the Civil War "the freedom war," and most people now remember it as the war that ended slavery in this country. But Abraham Lincoln's first priority was not to free slaves in the Confederate states, or even in the border states that had sided with the Union. Regarding slavery, all he had committed to was preventing the extension of slavery into the territories.

His first inaugural address stated as much. Speaking on a platform on the east portico of the Capitol, Lincoln tried to reassure Southerners that "their property, and their peace, and personal security" were not in danger. He quoted one of his previous speeches, repeating, "I have no purpose, directly or indirectly, to interfere with the institution of slavery in the States where it exists. I believe I have no lawful right to do so, and I have no inclination to do so." Regarding the controversial Fugitive Slave Law, which required Free State Northerners to return escaped slaves, he deferred to the Constitution, which required that slaves "shall be delivered upon claim of the party to whom such service or labor may be due."

To Lincoln, the war's primary aim was to preserve America's great political experiment. "The central idea pervading this struggle," he said in 1861, "is the necessity . . . of proving that popular government is not an absurdity." He believed that the fate of the American republic would have implications "to the whole family of man, the question, whether a constitutional republic, or a democracy" could persevere. "We must settle this question now, whether in a free government the minority have the right to break up the government whenever they choose," he said. "If we fail it will go far to prove the incapability of the people to govern themselves."

President Abraham Lincoln with his son Tad, taken on February 5, 1865, just two months before Lincoln's assassination. Tad was Lincoln's fourth and youngest son, eleven years old in this photo; he would later die at the age of eighteen in 1871. He got his nickname from his father, who found him to be "as wriggly as a tadpole" when he was a baby.

ABRAHAM LINCOLN

The War Changes—
and So Does Lincoln

WEEK 16

THE EMANCIPATION PROCLAMATION—
LINCOLN'S FINEST HOUR

Abraham Lincoln's Emancipation Proclamation, issued on New Year's Day, 1863, didn't free a single slave. The proclamation called for the freeing of slaves only in states still controlled by the Confederacy, not in slave states such as Kentucky, which were part of the Union, or even in territory that the Union army had occupied. Was Lincoln right to consider it the "central act of my administration, and the greatest event of the nineteenth century"?

African-American abolitionist Frederick Douglass said he "saw in its spirit a life and power beyond its letter," saying, "We shout for joy that we live to record this righteous decree." Douglass understood that the proclamation finally changed the meaning of the war from a contest between Union and division to a war of freedom. The proclamation might have been largely symbolic, but it was a symbol like few others in American history, marking the beginning of the end of slavery, an institution that had metastasized over the continent for over two and a half centuries. The Northern cause, Douglass said, was "now invested with sanctity." Lincoln knew what he'd done, and in the Gettysburg Address nine months later he spoke of "a new birth of freedom."

The proclamation also revealed Lincoln's commitment to end slavery. When he debated the institution with Stephen Douglas in the Illinois Senate race in 1858, he called for gradual emancipation that he believed wouldn't take place in "less than a hundred years at the least." He said he wouldn't interfere with slavery where it was rooted—the Constitution forbade him, he believed—a position he took into his presidency. With the proclamation, he declared that the special war powers granted a president gave him the power to overturn slavery, and he did so with the stroke of his pen. When Lincoln said, "If my name ever goes down into history, it will be for this act," his vision of history and his place in it was never more clear.

LINCOLN MYTHS

More myths swirl around Abraham Lincoln than around any president. Was Abraham Lincoln born in a one-room log cabin? Probably so; he certainly lived in one when he was a boy. Did the candidate who was given the title "The Rail-Splitter" during his election in 1860 really split fence rails? Honest Abe said that he didn't know if he'd split the two rails displayed at the Republican convention in 1860—but did confirm that he had worked as a day laborer when a young man, splitting trees into fence rails.

Did Lincoln carry things in his hat? He did.

As far as wearing a stovepipe hat, that's not a myth, but a mystery. "He was so tall, he stood out in any crowd, so why you would add another foot is beyond me," David Herbert Donald, one of the preeminent Lincoln scholars, has said, "except that he found it useful for storage. . . ."

Was Anne Rutledge rather than Mary Todd the love of Lincoln's life? This story was started by William Herndon, who was Lincoln's law partner. All we know for sure is that Rutledge died at age twenty-two and that Lincoln was depressed afterward. But Herndon's credibility is in doubt, since he didn't like Mary. And the love letters revealed in the 1920s between Lincoln and Rutledge turned out to be forged.

Did Lincoln write the Gettysburg Address on the back of an envelope on the train ride to Gettysburg? This myth was popularized in an article in *Scribner's* magazine in 1906, which stated that Lincoln wrote the speech on some brown wrapping paper, crumbled it up to throw it away, then retrieved it. But John Nicolay, one of Lincoln's secretaries who joined him on the trip to Gettysburg, doubted he wrote the speech on the train as "the rockings and joltings . . . [rendered] writing virtually impossible." Besides, it's unlikely that Lincoln would have tried to rush such an important speech. Perhaps the myth persists because we want to see Lincoln as a genius, not a man who thought, read, and learned until he could say what needed saying.

LINCOLN'S "TOTAL WAR" STRATEGY

On July 7, 1862, Union General George McClellan wrote a letter to Abraham Lincoln expressing his conviction that the war "should be conducted upon the highest principles known to Christian Civilization. It should not be a War upon population; but against armed forces. . . . Neither confiscation of property . . . nor forcible abolition of slavery should be contemplated for a moment."

But at that time, Lincoln was coming to believe all of that was necessary. Almost two years later Lincoln finally found the generals who could wage total war. The president liked what he'd seen from Ulysses S. Grant in his Vicksburg campaign in early 1863. Grant meant business: His army traveled light and fast, taking food from civilians in their approach to the key Mississippi city, and when a siege developed, he ordered the bombing of both soldier and civilian. The general's willingness to take the war to the enemy pleased Lincoln. "Grant is my man," Lincoln said, "and I am his for the rest of the war."

In the spring of 1864, Grant hammered Confederate General Robert E. Lee repeatedly and ordered his chief cavalryman Philip Sheridan to destroy Confederate General Jubal Early's army, which was loose in the Shenandoah Valley. "Take all provisions, forage and stock wanted for the use of your command," Grant told Sheridan. "Such as cannot be consumed, destroy." Grant wanted the valley left so barren that "crows flying over it . . . will have to carry their provender with them."

More infamous was William Tecumseh Sherman's march, which would cut a 225-mile wasteland through Georgia after Lincoln's reelection in the fall of 1864. Sherman started by pushing civilians out of Atlanta, making them refugees. When the city's leaders protested, he said, "War is cruelty; and you cannot refine it." Even without a battle, Sherman planned the "utter destruction of [Georgia's] roads, houses and people," acts intended to convince "sensible men" that further resistance was pointless. After four weeks, Sherman's army had completed its destruction.

"I beg to present to you as a Christmas gift," Sherman cabled Lincoln on December 22, 1864, "the city of Savannah."

LINCOLN'S DARK PREMONITION

A few days before Lincoln was assassinated, he had a dream, which he shared with his wife, Mary, and his aide and friend Ward Hill Lamon. Lamon later recounted what the president had described:

> There seemed to be a death-like stillness about me. Then I heard subdued sobs, as if a number of people were weeping. . . . [B]ut the mourners were invisible. I went from room to room; no living person was in sight. . . . I kept on until I arrived at the East Room, which I entered. There I met with a sickening surprise. Before me was a catafalque [a raised platform holding a coffin], on which rested a corpse wrapped in funeral vestments. Around it were stationed soldiers who were acting as guards; and there was a throng of people, some gazing mournfully upon the corpse, whose face was covered, others weeping pitifully. "Who is dead in the White House?" I demanded of one of the soldiers. "The President," was his answer; "he was killed by an assassin!" Then came a loud burst of grief from the crowd, which awoke me from my dream. I slept no more that night; and although it was only a dream, I have been strangely annoyed by it ever since.

Lincoln dismissed the idea that the dead man in the dream was himself. "For a long time you have been trying to keep somebody—Lord knows who—from killing me," Lincoln told his aide. "Don't you see how it will turn out? In this dream it was not me, but some other fellow, that was killed. It seems that this ghostly assassin tried his hand on someone else."

But Mary did not dismiss the dream: "I wish you had not told it," she said. "I am glad I don't believe in dreams, or should be in terror from this time forth."

WHAT LINCOLN CARRIED WHEN HE DIED

For his night at the theater on April 14, 1865, Abraham Lincoln put on his usual black suit, a white shirt, a black vest, and a black bow tie. And he gathered his belongings, putting them in his pocket. Into his vest pocket he had placed a gold watch he'd been given for donating the original Emancipation Proclamation to a charity event in Chicago. Into his coat pocket he had also slipped a pocketknife he might have used to peel an apple earlier in the day and a white Irish linen handkerchief that had the monogram "A. Lincoln" stitched in red thread.

He had two pairs of glasses, one he had repaired himself with a piece of string, and a piece of velvet he used to clean them. He also had a billfold. It contained no money except for a Confederate five-dollar bill, perhaps a souvenir from his trip to vanquished Richmond two weeks earlier, or a reminder of how different the world would be if the Union had lost the war.

Lincoln's family gathered these things after the assassination, and they disappeared from the public eye until 1937, when Lincoln's granddaughter presented a box wrapped in brown paper and tied with string to the Library of Congress for safekeeping. The box apparently got lost in the director's office for the next four decades. Then, when Library of Congress Director Daniel Boorstin walked into his office for the first time in 1976, he rummaged around and found it. On it, a notice said: "Do not open. Contents of the pockets of Abraham Lincoln on the night he was assassinated." Boorstin opened it.

He found the glasses, the handkerchief, the watch, and the pocketknife. He also found a few news clippings praising the Union cause and the president that Lincoln had stuffed into his billfold. One described a speech made by John Bright, from the House of Commons in England, praising Lincoln as one of the greatest men who ever lived. "It was rather well-worn," said Boorstin, "as if he'd taken it out many times to read."

LINCOLN'S GREATNESS—A CAPACITY TO GROW

Before the Civil War, and probably through the first year of the conflict, Abraham Lincoln believed that blacks were inferior to whites; that the war should not be fought over slavery; that blacks should not fight as soldiers; that emancipation should be gradual; and that when emancipation did occur, freed blacks should emigrate.

But the Civil War so drastically changed Lincoln's views on race that by the time the war ended, his views seemed those of another man. He was changed by abolitionists who educated him and by the entry of blacks into the army, which was necessary for Lincoln to achieve his first goal—to win the war to preserve the Union. By war's end, Lincoln saw blacks as equals and believed they should have the vote, a position that led the white supremacist John Wilkes Booth to vow to kill him.

The black scholar W.E.B. Dubois said Lincoln's outstanding ability was his capacity to grow. "Abraham Lincoln was perhaps the greatest figure of the nineteenth century. . . ." Dubois wrote. "I love him not because he was perfect, but because he was not and yet triumphed. The world is full of illegitimate children. The world is full of folk whose taste was educated in the gutter. The world is full of people born hating and despising their fellows. To these I love to say: 'See this man. He was one of you and yet he became Abraham Lincoln. . . .' [P]ersonally I revere him the more because up out of his contradictions and inconsistencies he fought his way to the pinnacles of earth and his fight was within as well as without. I care more for Lincoln's great toe than for the whole body of the perfect George Washington, of spotless ancestry, who 'never told a lie' and never did anything else interesting. . . . The scars and foibles and contradictions of the Great do not diminish but enhance the worth and meaning of their upward struggle: [It] was the bloody sweat that proved the human Christ divine; it was his true history and antecedents that proved Abraham Lincoln a Prince of Men."

THE LAST PHOTOGRAPH OF ABRAHAM LINCOLN

This image of Abraham Lincoln was taken on February 5, 1865, and was the last photo session the president gave before he was assassinated in April. Note that he was holding his spectacles and a pencil.

The Reconstruction Presidents—
Andrew Johnson, Ulysses S. Grant,
and Rutherford B. Hayes

FREDERICK DOUGLASS GETS A GLIMPSE OF ANDREW JOHNSON'S "REAL NATURE"

On March 4, 1865, the African-American abolitionist Frederick Douglass, then forty-seven years old, came to Washington for the second inauguration of Abraham Lincoln. Douglass had met Lincoln before and reported that the president, unlike other white men he'd met, "treated me as a man." They had disagreed about issues regarding blacks in the war, but Douglass had grown to respect the president.

As Douglass remembered it, there was one point in the inaugural festivities where Lincoln pointed Douglass out to his vice president-to-be, Andrew Johnson (for more on the speech Johnson gave this day, see page 337), and as Johnson looked over, Douglass thought he caught "a glimpse of the real nature of this man, which all subsequent developments proved true." Douglass wrote in his autobiography:

> The first expression which came to his face, and which I think was the true index of his heart, was one of bitter contempt and aversion. Seeing that I had observed him, he tried to assume a more friendly appearance, but it was too late; it is useless to close the door when all within had been seen. His first glance was the frown of the man; the second was the bland and sickly smile of the demagogue. I turned to Mrs. Dorsey and said, "Whatever Andrew Johnson may be, he is no friend of our race."

Douglass's intuition would be proven right. As Johnson biographer Annette Gordon-Reed writes, "an assassin's bullet would place the political fate of African Americans into the hands of a man who despised them. . . . It would be impossible to exaggerate how devastating it was to have a man who affirmatively hated black people in charge of the program that was designed to settle the terms of their existence in post–Civil War America."

ABRAHAM LINCOLN'S WORST DECISION?

The worst political decision Abraham Lincoln might have ever made was to choose Andrew Johnson as his vice president in 1864. Lincoln's choice in 1860 had been Hannibal Hamlin, a fierce abolitionist who had supported the Emancipation Proclamation and the arming of blacks during the war. But in 1864, Lincoln wanted to signal Southerners that he was amenable to conciliation if they surrendered sooner rather than later. Johnson, a Tennesseean who had freed his slaves in 1863 and the only senator from a seceding state who had stuck with the Union, was the signal Lincoln sent.

But Johnson had a deep animosity toward blacks and a mulelike stubbornness, two traits that would create what many consider the worst presidency in U.S. history. Johnson's term was dominated by Reconstruction, the period that included the return of Southern states into the Union after the Civil War. The only precondition that Johnson placed upon returning southern states was that they ratify the Thirteenth Amendment to the Constitution, which ended slavery. Otherwise, he believed the former Confederate states should do as they pleased.

He opposed the Fourteenth Amendment, which defined blacks as citizens. He acquiesced as southern states passed laws called black codes that established African Americans as second-class citizens, and also elected to Congress former Confederate leaders such as Alexander H. Stephens, who had been the Confederacy's vice president.

Congress, still dominated by northern so-called Radical Republicans, defied Johnson, trying to protect black political rights. The battle, often vicious, escalated to the point where the House of Representatives, wanting Johnson out of their way, impeached him. If Johnson was removed from office, he would have been replaced by Senator Benjamin F. Wade, who supported America's nascent labor movement and women's suffrage—forward-looking positions unpopular with most senators. Perhaps deciding on the devil they knew, the Senate fell just one vote short of the two-thirds vote they needed to remove Johnson from office.

Johnson's survival in many ways led to the national failure to bring blacks fully into the American political process for almost a century. As Johnson biographer Hans Trefousse put it, "He preserved the South as 'a white man's country.'"

GRANT'S TOLERANT INDIAN POLICY

When Ulysses S. Grant was elected president in 1868, the U.S. government had broken nearly all the 370 treaties it had signed with Native Americans, the people Grant called "the original inhabitants of this land." Former Civil War General William Tecumseh Sherman expressed the prevailing government attitude toward Indians when he wrote General Philip Sheridan: "I want you to go ahead, kill and punish the hostiles, capture and destroy the ponies . . . of the Cheyennes, Arahoes, and Kiowas. The more we kill this year, the less we would have to kill next year."

But Grant had long felt sympathy for the Indians. While serving in the army in the Northwest during the 1850s, he wrote to his wife, Julia, that the Indians he met "were the most harmless people you ever saw . . . the whole race would be harmless and peaceable if they were not put upon by whites." Grant's policy as president was to respect Indian treaties, encourage American citizenship, aid Indians financially, and move them to reservations to be educated and Christianized.

In 1870, Sioux leaders came to Washington to plead for aid from the "Great White Father." Grant, moved by their plight, convinced Congress to approve funding for their basic needs and education. In the West, Grant appointed "humanitarian generals" who believed Indian relations should be based on justice and honesty.

Leading up to Grant's reelection in 1872, some urged him to crack down on Indians to win Plains states votes. "If any change takes place in the Indian Policy of the Government while I hold my present office," Grant said, "it will be on the humanitarian side of the question."

Grant's relatively progressive policy survived until his last year in office, when white settlers poured into the Black Hills of Dakota in a gold rush, and Grant, deciding he had to move the Sioux off the land they considered sacred, sent in U.S. troops. Sioux soldiers wiped out George Custer and the Seventh Cavalry in the Battle of Little Bighorn. After that, a political backlash killed Grant's policy of toleration, his eight years in office only a brief interlude in the systematic government attacks on the American Indian.

ULYSSES S. GRANT—
THE FIRST CIVIL RIGHTS PRESIDENT?

Josiah Bunting III, a Ulysses S. Grant biographer, says the former general came into office during a period that was as challenging as faced by any president except for Abraham Lincoln and Franklin Delano Roosevelt. He struggled with economic policy and political corruption, but he took a stand on the major issue of his day: the rights of African-Americans.

After the war, Grant watched disapprovingly as President Andrew Johnson encouraged white Southerners to strip African-Americans of their political, civic, and economic rights. As President Grant, he proved as resolute in the political field as he'd been on the battlefield. Grant supported the Fifteenth Amendment, which granted blacks the vote and came up in his first term, as he had the Fourteenth Amendment, which gave blacks citizenship in 1866. "Treat the Negro as a citizen and a voter, as he is and must remain, and soon parties will be divided not on the color line, but on principle."

During Grant's first term, racist whites used terror, including kidnappings, beatings, arsons, and lynchings to keep blacks powerless. In March 1871, Grant called for a bill to curtail the violence, and Congress passed the Ku Klux Klan Bill in April. Two weeks later, Grant sent federal troops to various parts of the South, particularly South Carolina, to stop the violence. Federal grand juries indicted about three thousand Klansmen, and many were convicted. One scholar called the elections that followed the intervention "the fairest and most democratic presidential election in the South until 1968."

At the end of his term, when racist whites reasserted their power in the South, Grant backed off on northern intrusion into southern politics. Yet Frederick Douglass, a tough critic, wrote, "To Grant more than any other man the Negro owes his enfranchisement. . . . In the matter of the protection of the freedman from violence his moral courage surpassed that of his party. . . ."

GRANT—AS MUCH A VICTIM
AS A CAUSE OF CORRUPTION

Ulysses S. Grant presided over one of the most scandal-ridden presidencies in American history. But if the scandals are examined, it becomes apparent that Grant—considered honest and trustworthy—was more the victim of the corruption than its cause (for more on the Grant scandals, see page 352). This was certainly the case in his decision to invest $100,000 after he left the presidency in the New York City investment firm of Grant & Ward, named after Grant's son, Ulysses "Buck" Grant, Jr., and Ferdinand Ward, known as the "Young Napoleon of Wall Street."

Ward was delighted when Grant invested, aware that investors might infer that the "Grant" in the firm's name belonged to the former general. Over the next few years, the firm, rated "gilt-edged," paid investors as much as 40 percent in dividends annually. Grant believed himself a millionaire. But gilt edged turned out to be fool's gold.

In May 1884, Ward asked Grant for a loan of $150,000 to cover loans for a few days. The man who as president had significantly reduced the nation's debt, prevented the cornering of the nation's gold market, and had helped stabilize the dollar, asked few questions. He asked William H. Vanderbilt, a railroad investor, to provide a loan of $150,000, which he forwarded to Ward. Two days later the investment company went bankrupt. Apparently, Ward had engaged in a Ponzi scheme, paying old investors with money from new ones. The firm owed $16 million.

The following Tuesday morning Buck went to tell the news to his father. "Well, Buck, how is it?" Grant asked his son. Buck answered him directly: "Grant & Ward has failed, and Ward has fled." Grant's savings were gone and he was $150,000 in debt, with no pension. He went into his office without speaking a word. Later in the day, Grant sent for the firm's cashier, who had also been deceived. The cashier found Grant tightly gripping the arms of his chair, his face twitching.

"I have made it the rule of my life to trust a man long after other people gave him up," Grant admitted. "But I don't see how I can ever trust any human being again."

"THE DIRTY DEAL" ELECTS RUTHERFORD B. HAYES AND ENDS RECONSTRUCTION

The election of 1876 was the most controversial presidential contest in U.S. history—until 2000. And it too involved the state of Florida and a president who didn't win the popular vote.

The election was a contest between two reformers, Ohio Governor Rutherford B. Hayes and New York Democrat Samuel J. Tilden, who had jailed the corrupt "Boss" Tweed of Tammany Hall. In early counts, Tilden won 4.3 million votes to Hayes's 4 million, and 184 electoral votes, one short of victory, to Hayes's 165. To beat Tilden, Hayes would need the three undecided southern states—South Carolina, Louisiana, and Florida—as well as one remaining electoral vote in Oregon. Tilden went to sleep nearly certain of victory; Hayes wrote his son Ruddy at Cornell, "You will wish to know how we feel since the defeat. . . ."

But the next day, Democrats and Republicans both declared victory in the three outstanding states. Congress improvised, picking fifteen congressmen and Supreme Court justices to settle the election. Southern Democrats, not averse to Hayes, threatened to filibuster a Hayes victory unless he put a southern Democrat in his cabinet and fund infrastructure projects, including a railroad linking New Orleans to the West Coast. Hayes also agreed to remove federal troops from the statehouses in Louisiana and South Carolina, where President Grant had sent them to protect Republican officeholders and the civil rights of blacks. In return, southern Democrats made a promise—which would soon be broken—to respect the civil rights of blacks.

By an 8 to 7 vote, the commission gave Hayes all the undecided electoral votes—and the election—with a final 185 to 184 margin. But the price of Hayes's victory was the legitimacy of his presidency, as well as the rights of southern African Americans.

Reconstruction was over. The Fourteenth and Fifteenth Amendments, the former guaranteeing civil liberties to blacks and the latter affirming the right to vote in the South, would not be enforced. The *Nation* magazine made a prescient prediction: "The Negro will disappear from the field of national politics. Henceforth the nation, as a nation, will have nothing to do with him."

THE INAUGURATION OF
RUTHERFORD B. HAYES

The inauguration of Rutherford B. Hayes on March 5, 1877.

REFORMERS
(1881–1897)

Gilded Age Presidents—James A. Garfield, Chester A. Arthur, Grover Cleveland, and Benjamin Harrison

WEEK 18

JAMES A. GARFIELD—
HIS ASSASSINATION INSPIRES REFORM

James A. Garfield was born in a log cabin and grew up in poverty. His mother scraped together $17 to send him off to Geauga Seminary, where he discovered a love of learning, and he went on to become a teacher and preacher. Garfield soon saw politics as his path, and was elected a Republican state senator in Ohio in 1859.

He became an impassioned opponent of slavery, and campaigned hard for Abraham Lincoln in 1860. He welcomed the Civil War, and like many politicians, he recruited troops and was given an officer's commission. But when Ohioans elected him to the House of Representatives in 1862, President Lincoln, needing effective Republicans more than major generals, persuaded Garfield to become a full-time politician. He was a radical Republican who wanted to confiscate the estates of southern slave owners and execute or banish southern leaders. But after the war he called himself a "poor hater," and moderated his views, allying himself with liberal reformers who supported amnesty for ex-Confederates, free trade, and a gold standard.

During his eighteen years in the House, Garfield often commented on his trouble with seeing "too many sides of a subject." He was committed to free trade—except for many products made by his constituents, which he believed deserved protective tariffs. He supported civil service reform—but doubted the wisdom of merit exams and didn't consider it corrupt to have civil servants pay a percentage of their salaries to campaigns.

But after Garfield won the Republican nomination and the election in 1880, he lived up to expectations that he'd be a reformer, immediately bucking the corrupt New York political machine and appointing his own man as collector at the Port of New York, a plum position. On July 2, 1881, an attorney whom the White House had repeatedly turned down for a diplomatic position shot Garfield in the back at a Washington railroad station. Garfield died two months later. Reformers used Garfield's assassination by the deranged patronage seeker to gain sympathy for civil service reform. That would come from another unlikely reformer—Garfield's replacement, Chester A. Arthur.

CHESTER A. ARTHUR—THE HACK BECOMES A REFORMER

When Chester A. Arthur took office after the assassination of James Garfield in 1881, everyone assumed he'd stay true to his roots as a machine politician. Arthur's nickname was "The Gentleman Boss"; reformer Edward L. Godkin referred to him as a "mess of filth." He rose out of the corrupt New York State machine of Senator Roscoe Conkling, and just three years before he became president, President Rutherford B. Hayes had removed him from his lucrative job at the New York Custom House on suspicion of corruption.

When Garfield selected him as vice president in 1880, Godkin remarked casually, "There is no place in which [Arthur's] powers of mischief will be so small as in the Vice Presidency." But when James Garfield slowly died from an assassin's bullet, Godkin exclaimed, "Arthur for President! Conkling the power behind the throne!"

But in one of the greatest surprises in presidential history, Arthur didn't appoint Conkling men to his cabinet, and in 1883, he signed the Pendleton Act, which prevented forced contributions from government employees and replaced patronage appointments with a merit system based on competitive exams. Political reformers and machine politicians were both shocked.

Arthur didn't do too much else—he fought off a twenty-year ban on Chinese immigrants and pushed to reduce tariffs—but in the age of weak presidents, not much was expected. He worked from 10:00 A.M. to 4:00 P.M., and then enjoyed good food and lots of liquor, dressed impeccably, and was often the "last man to go to bed in any company." He burned his personal papers, and when his term drew to a close, few seriously considered nominating him for a second term. He died two years after leaving office and has since faded from presidential memory.

GROVER CLEVELAND—A MAYORAL VETO
LEADS TO THE VETO PRESIDENT

Grover Cleveland's rise to the presidency began with a single veto. He issued it as mayor of Buffalo, New York, an office he won because of a reputation for incorruptibility he'd earned as a lawyer and then sheriff of Erie County. In his mayoral run, he described public officials as "trustees of the people," and he called for clean and efficient government in what was a corrupt city.

The Buffalo Common Council tested Cleveland's convictions when they sent him a five-year street-cleaning contract with a local company totaling half a million dollars. Cleveland noticed that five other companies had bid less, and vetoed the bill, calling it the "most bare-faced, impudent, and shameless scheme to . . . worse than squander the public money." It was the kind of blunt message that Cleveland would send with his vetoes his entire political career. The shamed council revoted 23 to 2 to award the contract to the low bidder.

If the council had overridden his veto, he probably wouldn't have been elected governor on a reformer's platform that year or as twenty-second President of the United States in 1884. The veto mayor became the veto governor, and then the veto president.

Under Cleveland's predecessors, it had been common practice for the president to rubber-stamp Civil War pensions granted by Congress. But Cleveland stayed up long into the night reviewing each pension individually, rejecting two hundred. Congress retaliated by passing a bill that gave a pension to every veteran with at least three months of service, including those who weren't injured. Cleveland vetoed it as a raid on the treasury.

Cleveland's veto was often negative and obstructive (he used it to stop progressive legislation as well as public boondoggles), but in the age when corrupt machine politics dominated all levels of government, saying no was something of a virtue.

CLEVELAND—A PROBUSINESS POLITICIAN
DURING LABOR'S RISE

Grover Cleveland, a corporate lawyer, was as probusiness as any president of the Gilded Age—no easy achievement. After Cleveland was elected to his first term in 1884, financier Jay Gould sent him a telegram stating how sure he was that "the vast business interests of the country will be entirely safe in your hands."

To keep them safe, Cleveland often cracked down on workers during one of the most tumultuous periods in American labor history. Typical was Cleveland's reaction to an 1894 strike at the Chicago-based Pullman Company, ignited by a 30-percent wage cut for its railroad employees. The American Railway Union, with 150,000 members, joined the strike, ordering its members not to handle trains with Pullman cars, virtually halting railroad traffic to the West. Pullman then hooked up its cars to mail trains, hoping to elicit a government crackdown. It did.

Cleveland is said to have commented: "If it takes every dollar in the Treasury and every soldier in the United States to deliver a postal card in Chicago, that postal card should be delivered." The railroads got an injunction against the strike, and when the union violated it, the government arrested union leaders, including Eugene V. Debs. The strike was crushed.

The strike occurred during one of the worst depressions the country had suffered until that time. Thousands of businesses had failed, farm prices collapsed, and an estimated one out of every five factory workers lost their jobs. Cleveland rejected government aid for the suffering, believing it violated the Constitution as well as wasted government money. When a ragtag army of unemployed marched to Washington to encourage public works projects, Cleveland had police scatter the "petitioners in boots."

"While the people should patriotically and cheerfully support their Government," Cleveland wrote, "its functions do not include the support of the people." It would take a Democrat who came along nearly forty years later—Franklin Delano Roosevelt—to change that presidential perspective.

GROVER CLEVELAND—AN HONEST PRESIDENT
WHO STROVE TO "DO RIGHT"

We most often remember Cleveland for his stubborn vetoes, and as the presidential footnote to the question, "Who was the only president to hold two nonconsecutive terms in the White House?"

But he deserves better. His contemporaries saw him as a man of integrity, and he was. In the run-up to his first presidential election in 1884, he became the butt of the snickering rhyme, "Ma, Ma, where's my Pa? Gone to the White House, Ha, Ha, Ha." The rhyme referred to newspaper accounts that the bachelor candidate had fathered a child out of wedlock while in Buffalo. When a friend asked Cleveland how Democrats should respond, he replied with this telegram: "WHATEVER YOU DO, TELL THE TRUTH."

When the details came out—that there had been no adultery, no promise of marriage, and that Cleveland supported the child and mother financially for some time despite his questionable paternity—the public apparently forgave Cleveland, electing him president.

Cleveland's honesty carried into politics. His campaign slogan in 1884 was, "Public Office Is a Public Trust," and he meant it. Before he came into office for his second term, his predecessor, Benjamin Harrison, sent a treaty to Congress that annexed Hawaii, bowing to pressure from sugar planters who wanted the island to become U.S. property to avoid tariffs and also from imperialist-leaning Americans wanting to "civilize" the Hawaiians. Cleveland preferred the sentiment in the Declaration of Independence—that all people had a right to self-government—and yanked the treaty from the Senate, explaining in his annual message that "it seemed to me the only honorable course for our government to pursue was to undo the wrong that had been done by those representing us. . . ." His action, while just, only delayed Congress's annexation of Hawaii until after he'd left office.

But the stubborn defiance was in keeping with his character. As he lay dying at the age of seventy-one, his last words didn't refer to his personal life, but his political career, which included terms as mayor of Buffalo, governor of New York, and, twice, president: "I have tried so hard to do right."

BENJAMIN HARRISON—THE FIRST ACTIVIST
OF THE PROGRESSIVE ERA

Republican Benjamin Harrison, the twenty-third president, is sometimes consigned to "fun facts" in presidential history: the man who held office between two Grover Cleveland administrations, or one of four presidents to win the White House while losing the popular vote (along with John Quincy Adams, Rutherford B. Hayes, and George W. Bush).

But in an era when presidents were generally passive, Harrison worked aggressively with Congress to expand governmental budgets and extend U.S. power. Harrison pushed a foreign policy that expanded U.S. foreign markets. He built a navy that William McKinley would use in the Spanish-American War of 1898. He pressed for a canal in Central America, pushed for the annexation of Hawaii, sought navy coaling stations in the Caribbean and Pacific, and threatened a war with Chile when its leaders were reluctant to apologize over two Americans killed in a saloon brawl.

At home, Republicans passed the Dependent Pensions Act, which provided $160 million annually for Union veterans of the Civil War. The Sherman Antitrust Act also passed overwhelmingly; Theodore Roosevelt and William Howard Taft would later use it to break up monopolies. In the country's first billion-dollar peacetime budget, the government invested in harbor improvements, created several national parks, and began free rural mail delivery. They also raised tariffs by almost 50 percent. Harrison also tried to protect black voting rights by putting Southern elections under federal supervision, but Southerners killed that bill.

Such activism alienated many Americans. Critics called the Fifty-first Congress the "billion-dollar Congress." Immigrant laborers were angered by Harrison's crackdown on labor. Farmers, suffering from higher prices, denounced the tariffs targeted for eastern industries. Southerners were bitter because the military pensions didn't cover Confederate veterans.

In a presidential rematch in 1892, Cleveland beat Harrison. On March 4, 1893, Harrison and Cleveland rode in a carriage from the White House to the Capitol for the inauguration, just as they had four years before. Yet this time, the roles were reversed.

BENJAMIN HARRISON'S
INAUGURAL BALL

This picture depicts the inaugural ball of Benjamin Harrison in 1889, held in the Federal Pension Office. The menu for the dinner that evening included steamed oysters, pâté de foie gras à la Harrison, and terrapin, Philadelphia style.

TAKING *on the* WORLD *and* REFORM

(1897–1921)

McKinley Sails into War,
and Roosevelt Rides into Power

WEEK 19

THE MCKINLEY CAMPAIGN BRINGS BIG MONEY TO PRESIDENTIAL POLITICS

Until the 1880s, it was considered poor form for presidential candidates to admit they wanted the office; they would stay at home while their surrogates campaigned. Then it became acceptable for candidates to campaign—but only from their front porch. In 1888, roughly three hundred thousand visitors descended on the home of Republican candidate Benjamin Harrison.

But in 1896, Democratic candidate William Jennings Bryan broke all the rules of presidential campaigning by stumping nearly everywhere, championing the cause of farmers crushed by economic hardship. He delivered one of the most famous convention speeches in American history, calling for an end to the gold standard as a way to help farmers in debt. Bryan ended his speech, "You shall not press down upon the brow of labor this crown of thorns, you shall not crucify mankind upon a cross of gold," spreading his arms as if he were on the cross. It was the first time in his life, said a reporter, that a leader of a national party "had . . . unashamedly made his cause that of the poor and oppressed."

McKinley did not hit the campaign trail. Instead, he spoke to seven hundred thousand visitors who came to visit him at his home in Canton, Ohio. "I might just as well put up a trapeze on my front lawn and compete with some professional athlete as go out speaking against Bryan," he told McKinley. "I have to *think* when I speak."

But the money raised by the McKinley campaign spoke for him. Many businessmen and corporations, fearful of Bryan's Populist leanings, gave between $3.5 million and $16 million to McKinley's campaign. To reach 15 million voters, McKinley's campaign had 200 million pamphlets printed in fourteen languages. Teddy Roosevelt said the campaign "advertised McKinley as if he were a patent medicine." Bryan raised just $500,000—and lost the election by a wider margin than any candidate in a quarter century.

MCKINLEY TAKES THE PHILIPPINES—
AND INITIATES A WAR

When the United States defeated the moribund Spanish empire militarily in Cuba and in the Philippines in 1898, U.S. leaders had to make a decision: what to do with the Philippines. Debate at home was fierce, with many arguing that America had the responsibility to "take up the white man's burden" and bring democracy, civilization, and Christianity to the Filipinos, arguments similar to those that European colonialists had made for centuries. Businessmen pushed for annexation, well aware that Manila was a way station to the lucrative trade of Asia, and suspecting the islands might be a repository of valuable natural resources.

Those who opposed the annexation—including Andrew Carnegie and ex-presidents Benjamin Harrison and Grover Cleveland—argued that taking the territories contradicted the country's founding principles by imposing a government without the consent of the governed, and that it also took money and attention from problems at home—arguments that would arise in other U.S. interventions. "We said we are going to bring prosperity and democracy to the Filipinos," said William Jennings Bryan, McKinley's presidential opponent in 1896 and 1900. "But we had better not educate them, because they might learn to read the Declaration of Independence."

At first, McKinley resisted the push toward war, but he later said his decision on how to handle the islands came to him one night when he "went down on my knees and prayed to Almighty God for light and guidance." There, he decided that to give back the islands to Spain would be "cowardly and dishonorable"; to turn them over to commercial rivals France or Germany would be "bad business"; to allow them to govern themselves would lead to "anarchy and misrule." "[T]here was nothing left for us to do but to take them all, and to educate the Filipinos, and uplift and civilize and Christianize them, and by God's grace do the very best we could by them, as our fellow men for whom Christ also died. And then I went to bed and . . . slept soundly."

The United States offered $20 million for the Philippine islands, and the nearly bankrupt Spanish leaders agreed to the sale. That ended the "splendid little war" with Spain—but it soon launched a brutish one with the Filipino nationalists seeking independence (for more on the U.S. intervention in the Philippines, see page 375).

"TEEDIE" ROOSEVELT, CHILD NATURALIST

In his autobiography, Theodore Roosevelt wrote about a moment when he was eight years old: "I remember distinctly the first day that I started on my career as a zoologist. I was walking up Broadway, and as I passed the market to which I used sometimes to be sent before breakfast to get strawberries, I suddenly saw a dead seal laid out on a slab of wood. That seal filled me with every possible feeling of romance and adventure." He came back again and again to measure the animal and ask how it had died. He asked for the animal for his bedroom "museum," and was eventually given its skull.

At about the same time the boy, homeschooled, got a journal in which he drew mice and especially birds, and wrote about ants, spiders, beetles, and dragonflies. It wasn't long before he was stuffing birds, and at age eleven, he bragged about a menagerie of a thousand specimens in his bedroom. He was soon writing natural histories on the creatures that most beguiled him, including "The Foraging Ant." In the fall of 1871, the American Museum of Natural History logged that it had acquired one bat, twelve mice, a turtle, a squirrel's skull, and four bird eggs from Theodore Roosevelt, Jr., age thirteen.

At fourteen, he realized that he couldn't see the things his friends saw, and requested a pair of glasses. "I had no idea how beautiful the world was," he wrote afterward. It was also the year he learned to shoot a gun, which he immediately aimed at birds, the first of many creatures around the world who would eventually fall to Roosevelt the hunter.

FROM INVALID TO PUGILIST

When "Teedie" was ten, his parents took the family on a trip to Europe, and in his diary the sickly boy chronicled his health issues—stomach upsets, headaches, and bronchial asthma, which had plagued him since he was three. While he gasped for air, his father would provide his own medicine—a cigar to smoke—or his mother rubbed his chest. He once wrote: "I was rubbed so hard on the chest this morning that the blood came out."

During his childhood, he would be stricken with numerous attacks every month, and the family would try to cure him with vacations, sulfur baths, the lancing of swollen lymph glands (without anesthesia), medicines such as ipecac and magnesia, mustard plasters applied to his chest, and even electrical charges. Years later, Roosevelt wrote: "Nobody seemed to think I would live."

When Theodore approached his fourteenth birthday, his father, whom Theodore admired deeply, told him he must overcome his invalidism. "Theodore, you have the mind but you have not the body, and without the help of the body, the mind cannot go as far as it should." According to his sister Corinne, Theodore said, "I'll make my body."

First the boy went to a gym, and then his father built one on the second floor of their home. Teedie built up his chest and arms with monotonous repetitions on dumbbells, horizontal bars, and a punching bag. He then took boxing lessons with an ex-prizefighter, and surprised all with his ability to take a beating. It would take years, but the weak boy became a strong young man. His asthma attacks became less frequent, to the point where he could hide the episodes.

After boxing, he said, he began "constantly forcing himself to do the difficult and even dangerous thing" in all of life's arenas to overcome fear. He would box at Harvard, wrestle his cabinet members, and embody the life lesson that "man does in fact become fearless by sheer dint of practicing fearlessness."

RIDING UP SAN JUAN HILL
LAUNCHES A POLITICAL CAREER

When war between the United States and Spain loomed in 1898, Theodore Roosevelt resigned his post as assistant secretary of the navy to become a lieutenant colonel. He recruited a regiment of one thousand soldiers he called the Rough Riders to fight in Cuba. The charge he led up San Juan Hill boosted his political prospects and earned him a cover story in *Harper's Weekly*.

Many politicians, aware that Civil War records had elected the Gilded Age presidents, were envious of Roosevelt's instant celebrity and blocked a medal of honor Roosevelt wanted. The ambitious William Randolph Hearst was angry at himself for "not raising the cowboy regiment I had in mind before Roosevelt raised his." After the war, Buffalo Bill Cody hired sixteen Rough Riders for his Wild West show. Roosevelt fueled his fame by dashing off a book, *The Rough Riders*.

Still, the future was uncertain for the thirty-nine-year-old. His career, while successful, had consisted of a series of appointed posts. His electoral record was slight, as he had lost the New York City mayor's race in 1866 and had only managed to win election to the state assembly. Now some reporters asked Roosevelt if he'd run for governor; others asked him when he'd run for president.

New York Republican bosses were lukewarm on Roosevelt—they pegged him, correctly, as his own man—but had little choice but to nominate the war hero. One of the Rough Riders blew his bugle from the back of a campaign train that cut across the state as Roosevelt addressed crowds sometimes numbering twenty thousand people. Hearst turned his newspapers against Roosevelt, attacking him as a political fake.

In November—three months after he had returned from Cuba—the man they called the "Colonel" was elected governor by a narrow 17,794 votes. He served the two-year term, accepted the nomination as William McKinley's new vice president in 1900, and became president when McKinley was shot in September 1901, just three years after he rode up San Juan Hill.

A NEW PRESIDENTIAL ROLE—TR MEDIATES
THE COAL STRIKE OF 1902

In 1901, 513 men died in coal mine accidents. In 1902, the United Mine Workers went on strike to demand recognition of their union and to protest unsafe working conditions, low wages, and long hours—the men worked twelve hours a day, six days a week. They also were unhappy with the company town, which forced them to purchase overpriced food and housing.

The six mine owners refused to budge. George F. Baer of the Reading Railroad managed to offend workers all over the country when he said, "The rights and interests of the laboring man will be protected and cared for, not by the labor agitators, but by the Christian men in whom God in His infinite wisdom has given the control of the property interests of the country, and upon the successful management of which so much depends."

In the fall of 1902, schools began closing because they were without coal and Roosevelt worried that Americans in colder climates would be without coal come winter, causing "terrible suffering and a grave disaster." Coal prices spiked from $5 to $14 a ton.

Earlier presidents almost always crushed such strikes, and businessmen pressured Roosevelt to send in federal troops on the grounds the strike was an illegal restraint of trade. Socialist Victor Berger and labor leaders wanted Roosevelt to nationalize the mines for the good of the public. Instead, Roosevelt created a commission to resolve the dispute, but the owners were still recalcitrant. He leaked to newspapers that he would have the army take over the mines and run them. The mine owners agreed to the commission, and the president appointed one that included people from the miners' union and the community. Within weeks, they gave their recommendation: The union would get a 10 percent wage increase and nine-hour days, but not union recognition or a more accurate coal weighing. Labor had gained more leverage in its relationship with capital—and Roosevelt was responsible. Roosevelt biographer Edmund Morris points out, "Theodore Roosevelt's mediation between capital and labor earned him fame as the first head of state to confront the largest problem of the twentieth century."

This photo shows the dynamic Theodore Roosevelt speaking to a crowd from the back of a railroad car in 1907. Roosevelt held the presidency from 1901, following the assassination of William McKinley, until 1909. He declined to run for reelection in 1908, but ran as a third-party candidate in 1912 (for more on the election of 1912, see page 345).

Roosevelt—Reformer, Conservationist, Internationalist—and William Taft

WEEK 20

THE OPPORTUNIST REFORMER—
TR REGULATES FOOD AND DRUGS

Roosevelt is often seen as a reformer, but he was wary of most progressives and actually felt more comfortable with business tycoons. In a dinner speech at the Gridiron Club in 1906, the president mocked an investigative journalist as the generic "man with the Muckrake, who could look no way but downward with muckrake in his hand; who was offered a celestial crown for his muckrake, but who would neither look up nor regard the crown he was offered, but continued to rake to himself the filth of the floor." From the speech, the word *muckraker* was born, which popular usage turned from an epithet into a badge that described investigative journalists, who would publicize numerous social injustices that Roosevelt would ride into legislation.

One of the muckrakers was twenty-seven-year-old Upton Sinclair, who wrote *The Jungle*, which described the filthy factory production of contaminated meat in the Chicago meatpacking industry, dangerous to both workers and consumers. Sinclair was a Socialist, made clear in his dedication "To the Workingmen of America" and to the book's last words—"Organize! Organize! Organize!" But Roosevelt didn't believe that government should take over business. Instead, he wanted businesses, even the large trusts, to thrive. "Our aim is not to do away with corporations," he said in 1902, "on the contrary, these big aggregations are the inevitable development of modern industrialism." He was a capitalist with a conscience who wanted to curb corporate excesses, what he called the "vital work" of his presidency, and thus prevent socialism from getting a foothold in capitalism. "We draw the line against misconduct, not against wealth."

Roosevelt saw *The Jungle* as the kind of publicity that could jostle his Meat Inspection Act out of committee, and with grassroots agitation, it did. Congress passed it in June 1906. The imperfect bill—Roosevelt was always willing to compromise—restored the public's confidence, thereby increasing meat makers' profits. On the same June day, Congress also passed the Pure Food and Drug Act, which regulated both those products for the first time. The bill took medicines out of the control of quacks, and banned the addition of one drug often added to medicines and Coca-Cola—cocaine.

THEODORE ROOSEVELT—
THE CONSERVATIONIST PRESIDENT

By 1907, President Theodore Roosevelt and Gifford Pinchot, first chief of the U.S. Forest Service, had made tremendous strides in officially placing millions of acres of American forests off-limits to strip miners and lumbermen. But that year, Republican Senator Charles W. Fulton of Oregon proposed an amendment to the agricultural appropriations bill that would take away the president's power to put aside land in Oregon, Washington, Idaho, Montana, Colorado, or Wyoming.

The bill passed Congress, and on February 25, it was waiting on Roosevelt's desk for his signature. To veto the agriculture bill would have been political suicide, so instead, Pinchot's forestry men worked in twenty-four-hour shifts to map the most important tracts in the region. A week later, the paperwork had been completed on twenty-one new forest reserves and eleven enlarged ones in the northwestern states. Roosevelt then used his executive power to establish them, knowing that Congress would have to vote to stop him and then muster even more votes to override his veto—votes they didn't have.

His executive orders created 16 million acres of national forests, including Toiyabe, Nevada; Holy Cross and Montezuma in Colorado; Priest River in Idaho and Washington; Bear Lodge, Wyoming; Big Belt, Big Hole, and Otter Forest, Montana; Blue Mountain, Oregon; Olympic Forest, Cascade, and Rainier, Washington. With the lands safely sequestered, Roosevelt happily signed the agricultural bill, replete with Fulton's now useless amendment.

Over two terms, Roosevelt created five national parks, doubling the number that he'd inherited in 1901, and eighteen national monuments, which included a crater lake, a rain forest, a petrified forest, sequoia stands, and the Grand Canyon. Roosevelt would increase the country's national forests from 42 million acres to 172 million acres, and he would create the country's first fifty-one wildlife refuges. The first one was a tiny island off the coast of Florida. "Is there any law that will prevent me from declaring Pelican Island a Federal Bird Reservation?" he asked rhetorically. "Very well, then I so declare it."

TR'S GUNBOAT DIPLOMACY—THE PANAMA CANAL

Theodore Roosevelt's powerful will, fearless decision making, and his adamant desire to create a world-class navy capable of projecting U.S. power around the world all came together in his successful effort to build the Panama Canal, what he believed was his grandest achievement as president.

The first hurdle was getting access to the land to build the canal. The preferred six-mile crossing site was in Panama, which had long been controlled by Colombia. But in 1903, with an agreement close, Colombian leaders balked on a potential one-hundred-year canal lease with the United States. Roosevelt, who called the Colombian leaders "foolish and homicidal corruptionists," told his secretary of state, "I am not inclined to have any further dealings whatever with those Bogotá people."

Soon after, Panamanian revolutionaries moved, and Roosevelt sent a gunboat—the "big stick" he liked to use—to protect Panamanian nationalists from Colombian forces. Two weeks later, the quickly recognized Panamanian government signed the canal lease with the United States. Panama got $10 million, and the bondholders of the New Panama Canal Company got $40 million more.

As the canal was built—it would take a decade to finish—Roosevelt insisted on a world-class navy. "Our justification for upholding the Monroe Doctrine, and for digging the Panama Canal, must rest primarily upon our willingness to build and maintain a first class fighting fleet." Many have claimed that Roosevelt wanted the armada to protect American business interests and expand U.S. power, but Roosevelt insisted the fleet was "by far the most potent guaranty of peace which this nation has or can ever have." He had to fight for funds from a suspicious Congress, but by the end of his term, he had nearly doubled the size of the navy.

The canal saved billions of dollars in transportation costs to private businesses, and allowed the United States to create a one-ocean navy instead of two. Before he left office, Roosevelt sailed the so-called Great White Fleet around the world. He called it a "goodwill" tour, but it was also a statement heard around the world: For better and for worse, the American navy had arrived.

ROOSEVELT IS SHOT IN THE CHEST—
AND THEN DELIVERS A SPEECH

The most memorable event in the 1912 presidential campaign was not a misstatement, a debate, or a dirty trick, but the bullet Theodore Roosevelt took to his barrel chest.

Roosevelt was running as a third-party candidate with the Progressive Party against Woodrow Wilson, the Democratic choice, and Howard Taft, who had outmaneuvered Roosevelt for the Republican nomination. In October 1912, Roosevelt was campaigning more like a gazelle than a Bull Moose, giving as many as twenty speeches a day. Outside the Gilpatrick Hotel in Milwaukee, Roosevelt was waving to people on the sidewalk when a paranoid schizophrenic shot him in the chest. "They have pinked me," Roosevelt said, and then told the crowd not to hurt the man, who'd been wrestled to the ground.

The bullet had pierced his coat, a steel eyeglass case, his suspenders, and his speech, folded up thickly in his breast pocket. It broke a rib and lodged in his chest. For all his rough riding, it was the first time Roosevelt had ever been shot, except for the bullet that skimmed his elbow in Cuba.

Roosevelt surmised that since he was not coughing up blood, the bullet had not pierced his lung. He decided to "make that speech if I die doing it." He showed the mortified crowd his bloody shirt and pulled out his bloody speech. Because of the bullet in his chest, he told them he'd have to speak less forcefully than usual. He then spoke for an hour and a half. Later, at Mercy Hospital in Chicago, his wife, Edith, tried to keep visitors away, but Roosevelt insisted on talking to reporters.

The campaign hoped that Roosevelt's heroics and the sympathy that followed the assassination attempt would lead to victory, but the Bull Moose lost to Wilson. Afterward, he explained why he'd insisted on making the speech after he was shot. "There was then a perfectly obvious duty," he explained to a friend, deciding that "in the very unlikely event of the wound being mortal, I wished to die with my boots on."

ROOSEVELT'S FOUR SONS JOIN THE WAR, AND TRAGEDY FOLLOWS

Theodore Roosevelt believed that physical strength and bravery were the measure of a man, and that both traits were tested by war. He had passed the test on San Juan Hill in Cuba, and when World War I broke out, he wanted to enlist as an officer and bring in another division of Rough Riders. But Woodrow Wilson's administration refused his offer.

Roosevelt's four sons had absorbed their father's values and, with their father's help, sought the war's battlefronts with the heaviest fighting. Roosevelt's son Ted was hit by gas and hurt by shrapnel, and both parents were proud to learn that their son Archie had also survived a wounding and won the Croix de Guerre.

When the news came in May 1918 that Quentin, the youngest, who served in the air corps, had shot down his first German airplane, Roosevelt said, "The last of the 'lion's brood' has been blooded." But less than two weeks later, a cable came that Quentin had been shot down behind enemy lines and killed.

Americans sent two thousand condolence letters to the Roosevelts, and TR wrote back to one woman: "To feel that one has inspired a boy to conduct that has resulted in his death, has a pretty serious side for a father,—at the same time I would not have cared for my boys and they would not have cared for me if our relations had not been just along that line." That fall, Roosevelt confessed to a "sickening feeling" that he had played a part in Quentin's death. "Just because they are my sons, they feel they must be extra brave," he told a friend. " They take chances they wouldn't perhaps otherwise take."

Some say that Roosevelt never recovered from Quentin's death. James Amos, Roosevelt's butler and bodyguard since 1901, said, "It was plain that he was a changed man." Roosevelt admitted his grief in a letter to writer Edith Wharton, a relative of his wife's. "There is no use of my writing about Quentin; for I should break down if I tried."

WILLIAM H. TAFT—ADRIFT AT THE HELM

The failure of William Howard Taft's presidency had not as much to do with his capabilities—he graduated second in his class at Yale and served ably as Theodore Roosevelt's right-hand man—but with his ambitions. Most politicians seek the limelight that accompanies the presidency. (Roosevelt's family sometimes joked that he wanted to be the bride at every wedding and the corpse at every funeral.) But Taft preferred the anonymity of the crowd.

Taft was a good-natured man, and he apparently acquiesced to Roosevelt's designation as his successor because he wasn't quite sure how to decline the honor. He called the campaign of 1908 "one of the most uncomfortable four months of my life." He retreated to Hot Springs, Virginia, where he lost himself in golf.

Once elected, Taft seemed overwhelmed. He began in his inaugural: "Any one who has taken the oath I have just taken must feel a heavy weight of responsibility." He tried to comfort himself by eating, and while he was already a very large man—weighing three hundred pounds at his inauguration—he gained fifty pounds more over four years.

The lawyer resisted Roosevelt's cowboy-like activism, and was criticized for his passivity. His presidency drifted to the right, and he offended Roosevelt—and conservationists—by firing one of TR's favorites, Gifford Pinchot, the chief of the forest service. He also angered TR by having his attorney general bust U.S. Steel, a corporation that Roosevelt had allowed to form. (Taft isn't usually given credit for the eighty antitrust suits initiated under his administration, or his other liberal stands, such as endorsing direct elections of U.S. senators and a federal income tax.) Roosevelt took it as a slap in the face—and an opportunity to renew his campaign to take back the White House in 1912. Taft fought back, but confessed privately that "in my heart I have long been making plans for the future." (For more on Taft's postpresidency, see page 385.)

After losing the 1912 election badly, Taft would later write: "I don't remember that I ever was President."

WILLIAM H. TAFT PLAYS GOLF

William H. Taft playing golf at Hot Springs, Virginia. He was the first president to openly take up golf, a sport considered for the rich and rather effeminate at the time. His love for the sport caused a golf boom in the United States, doubling the number of players on public courses.

Woodrow Wilson—More Reform, and Then World War

WOODROW WILSON: TRULY MORAL—
OR MORAL HYPOCRITE?

Born December 28, 1856, in Staunton, Virginia, Thomas Woodrow Wilson had a strict, caring, and enlightened religious upbringing. He loved and respected his "incomparable father," a Presbyterian minister, who took the primary hand in directing his studies. Woodrow would sit in church and listen with awe while Joseph Wilson preached, and the boy dreamed of one day speaking from his own pulpit.

In 1874, Woodrow entered Davidson, a Presbyterian college, but left within a year in part because of illness. As religious as ever, he nonetheless started having doubts about his calling, even considering joining a ship's crew. He eventually enrolled at the College of New Jersey (later renamed Princeton), where he was happiest debating national issues. No longer interested in preaching religious morality, he had begun preaching civic morality.

Religious belief remained inseparable from Wilson's politics. Later, he indicated that the United States had been chosen by Providence "to show the way to the nations of the world how they shall walk in the paths of liberty." Europeans were shocked by this attitude. Sniffed France's president, "He thinks he is another Jesus Christ come upon the Earth to reform men."

Did Wilson's politics live up to his lofty morality? Wilson insisted that morality demanded equality, civil liberties, and democracy. But he racially segregated federal departments and drastically curtailed free speech (for more on his Palmer raids, see page 364). He argued fervently to end the scourge of warfare, but led the United States into war, sending troops to Haiti, the Dominican Republic, Nicaragua, Mexico, Cuba, and other nations. While his motives for these military actions have been debated, the fact remains that they "formed the high-water mark of United States intervention in the Caribbean" and elsewhere.

Wilson himself "look[ed] upon his own inconsistencies as mere transient details in the one great impulse towards right and justice," wrote one early observer. Whether that made him genuinely moral—or morally fraudulent—is debated to this day.

THE DOCTORAL—AND DYSLEXIC?—PRESIDENT

Thomas Woodrow Wilson—the only president to have earned a doctoral degree—was unable to read until he was about twelve years old, perhaps due to dyslexia. To make work easier, he taught himself shorthand and planned much of what he wanted to say before writing it down.

While he was in graduate school at Johns Hopkins, Wilson excelled as an orator and debater. He became fascinated by history and government and began to write; his first book was *Congressional Government*. But still he complained: "I have no patience for the tedious toil of what is known as 'research'; I have a passion for interpreting great thoughts to the world."

With a doctorate in political economy, he taught at Bryn Mawr, Wesleyan, and Princeton. He was soon known for his scholarship on governmental systems and his energetic, challenging teaching style. He chose among many offers to become Princeton's first nonclergy president in 1902.

Wilson was determined to make the school an intellectual model. "If the thing keeps up," joked one student, "Dr. Wilson will make Princeton an educational institution!" Yet education, believed Wilson, was meaningless if it simply improved the individual. The critical goal of education was to improve the broader society.

One afternoon, the mother of a Princeton student came to see Wilson because her son was being expelled for cheating. She begged Wilson for leniency, asserting that the expulsion might kill her. "But if I had to choose between your life or my life or anybody's life and the good of this college," Wilson said softly, "I should choose the good of the college."

ATTACKING TARIFFS:
WILSON OUT-ROOSEVELTS ROOSEVELT

On April 8, 1913, one month into his presidency, Woodrow Wilson declared his intention to speak to a joint session of Congress—the first president to do so since John Adams. Some horrified congressmen felt this was a violation of the separation of powers, but Wilson believed that the president "must be prime minister, as much concerned with the guidance of legislation as with the just and orderly execution of law."

Wilson's intended subject was tariffs (taxes on imported goods), an issue that for years had divided the nation. Wilson agreed with progressives that, as Representative Joseph Bailey put it, tariffs were license to "rob and plunder industrious consumers." Representative Cordell Hull declared that tariffs indirectly taxed the vast majority of Americans while "virtually exempting the Carnegies, the Vanderbilts, the Morgans, and the Rockefellers, with aggregated billions of hoarded wealth."

The wealthy, protariff lobby fought back, pressuring congressmen to keep tariffs high. Wilson charged that "[a] brick couldn't be thrown without hitting [a lobbyist]," and he urged citizens to contact their representatives: "[I]t is of serious interest to the country that the people at large should have no lobby and be voiceless in these matters, while great bodies of astute men seek to create an artificial opinion and to overcome the interests of the public for their private profit. Only public opinion can check and destroy it."

Wilson's historic address to Congress was brief and mild. But Congress subsequently voted to reduce tariffs by over 25 percent and institute the first graduated income tax to replace the lost tariff revenue. Despite predictable opposition from the rich, Wilson signed the tariff/tax bill into law on October 3, 1913.

On the ride home from the Capitol after the joint session of Congress, Wilson's wife, Ellen, said, "That's the sort of thing Roosevelt would have loved to do if he had thought of it."

"Yes," Wilson replied, "I think I put one over on Teddy."

REGULATING THE BANKS, OR NOT?
THE FEDERAL RESERVE

Wilson's reform of the nation's banking system, embodied in the Federal Reserve Act, is generally considered his most important legislative accomplishment. The act kept faith with progressivism by creating a national banking system owned and formally controlled by the government, but appeased Wall Street by insulating the new system from direct political influence, thereby rendering it unresponsive to popular sentiment.

The new central bank would have enormous power over the economy through its ability to control the money supply and influence interest rates, but the elected representatives of the people would have very little power over it. Instead, power would rest with twelve regional Federal Reserve Banks directly controlled by the private banking sector, and with a Federal Reserve Board composed of two government officials and five members appointed by the president and confirmed by Congress to serve ten- (subsequently fourteen-) year terms whose length would insulate the appointees from popular pressure.

Wall Street initially attacked Wilson's proposed reform, and the American Bankers Association convention adopted a resolution condemning it as a form of socialism. But in the end, most of the banking industry supported the bill as it came to understand that it could capture the Federal Reserve System, and would.

Proof that the new Federal Reserve System would serve the interests of banks rather than the public was not long in coming. In the recession of 1920–21, the Federal Reserve Board chose to fight inflation rather than provide the credit needed to revive the economy and put people back to work. It raised interest rates sharply, effectively doubling the cost of money. By insulating the Federal Reserve System from public pressure, Wilson had allowed the big banks to turn it into a potential tool for their own profitability.

GERMAN SUBS SINK U.S. NEUTRALITY

When the German army rolled through neutral Belgium in 1914 to ignite World War I, Wilson hoped that the United States could stay out of it. But when Germany—itself blockaded by the Allies—used submarines to blockade England and France, its U-boats torpedoed not only ships, but also Wilson's hopes for U.S. neutrality.

In 1915, a U-boat sank the British passenger ship *Lusitania*, killing 128 Americans and 1,170 others. Though many Americans urged war against Germany, Wilson resisted such calls. Wilson demanded—and got—an apology and reparations from Germany.

After several more submarine attacks, Wilson issued an ultimatum: No more attacks on nonmilitary shipping, or the United States would sever diplomatic relations, a step that is often a prelude to war. Germany agreed, and Wilson ran for reelection in the fall of 1915 on the slogan "He kept us out of war."

In February 1917, however, German leaders changed their minds, in the belief that stopping all supplies to the Allies and then quickly defeating them before U.S. troops reached Europe was Germany's only chance for victory. Wilson broke off diplomatic relations but declared that he would not go to war absent "actual overt acts." In March, Germany sank five U.S. merchant ships, and Wilson reluctantly called Congress into special session to ask for a declaration of war.

For Wilson, this was not a war of choice. As he went before Congress on April 2, 1917, he said, "[W]e are clearly forced into it because there are no other means of defending our rights." His speech was greeted with wild, prolonged applause, and even an enemy congratulated him, telling Wilson, "Mr. President, you have expressed the sentiments of the American people in the loftiest possible manner." Later that night, however, Wilson confided to his private secretary, Joseph Tumulty, "My message tonight was a message of death for our young men. How strange it seems to applaud that." Then he put his head on his desk and wept.

WILSON LEADS A CRACKDOWN AGAINST
WAR DISSENTERS

Wilson himself set the tone for a wartime assault on tolerance and civil liberties by publicly promising that disloyalty "will be dealt with a firm hand of stern repression." He unleashed a vitriolic propaganda campaign, directed by the Committee on Public Information, against anyone less than enthusiastic in supporting the war.

Wilson also prevailed upon Congress to pass several laws curtailing free speech. The Sedition Act made it a crime (punishable by up to twenty years' imprisonment) to "willfully utter, print, write or publish any disloyal, profane, scurrilous or abusive language about the form of government of the United States, the Constitution, . . . or the flag." Hundreds of people were convicted under the act, including one clergyman who was sentenced to fifteen years in jail for saying that Jesus was a pacifist. Eugene Debs, a labor leader who had gotten 6 percent of the vote in the 1912 election, received a ten-year sentence (and served nearly three) for an antiwar speech. Calling him a "traitor," Wilson refused three times to pardon him.

"Slacker brigades" organized by the justice department stopped draft-age men on the streets, detaining without warrant anyone suspected of draft evasion. The post office refused to send any publication it deemed subversive of the war effort. And under the Alien Act of 1918, the immigration department deported thousands of legal, noncitizen residents that it considered insufficiently patriotic.

The justice department recruited the American Patriotic League's quarter million members to spy on their neighbors and report their neighbors' patriotic deficiencies. Police looked the other way as mobs broke up antiwar meetings, tarred and feathered "agitators," and lynched labor organizers. Wilson took the country to war to "make the world safe for democracy," but in doing so, he damaged democratic institutions at home.

President Woodrow Wilson in June 1920, with his wife, Edith Bolling Galt, at his side. This is Wilson's first posed photograph after he suffered a severe stroke in 1919. He was paralyzed on his left side, and Edith is seen here holding a document steady while he signs it.

BOOM *and* BUST
(1921–1941)

Big-Business Presidents— Warren G. Harding, Calvin Coolidge, and Herbert Hoover

WEEK 22

WARREN G. HARDING—NOT AS BAD AS THEY SAY

It's often forgotten that Warren G. Harding, the man often plunked near the bottom of the presidential rankings, was elected in 1920 by what was then the largest popular majority in American history. He was so well liked going into his third year that it was assumed he would be renominated in 1924.

Harding's friendliness was an antidote to Woodrow Wilson's haughtiness, and Harding's presence alone reassured the country after Wilson's invalidism. After a brutal world war and the economic panic in 1920, most Americans yearned for peace and prosperity, just what Harding promised. "America's need is not heroics but healing," he said, "not nostrums but normalcy; not revolution but restoration; not agitation but adjustment; not surgery but serenity; not the dramatic, but the dispassionate; not experiment but equipoise. . . ."

Not altogether inspiring, but classic Harding, who ushered in the Age of Normalcy. He generally pushed pro-business policies, including lower taxes and smaller government, and did little to help farmers hurt by falling crop prices and workers whose wages were cut. He was the only postwar president in U.S. history to cut federal expenditures below prewar levels.

In international affairs, he backed away from the League of Nations for fear it might drag the nation into another world war. But he did support U.S. involvement in the World Court and signed the Washington Naval Treaty with Great Britain, France, and Japan, which prevented an expensive naval arms race.

Harding also quietly reinvigorated democracy at home by freeing labor leaders and socialists imprisoned during the Red Scare of 1919, including Eugene Debs, who had been sentenced to ten years in prison for opposing World War I.

Why then have so many historians damned him? Harding has been hurt by his knack for appointing corrupt officials, whose deeds were largely revealed after Harding died in August 1923 (for more on this corruption, see page 353). He also wasn't around to defend his reputation, and many thought the worst until his presidential papers were opened to scholars in 1964, which buoyed his standing. Harding was "neither a tool," concluded one Harding biographer, "nor a fool."

CONSERVATIVE, VIRTUOUS, AND FRUGAL—
CALVIN COOLIDGE

Warren G. Harding was lazy, and his hard-drinking, poker-playing cabinet seemed to specialize in robbing the public treasury. Calvin Coolidge, who took office when Harding died in 1923, was an accidental antidote, a man with puritanical virtues that contrasted with the libertine 1920s. In a country shaken by graft, sloth, and immorality, Coolidge quickly restored faith in the government and in the presidency by cleaning house and prosecuting corrupt officials. He was frugal, prompt, conservative, and austere; one observer said he looked like "he'd been weaned on a pickle."

He woke at 6:30 A.M., and was at his desk by eight. At exactly 12:30, he shook hands with hundreds of White House visitors. He'd eat, nap for two hours, and then work into the evening as well as on weekends.

He was not a great communicator (he was the last president not to have a telephone), but a frequent one, holding two press conferences a week. Robert Cowley, an expert on the 1920s, has written that Coolidge's four years "were notable more for what he refused to do than for what he accomplished." What he refused to do was spend much government money. As one of the strongest presidential defenders of limited government in the twentieth century, he succeeded in cutting spending, taxes, and the national debt.

To this end, he vetoed all sorts of popular legislation—raises for postal workers, bonuses for World War I veterans, and price supports for desperate farmers. He did what he set out to do: He squeezed the federal budget, which spent just $4 million more when he left office in 1929 than when he entered in 1923. He also let business run loose ("The chief business of the American people is business," he said), a strategy that nurtured both the Roaring Twenties and then the crash on Wall Street.

Coolidge escaped being in office when the boom went bust by walking away from power, announcing his abrupt decision not to seek a second term in 1927, showing a restraint and humility hard to find among U.S. presidents. "Isn't that just like the man," his wife, Grace, said. "I had no idea."

HOW DID HERBERT HOOVER GET IT SO WRONG?

Herbert Hoover, it is often noted, had a reputation as a humanitarian when he stepped into the White House in 1928. When World War I broke out in 1914, the successful businessman oversaw the flight of a hundred thousand Americans from the European continent. And when it became clear that the war might lead to the starvation of Belgium, Hoover raised and spent millions of dollars to feed the Belgian people. The efficient Hoover, one British editor said, "won admiration from most and extorted respect from all." When the United States entered the war, an impressed President Woodrow Wilson appointed Hoover as his food czar.

With such a record, how did Hoover fail so miserably to respond to the suffering of the Great Depression?

Hoover is sometimes condemned as standing idly by when the stock market crashed, but that wasn't so. He immediately called on industry leaders to preserve wage levels and asked unions to avoid strikes. He wired states to expand construction, called on Congress to pass a $150 million public works project and a tax cut, and convinced the Federal Reserve Board to expand the money supply to make credit more available. He tried to calm the nation by replacing the word *panic* with the less frantic word *depression,* a coinage that would be linked to his name forever.

But while Hoover called for a larger government role than had any former president facing an economic crisis, the scale of his response was curtailed by his ideology. He believed government response should be small—he called for "energetic yet prudent" public works projects. And he believed that local entities, or better yet, private relief organizations, should take the lead, not the federal government. At the end of 1930, after six hundred banks failed, Hoover retreated to balancing the budget, seeking to curtail "big government" spenders.

He couldn't have made a worse decision.

As the economy collapsed—about one in four Americans were out of work by Hoover's last year in office—the American people looked to their leader for hope, but found none. "If you want to get the gloomiest view of any subject on earth," his wife once noted, "ask Bert about it." Instead, Americans turned to FDR.

HOOVER BOTCHES THE RESPONSE TO THE BONUS ARMY
AND SEALS HIS REPUTATION

In May 1932, the Great Depression over two years old, upward of twenty thousand desperate World War I veterans and their families descended on Washington, D.C., to convince Congress to dispense a bonus not due them until 1945. Washington Police Superintendent Pelham D. Glassford treated this Bonus Army with consideration, bringing in straw mattresses for women and children.

But President Herbert Hoover refused to speak with them. He ordered police officers stationed around the White House and had surrounding streets blockaded. When Hoover had the gates to the White House chained, a headline proclaimed HOOVER LOCKS SELF IN WHITE HOUSE.

In June, the Senate overwhelmingly rejected the veterans' request. Many went home, but thousands remained in empty buildings on Pennsylvania Avenue and at a shantytown built on flats along the Anacostia River in sight of the Capitol. Finally, Hoover ordered Glassford to move the squatters, beginning with the Pennsylvania Avenue buildings. When the crowd pelted the policemen with debris, Hoover sent in the U.S. Army.

Onlookers mistook the six hundred soldiers and five tanks marching down Pennsylvania Avenue for a parade and cheered them until the horses charged the buildings. That night, General Douglas MacArthur planned to sweep through the Anacostia encampment. But Hoover, having second thoughts, twice ordered MacArthur to hold off. The general instead gave the shanty dwellers a few hours to evacuate, and then sent his men, with tear gas canisters and bayonets, into the encampment, burning it down, a sweep that injured hundreds of people.

Hoover never disciplined MacArthur, insisting, as MacArthur had, that the Bonus Army didn't consist of veterans, but "Communists and persons with criminal records," although an army investigation conducted afterward found otherwise. After the assault, the grim president became the face of callous indifference to the Depression and the suffering it spawned.

"I voted for Herbert Hoover in 1928," wrote one woman in a letter to the editor. "God forgive me and keep me alive at least until the polls open!" "Well," said Franklin Roosevelt, the Democratic nominee who read the accounts with a "feeling of horror" with his wife Eleanor, "this elects me."

THE STRUGGLE TO WALK—
AND RELAUNCH A POLITICAL CAREER

When Franklin Roosevelt contracted polio in 1921, he vowed to return to politics, but only once he could walk again. For the next half dozen years, sunlamp treatments, deep massages, electric belts, and pulleys for his legs did not help. In 1926, a physical therapist taught Franklin how to use crutches, which Roosevelt knew to be political suicide.

In the summer of 1928, New York Governor Al Smith asked Roosevelt to give a nominating speech for his presidential run at the Democratic convention in Houston. Before fifteen thousand people, Roosevelt began the most important walk of his life. With one hand, he gripped a cane. With the other, he held tightly to the muscular arm of his son Elliott. Although both men strained, they chatted and laughed on their way to the dais.

The speech launched Roosevelt's political comeback. Someone asked Smith whether he erred in thus elevating a potential rival. "No," Smith replied. "He'll be dead within a year." But six months later, Smith was a badly beaten ex-presidential candidate and Roosevelt was New York governor.

For the rest of his life, Roosevelt kept up what writer Hugh Gallagher has called "a splendid deception," one the press corps complied with. The American public never learned that their president relied on a wheelchair, was carried up and down stairs, and was lifted into bed at night. Only once would Roosevelt reveal his condition on the public stage.

On March 1, 1945, six weeks before he died, Roosevelt returned from the Yalta Conference and went to the Capitol to address Congress. Instead of making his way to the podium using a cane, he rolled down the aisle in a wheelchair. Instead of standing at the lectern, he sat in a soft chair.

"I hope you will pardon me for the unusual posture of sitting down . . ." he said, "but I know that you will realize that it makes it a lot easier for me in not having to carry about ten pounds of steel around on the bottom of my legs. . . ." The applause was sustained.

"He did it with such a casual, debonair manner," Roosevelt's Secretary of Labor Frances Perkins said later, "without self-pity or strain that the episode lost any grim quality, and left everybody quite comfortable."

PRESIDENT HOOVER WAITS, GOVERNOR ROOSEVELT ACTS

The stock market collapsed a year after Franklin Roosevelt was elected New York's governor, putting homeless people on the street not far from Franklin and Eleanor's posh Sixty-fifth Street townhouse.

At first, the patrician Roosevelt sounded like President Herbert Hoover, referring to the Wall Street collapse as "that little flurry downtown." But the governor's path soon veered. Hoover believed the federal government should play a limited role in righting the economy and providing relief. Roosevelt's response foreshadowed the New Deal.

The governor asked for $20 million from the legislature to create jobs and to provide the needy "with food against starvation and with clothing and shelter against suffering." At home, Eleanor gave their cook instructions to provide hot coffee and sandwiches to anyone who came to the door.

Roosevelt also proposed old-age pensions and became the first state governor to endorse unemployment insurance. He also proposed tax relief for farmers and the establishment of a dairy cooperative that would help stabilize milk prices. "If the farmer starves today," Roosevelt said in a speech in December 1929, "we will all starve tomorrow."

"The important thing," he told the New York State Assembly, "is to recognize that there is a duty on the part of government to do something about this."

In 1932, President Hoover invited the nation's governors to a White House dinner, wanting to size up the governor who was the Democratic presidential front-runner. "[W]ith a cane in his hand, he started going to the dining room, dragging his legs from his hips and supporting himself on the cane and his bodyguard's arm," remembered Alonzo Fields, the White House butler. "And he walked at the angle, a forty-five-degree angle, to the table." Roosevelt fell into his seat, and "that scene was witnessed by all the guests at the dinner table. And everybody said, 'Well, that man, what is he thinking about? How is he going to be president? He's only a half-man.'"

On November 8, 1932, Roosevelt, promising a "new deal for the American people," beat Hoover in a landslide.

HOOVERVILLES RISE DURING THE DEPRESSION

This 1938 photo depicts a shantytown in Circleville, Ohio. Called Hoovervilles as a slap at President Herbert Hoover and his inability to take the country out of economic crisis, such homes were often built out of boxes, wood, cardboard, or scrap metal.

Franklin D. Roosevelt
Tries a New Deal

THE FIRST HUNDRED DAYS

In his first inaugural in March 1933, Franklin Roosevelt stated, "The nation asks for action, and action now." Roosevelt and his New Dealers delivered, passing everything the president tossed their way from March to May, mythologized in American political history as the Hundred Days.

Between 1930 and 1933, nine thousand banks had failed. Using long-forgotten legislation from World War I, Roosevelt declared a bank holiday to calm the run on banks. Congress established the Federal Deposit Insurance Corporation (FDIC), insuring deposits up to $5,000, which convinced skittish depositors to return their money to banks. The Home Owners' Loan Corporation (HOLC) refinanced mortgages at lower interest rates, saving almost a million homeowners from foreclosure.

Mainly, the Hundred Days provided relief, sending $500 million in direct grants to cities and paying farmers to reduce their yield to stop falling produce prices. The administration launched an alphabet soup of government relief efforts, such as the Civilian Conservation Corps (CCC), which employed single young men at a dollar a day to build America's parks and reforest. The Civil Works Administration (CWA) put more than 4 million people to work building over 1 million miles of roads, forty thousand schools, and one thousand airports in just one year. The CWA's work overlapped with the Public Works Administration (PWA), with projects as diverse as the bridge linking Key West to the Florida mainland, and the aircraft carriers *Yorktown* and *Enterprise*.

Work, thought the New Dealers, was better than charity, and many Americans agreed. "I'd rather stay out here in that ditch the rest of my life," said one out-of-work accountant hired under the CWA, "than take one cent of direct relief." Roosevelt justified it another way: "You cannot let people starve."

The first hundred days, as Roosevelt said, were marked by "bold, persistent experimentation." His measures were often politically inconsistent, and many failed. But he convinced the people that they had a captain at the helm of the ship, and one who cared. "The accomplishments of the Hundred Days," writes David M. Kennedy in *Freedom from Fear*, "constituted a masterpiece of presidential leadership unexampled then and unmatched since."

THE "CONFIDENCE-GIVING CONFIDENCE" OF FRANKLIN ROOSEVELT

Franklin Roosevelt's inaugural declaration—"the only thing we have to fear, is fear itself"—was not just a tonic Roosevelt delivered to a worried nation. It expressed Roosevelt's inherent optimism, as obvious as his turned-up chin. One White House dinner guest remarked afterward that Roosevelt's high-test optimism "seemed to generate from him as naturally as heat from fire."

Biographer Roy Jenkins wrote that Roosevelt had a "confidence-giving confidence," likely instilled by his aristocratic upbringing. He came from a well-to-do family. His father, James Roosevelt, inherited a good deal of money and made more from coal and transportation holdings. His mother, Sara, inherited money from her father, a magnate in the China trade. But Roosevelt's riches were emotional as well. Sara adored her only son.

"Granny [Sara] was a martinet," said Franklin's daughter Anna, "but she gave Father the assurance he needed to prevail over adversity. Seldom has a young child been more constantly attended and incessantly approved by his mother." Sara said that she expected he would "grow up to be like his father, straight and honorable, just and kind, an upstanding American."

At Harvard, Roosevelt mapped out a career path that would have seemed delusional if it hadn't been prescient. He told his friends that he would, like his fifth cousin, Theodore Roosevelt, become president. Franklin would also follow many of the steps that Teddy had taken—Harvard, the New York State legislature, assistant secretary of the navy, and governor of New York.

Franklin was undoubtedly smitten by Eleanor's charms. She was bright, educated, moral, and had a character that went far deeper than most of the debutantes of her class. Yet the enchantment might also have been dusted by her lineage: She was the daughter of Theodore Roosevelt's younger brother Elliott. In fact, Eleanor, an orphan, was given away by President Roosevelt at her 1905 wedding, and afterward TR quipped to the groom, "Well, Franklin, there's nothing like keeping the name in the family."

Roosevelt's confidence fostered a willingness to experiment. Eleanor observed that he would often quell others' uncertainty, saying, "There are very few things we can know beforehand. We will try and if we find we are wrong, we will have to change."

KNOWING WHEN TO FOLLOW—
ROOSEVELT'S SOCIAL SECURITY PLAN

History often portrays Franklin Roosevelt as one of America's great leaders, but in fact, he was often one of America's most adept followers—of the American public and political rivals.

In 1934, Huey Long, the Louisiana senator, began barnstorming the nation to boost his "Share Our Wealth" program, which proposed taking money from the rich and redistributing it to all American families so they'd receive $2,500, double the national median income. To round out his program to make "every man a king," the young would get free education and the old would receive pensions. Many expected Long would run for president in 1936, and Roosevelt feared it could split his support and lose him the election.

Dr. Frances Everett Townsend, a physician in Long Beach, California, put forward a cousin to Long's plan. The Townsend Plan called for a monthly pension of $200 for everyone over sixty financed by a 2 percent business tax. The pensioners would have to retire, opening up jobs to the young, and spend their pension checks in a month, juicing the economy. While the plan was likely unworkable, 20 million people signed petitions for it.

Sensing the momentum, Roosevelt asked his Secretary of Labor, Frances Perkins, to come up with an administration plan. "Keep it simple," he told her. Perkins's plan provided an economic umbrella for children, the handicapped, the unemployed, and senior citizens. The proposal would be self-funding, supported by contributions from employees and employers, so that "no damn politician can ever scrap my social security program," Roosevelt said.

In 1935, the House of Representatives passed the Social Security Act by a bipartisan vote of 371 to 3; the Senate, 76 to 6. The United States was the last major industrial nation to establish unemployment insurance and pensions for the elderly and Perkins said Roosevelt saw it as the capstone of his New Deal agenda. "I think he took greater satisfaction from it than from anything else he achieved on the domestic front."

FRANKLIN AND ELEANOR—
A REMARKABLE POLITICAL MARRIAGE

In September 1918, Franklin Delano Roosevelt, a thirty-six-year-old assistant secretary of the navy, came home from Europe. His wife, Eleanor, unpacked his suitcase and found a packet of love letters from her social secretary, Lucy Mercer. The infidelity shattered Eleanor and she offered a divorce. But Franklin's mother, Sara, warned that if he divorced she "would not give him another dollar." Louis Howe, Roosevelt's longtime political advisor, told them both that divorce would end Franklin's political career.

Both agreed to stay. Though physical intimacy apparently ceased, what developed was one of the most remarkable marital partnerships in American political history.

Eleanor became part aide, part confidante, part social conscience; he and the offices he held provided her a prominent platform to voice her progressive ideals. After Franklin contracted polio in 1921, Eleanor insisted he reenter politics and pursue his presidential ambitions. He became governor of New York in 1928. In 1929, Franklin encouraged her to become his "eyes and ears" in the world. He first sent her to inspect an insane asylum. When Eleanor returned with a menu, he asked, "Did you lift a pot cover on the stove to check whether the contents corresponded with this menu?"

In her husband's first year in the White House, she traveled forty thousand miles. For most of his presidency, Roosevelt always cleared his calendar on the night of Eleanor's return so she could debrief him over dinner.

"Much of what she learned and what she understood about the life of the people of this country rubbed off onto FDR," Labor Secretary Frances Perkins said. Eleanor inspected mines; she also investigated poverty in Appalachia and the exploitation of child laborers in Puerto Rico. She pushed him to move faster than he thought politically possible and wrote him so many memos Franklin told her she would have to limit herself to three a night.

"I was the agitator," Eleanor said. "He was the politician."

ROOSEVELT LAUNCHES THE WPA—
INCLUDING WORK FOR ARTISTS

In 1935, President Franklin Roosevelt launched the Works Progress Administration (WPA), which over eight years would employ 8.5 million Americans at a cost of $11 billion and provide "permanent improvement in living conditions or create future new wealth for the nation." Most of the money would go to major construction projects, such as the building of half a million miles of highways and nearly a hundred thousand bridges, but a small percentage was designated for Federal One, a project designed to hire painters, musicians, actors, and writers who were charged with bringing arts to the people. Broadway plays at the time cost between $2 and $5, but many WPA plays, performed in parks, schools, barns, churches, and community centers, were free, and no tickets cost more than a dollar.

The Federal Theater Project was the most politically edgy of the four WPA arts programs. It produced *Macbeth*—with an all-black cast. By the time the theater project closed, 30 million people had seen one of its performances. The Federal Arts Project hired sculptors, glassblowers, poster artists, art teachers, and painters such as Ben Shahn, Stuart Davis, and Jackson Pollock to produce public art. One Portland artist who had been painting backdrops for department store displays said it was as if "we artists had received a commission from the Medicis."

The Federal Music Project hired fifteen thousand musicians to give some two hundred twenty-five thousand performances in symphony halls, parades, baseball stadiums, and schools. Writers were the last group hired, and one writers' union marched in New York City carrying a placard that read CHILDREN NEED BOOKS, WRITERS NEED JOBS, WE DEMAND PROJECTS. They got them, and among the 6,500 writers employed were James Baldwin, John Cheever, Saul Bellow, and Richard Wright. Some writers were hired to record American folklore; others took testimonies from former slaves; others penned the American Guide Series, popular guidebooks on American cities, states, and highway routes.

President Franklin Roosevelt noted that he found some of the art good, "some not so good, but all of it native, human, eager, and alive—all of it painted by their own kind in their own country, and painted about things that they know and look at often and have touched and love."

ROOSEVELT'S FAILED ATTEMPT
TO PACK THE SUPREME COURT

One of Franklin Roosevelt's biggest frustrations in his first term was how often the U.S. Supreme Court knocked down his New Deal legislation. By the end of 1936, the Supreme Court had ruled seven of the nine New Deal programs unconstitutional, challenging the right of government to intervene in the free market. Roosevelt feared that his New Deal would be completely destroyed by a group of nine men with an average age of seventy-one, none appointed by him. "When I retire to private life on January 20, 1941," he said, "I do not want to leave the country in the condition Buchanan left it to Lincoln."

His administration considered and then abandoned pursuing a constitutional amendment to redefine federal powers. Instead, Roosevelt decided to spend his vast political capital—he'd won the 1936 election by the second most lopsided election victory in U.S. history—to reconfigure the makeup of the Supreme Court.

The proposal was not subtle. For every justice over seventy years old who refused to retire, he'd be given the power to appoint an additional justice until he reached a total of fifteen. Roosevelt gave a flimflam reason for the measure: It would speed the court's progress through its overcrowded dockets. The Roosevelt team also insinuated that some of the older justices were senile.

The action was roundly denounced as "court packing" and an attack against the Constitution's separation of powers. "If the American people accept this last audacity of the President without letting out a yell to high heaven," wrote columnist Dorothy Thompson, "they have ceased to be jealous of their liberties and are ripe for ruin."

The fight had derailed the New Deal's momentum, and unnecessarily. Even before Roosevelt abandoned the battle, the justices, perhaps chagrined by denunciations against its conservatism, began backing New Deal legislation. Soon after, the justices began to fall from office with the regularity of autumn leaves, and in the next eight years, Roosevelt would make seven appointments to the Supreme Court.

ROOSEVELT GIVES A FIRESIDE CHAT

Franklin Delano Roosevelt is shown here giving one of his "fireside chats" in 1937. Roosevelt gave thirty of these radio addresses between 1933 and 1944 to reassure and educate the nation during the Great Depression and World War II.

WORLD WAR *and* THEN COLD WAR

COLD WAR

(1941–1960)

Franklin D. Roosevelt Becomes Commander in Chief

WEEK 24

A BALANCED BUDGET, AND THEN
A SECOND ECONOMIC COLLAPSE

In 1943, at his 929th press conference, Franklin Roosevelt was asked how his New Deal had come into existence. "It was because there was an awfully sick patient called the United States of America, and it was suffering from a grave internal disorder. . . . Old Doctor New Deal" had "saved the banks" and "set up a sound banking system." It "was saving homes from foreclosure . . . rescued agriculture from disaster . . . protected stock investors through the S.E.C." Further prescriptions included Social Security and unemployment insurance; minimum wage and maximum hours legislation; and public works projects. "I probably left out half of them," he said.

Roosevelt's look back made it sound like he and his New Deal had cured the Depression, but that's not what happened. The New Deal had improved the health of the economy, but by 1937 unemployment still stood at 14 percent. The thrifty Roosevelt had tolerated deficits to prime the economy's pump, but he still wanted a balanced budget and pursued one. He slashed funds. A deficit of $4.3 billion in 1936 was cut to $2.7 billion in 1937. By 1939, projections showed a balanced federal budget.

It might have been Roosevelt's worst decision as president. In October, the stock market had its most precipitous drop since 1929. Industrial activity showed its greatest decline in the nation's history. Between Labor Day and Christmas, more than 2 million people lost their jobs; another 2 million became unemployed the first three months of 1938. Roosevelt froze, then backtracked, calling for an infusion of $3.4 billion into the economy, but it gained only half the ground it had lost. As one writer put it, "[I I]e kept injecting maintenance doses that kept the patient alive but allowed the sickness to continue."

The country's entrance into World War II provided the right dose of financial medicine. Although the nation's debt doubled in the war, the war economy eliminated unemployment and wages in some industries jumped 70 percent. Neither the New Deal nor war, in fact, had ended the Great Depression. What had was lots of government spending.

AN UNPRECEDENTED THIRD TERM

As Franklin Roosevelt approached the end of his second term, Eleanor encouraged her husband to groom a successor for the presidency. "Franklin always smiled and said he thought people had to prepare themselves," she said. "[S]o long as he was in the picture, it was very hard for anyone to rise to a position of prominence."

Yet Roosevelt, fifty-eight, seemed to want out. "I am tired. I really am. I can't be president again," he told Teamster president Daniel Tobin just after Christmas, 1939, referring to a third term. "I want to go home to Hyde Park. I want to take care of my trees. I want to make the farm pay. I want to write history." Besides, he noted another time, "I would have much more trouble with Congress in my third term and much more bitterness to contend with as a result of my running for a third term. . . ."

In January 1940 he signed a contract with *Collier's* magazine to write twenty-six articles a year for three years for a sum of $75,000. "The role of elder statesman appealed to him," Eleanor said. He had begun to pore through his papers and started building a presidential library, the first ever, at his beloved Hyde Park. Through the spring of 1940, said his housekeeper Henrietta Nesbitt, "The Roosevelts were closing up."

For 144 years, the two-term limit established by George Washington had been sacrosanct. "This is a government of law, and not one man, however popular," said Senator Patrick McCarren as the election approached. Eleanor advised her husband that he "might have served his purpose in history" unless "the international crisis made him indispensable."

And it would. By July 1940, most of Europe had fallen to Germany. Roosevelt would win election in the fall of that year, and a fourth term in 1944. When he died five months later, many Americans grieved for the only president they'd ever known.

His four terms did not set a precedent. Congress passed the Twenty-second Amendment to the Constitution in 1951, establishing a two-term limit. Roosevelt would be the first four-term president—and the last.

THE GREAT ARSENAL FOR DEMOCRACY—LEND-LEASE

In 1940, Franklin Roosevelt desperately wanted to help the English against the Nazis in Germany, but the American people were torn. Some sympathized with groups such as the Committee to Defend America by Aiding the Allies; others, including aviation hero Charles Lindbergh, organized the group America First, urging Americans to defend only the United States. Congress, sensing a divided American people, forbade Roosevelt to send weapons to the English unless they paid in cash.

But England had none. In December, while on a Caribbean cruise, Roosevelt figured a way out: The United States would neither lend money nor sell arms to the British. Instead, it would provide weapons on a "lend-lease" basis.

To explain what that was to confused reporters, the president then provided one of the most famous analogies in the history of American foreign policy: "Suppose my neighbor's home catches on fire, and I have a length of garden hose four or five hundred feet away. If he can take my garden hose and connect it up with his hydrant, I may help him put out his fire. Now what do I do? I don't say to him before that operation, 'Neighbor, my garden hose cost me $15, you have to pay me $15 for it.' . . . . I don't want $15—I want my garden hose back after the fire is over."

The analogy was as folksy as it was absurd: Win or lose, most of the weapons sent to England would likely never be seen again. But most Americans seemed to approve and agreed with what Roosevelt said in a follow-up fireside chat: "We must be the great arsenal of democracy." Congress approved an unprecedented $7 billion to pay for it. American neutrality in Europe had ended.

Most Americans had their attention on Germany when on December 7, 1941, the Japanese air force destroyed the American Pacific fleet docked at Pearl Harbor in the Hawaiian Islands. Roosevelt called it "a date that will live in infamy" and asked Congress to declare war on Japan. Three days later Japan and its allies—Germany and Italy—declared war on the United States.

ROOSEVELT IMPRISONS JAPANESE AMERICANS

After the Japanese air force destroyed the American navy at Pearl Harbor on December 7, 1941, anti-Japanese sentiment on the West Coast boiled. The Roberts Commission, appointed by Roosevelt to investigate, concluded in January 1942 that Japanese Americans in Hawaii had aided the attack. No evidence was offered.

Newspapers and politicians stumbled over each other to call for the relocation of Japanese Americans from the West Coast. This included California Governor Culbert L. Olsen, Republican Attorney General Earl Warren, and the entire California congressional delegation.

Some generals didn't think a Japanese invasion of the West Coast was imminent; those who did argued for quarantining Japanese Americans. "If it is a question of safety of the country or the Constitution of the United States," said John J. McCloy, the war department's point man on domestic security, "why, the Constitution is just a scrap of paper to me."

In February 1942, Secretary of War Henry Stimson called Roosevelt about what to do. Roosevelt threw the question back to Stimson, who deferred to McCloy, who made the decision. Roosevelt signed Executive Order 9066. Approximately 110,000 Japanese Americans, about two-thirds of them American citizens, were moved to primitive dormlike war relocation camps in remote and often arid sections of the West. It was an imprisonment that would last the rest of the war.

They were allowed to bring nothing with them. They sold their belongings at fire-sale prices. Some suggested the U.S. government insure fair prices, but Roosevelt said, "I am not concerned about that." Properties were sold or taken. The estimates of Japanese property losses were some $400 million in 1942 dollars—well over $5 billion today. Congress approved $37 million in reparations to the interned Japanese after the war; in the Civil Liberties Act of 1988, every surviving detainee was awarded $20,000.

Shocked by her husband's decision to approve what the Civil Liberties Union would call the "worst single wholesale violation of civil rights of American citizens in our history," Eleanor Roosevelt argued that Americans' civil rights must be preserved in wartime (for more on Eleanor Roosevelt, see page 330). Franklin gave her a chilly response, then told her that he didn't want the issue mentioned again.

ROOSEVELT MOBILIZES FOR WAR— WITH BIG BUSINESS AS HIS PARTNER

During his second term, Franklin Roosevelt had veered to the left—a "traitor to his class," other well-to-do Americans called him—and antagonized businessmen with his New Deal policies and his call for a more progressive tax code. After Pearl Harbor, however, Roosevelt embraced the business community. "The New Dealers are a vanishing tribe," complained one of Roosevelt's former supporters, "and the money-changers who were driven from the temple are now quietly established in government offices."

Roosevelt appointed Donald Nelson, executive vice president of Sears, Roebuck and Company, to oversee the War Production Board.

"If you . . . go to war . . . in a capitalist country," Secretary of War Henry Stimson remarked, "you have to let business make money out of the process or business won't work." Roosevelt agreed. The government awarded contracts on a cost-plus basis, guaranteeing corporate profits, which would soar from $6.4 billion in 1940 to $11 billion in 1944.

Roosevelt called for a "crushing superiority" of American weapons over those produced by Axis powers, setting war production goals so high they "startled and alarmed" Nelson and military leaders. From 1942 to 1943, Roosevelt ordered aircraft production to double from 60,000 to 125,000 and tank production to triple from 25,000 to 75,000. He called for the number of merchant ships to increase from 1.1 million tons in 1941 to 10 million tons in 1943.

The country would meet Roosevelt's ambitious goals, and in some cases, exceed them. In so doing, the country lifted itself out of the Great Depression. At the end of the 1930s, nearly one in seven Americans were unemployed. By war's end, the U.S. economy was at full employment, creating jobs for over 3 million Americans who reached working age during the war and 3.5 million women as well. Unions and greater demand for workers lifted wages higher than ever before. Those in war-torn countries suffered severe deprivations. But not Americans. On December 7, 1944, the third anniversary of the attack on Pearl Harbor, Macy's rang up its highest sale day ever. Wartime, it turned out, was also a boom time.

ROOSEVELT'S YALTA CONCESSIONS:
A FAILURE OR A NECESSITY?

Franklin Roosevelt would make many controversial decisions during his presidency, but the one that elicited the most criticism was his last: how to shape the postwar world. In February 1945, at Yalta, a resort on the Black Sea, he met with the Soviet Union's Joseph Stalin and Britain's Winston Churchill. Critics would accuse Roosevelt of giving away Poland and the Balkan states to the Soviets, as well as parts of Asia, in return for their participation in the United Nations and in the war against Japan, which critics said wasn't needed.

Roosevelt came to the conference visibly gaunt. Ten months earlier, his cardiologist diagnosed him with hypertension, heart disease, and failure of his left ventrical chamber, calling his health "god-awful." But Roosevelt went anyway, his primary goal to convince the Soviets to join the war against the Japanese. The atomic bomb had not yet been tested, and U.S. leaders feared that an invasion of Japan would lead to catastrophic American losses. Stalin agreed to open up a second front three months after the war against Germany ended, but in return, he wanted concessions such as the Kurile Islands, and the restoration of Soviet territory lost in its 1904 war against Japan: the southern half of Sakhalin Island, as well as railroads and ports in North Korea, Manchuria, and Outer Mongolia. Roosevelt agreed.

The Soviets also wanted Poland as a buffer against future invasions, and had already installed a pro-Soviet government there. Stalin said that control of Poland "was a matter of life and death." Roosevelt and Churchill sought a commitment to free elections down the road, and Stalin gave it, but they knew the commitment was weak. Roosevelt conceded Poland and the Asian territories in large part because the Soviets already occupied them.

Roosevelt was also pleased when Stalin accepted his general outline for the United Nations, which Roosevelt believed was the best guarantee of peace. Stalin held out for a single-power veto on the Security Council, which was hardly ideal, but Roosevelt accepted it as the price for Soviet participation.

"I didn't say that the result was good," Roosevelt told one aide afterward. "I said it was the best I could do."

The aim of the Tehran Conference in December 1943 was to plan the final
strategy to defeat Nazi Germany. Seated in this photo from the conference, held
at the Soviet Embassy in Tehran, Iran, are Joseph Stalin, Franklin Roosevelt, and
Winston Churchill. The men would meet again in Yalta, on the Black Sea, in
February 1945.

HARRY S TRUMAN

Farmer, Soldier, Machine Politician

WEEK 25

AN INAUSPICIOUS START TO A POLITICAL CAREER

For most of Harry Truman's life, no one expected he'd become anything out of the ordinary, much less President of the United States. He did have a proclivity for the piano, which he played two hours every morning before school (Chopin was his favorite), and considered becoming a concert pianist.

He had poor eyesight, which precluded sports and kept him from pursuing another dream: that of going to West Point and becoming a soldier. He was bookish and wanted to go to college, but his family couldn't afford it.

To help support his family, who were farmers, he worked in the mailroom of the *Kansas City Star* in the summer of 1902, then for a construction company, and eventually as a bank clerk, making $100 a month, the most he ever had. It was here he had the first photograph of himself taken.

But when his father's farm had a flood that destroyed his entire corn crop and Harry was called home to help, he lived with his extended family in a house that lacked electricity, running water, or plumbing. He did "everything there was to do"— cared for horses, fixed tractors, sharpened hoes, mended fences, and did the bookkeeping. His day would start at 5:00 A.M. and he wrestled plows pulled by horses. The work was second nature to his father, but Harry didn't like it. He found milking cows, putting rings in hogs' noses, and husking corn disagreeable work, although he rarely complained.

When Truman realized his work on the farm would never provide a good income, he grew restless, investing thousands of dollars in a zinc mine, and then investing in an oil company. "I don't suppose I'd ever have been real pleased if I hadn't tried just once to get rich quickly," he admitted. But Harry wanted the money for more than himself. He also thought financial success might make him more attractive to the childhood sweetheart he called "the most beautiful person on earth": Elizabeth Virginia Wallace.

BESS

Harry S Truman was six years old when he met Elizabeth "Bess" Wallace at the Presbyterian Church's Sunday school in Independence, Missouri, and he would remember the meeting for the rest of his life. "I thought (and still think) she was the most beautiful girl I ever saw," he wrote later. "She had tanned skin blond hair; golden as sunshine, and the most beautiful blue eyes I've ever seen, or ever will see."

The two lost touch after high school, and in 1910, after Truman came back to help on his family's farm, his Aunt Ella asked him to return a cake plate that belonged to Bess's mother. He knocked on the door, Bess answered, and an old-fashioned courtship began that was complete with sitting room visits, picnics, talk of books, letters, and fishing with friends.

In June 1911, Harry wrote Bess an awkward letter proposing marriage. "You may not have guessed it but I've been crazy about you ever since we went to Sunday school together. But I never had the nerve to think you'd even look at me. . . ." She said no, and he wrote back, "You turned me down so easy that I am almost happy anyway. . . . I really never expected any reward for loving you. I shall always hope though."

For seven years he would court her. Finally they promised themselves to each other, but then Harry decided to enlist for World War I. He visited Bess's house on the Fourth of July, 1917, wearing his new uniform. She cried on his shoulder, tears, he later wrote, that were "worth a life time on this earth."

Bess wanted to get married immediately, but he refused, saying he didn't want her to tie herself to "a prospective cripple—or a sentiment. . . ." He carried Bess's oval portrait in his shirt pocket until he returned home two years later. "It has never left me . . . ," he wrote, "nor will it ever." They married on June 28, 1919, twenty-nine years after they first met.

HARRY GOES TO WAR

When Harry S Truman decided to enlist, he organized an artillery battery and was elected first lieutenant by the men. He was fit, except for his eyes; according to his brother Vivian, he only was able to pass the eye exam by memorizing the chart first.

In July 1918, he was given charge of Battery D, 194 men and four guns, of the Second Battalion, 129th Field Artillery, informally known as "Dizzy D" because of the reputation of the Irish Catholics from Kansas City who belonged to it. The men liked him for his friendliness. "You soldier for me," Truman told his men, "and I'll soldier for you."

In his first engagement, Truman was ordered to shell the enemy, German batteries four miles away, with poison gas. The firing commenced at 8:00 P.M., Battery D firing five hundred rounds. But the attack apparently "woke somebody up over there." Truman's battalion was supposed to retreat out of range, but the first sergeant in charge of bringing the horses up didn't arrive. Truman's men feared they'd be hit by poison gas, and struggled to put gas masks on their horses and themselves. Then the German shells hit. Truman's horse was knocked on top of him, and he was pulled out before he was suffocated underneath it.

The men panicked and scattered in the rain. Truman stayed. "I got up and called them everything I knew," he remembered. The men settled and he marched them down to the base position through the dark. It was one of the events of the war, says historian Alonzo Hamby, a Truman biographer, that "established [Truman] as a leader of men."

The night after the artillery barrage, he understood what had happened. "The men think I am not much afraid of shells," he wrote Bess, his confidante, "but they don't know I was too scared to run and that is pretty scared."

TRUMAN ENTERS POLITICS—WITH THE HELP OF A POLITICAL MACHINE

In 1919, like so many soldiers home from war, Harry S Truman was in search of a job. Eddie Jacobson, an old army buddy, suggested they start up a haberdashery in downtown Kansas City to sell "gents' furnishings." Harry did the selling, and for a while the selling was good.

As usual, Harry worked hard, but the haberdashery got crushed in a postwar recession. Truman was thirty-eight, out of work, and feeling "fairly blue." He wrote: "Lost all I had and all I could borrow." Staring failure in the face again, he made a decision that would change his life—and the course of American history.

Jim Pendergast, an army buddy, thought Truman's war record might be a good platform for political office. Pendergast's uncle Tom was such a powerful political operative in Kansas City that they called it "Tom's Town." The Pendergast political machine was involved in bootleg liquor, prostitution, and gambling, and Tom also took kickbacks for his county concrete and real estate business.

In 1922, the Pendergast machine needed a candidate for county commissioner—and saw a good one in Truman, with his farmer stock and war record. Truman's reputation for integrity also put a shine on their less respectable one. When someone told Truman he wasn't the political type, he responded, "Well, I've got to eat."

Truman was in a five-way race and won by 279 votes, possibly with the help of some tampering by Pendergast's organization. For the rest of his life, Truman was tainted with the charge of being a Pendergast man. He vowed never to take a bribe or a kickback, but at one point was plagued by headaches and insomnia because of the ethical implications of his association.

"I wonder if I did right . . . ," he wrote in his diary while county commissioner. "[I saved $3,500,000] but I had to put a lot of no good sons of bitches on the payroll and pay other sons of bitches more money for supplies than they were worth in order to satisfy the political powers. I believe I did do right."

WARTIME WATCHDOG—THE TRUMAN COMMITTEE

In early 1941, Senator Harry S Truman heard accounts that the production of armaments across the country to supply the Allies in the war against Germany was rife with waste. Deciding to investigate, he set out in his old Dodge on a three-thousand-mile trek down to Florida, through Texas, and north again to Michigan, stopping along the way at army bases and defense plants.

In one plant, he saw hundreds of men standing around idle; in another, he saw millions of dollars of equipment rusting in the rain. He also discovered that most of the military work was going to a small number of large corporations, and that the companies received a percentage of profits above costs, no matter how excessive their cost overruns.

At Truman's urging, the Senate established the Senate Special Committee to Investigate the National Defense Program, or the Truman Committee. Truman felt part of history for the first time since his service in the First World War. "Looks like I'll get something done," he wrote Bess.

Truman told his staff that their purpose wasn't to grab headlines or to witch-hunt. "There is no substitute for facts," he would say. And hard work: He told his staffers, "Give the work all you've got." The committee undertook five to fifteen investigations at a time, and the work would take them across the country in the sleeper cars of trains to pursue investigations. He found the work exhausting and in one letter to Bess he wrote of wanting to go away to read Shakespeare and Plutarch. Meanwhile, he earned a reputation for tough but fair treatment of witnesses.

On March 8, 1943, *Time* magazine put "Investigator Truman" on its cover and called his committee the "watchdog, spotlight, conscience and spark plug to the economic war-behind-the-lines." Truman saved taxpayers billions of dollars and prevented shoddy materials from going to the front lines—this from the man the corrupt Pendergast machine of Kansas City had elected to the Senate.

"The sudden emergence of Harry Truman in the Senate," *Time* magazine wrote, "is a queer accident of democracy."

BACKING INTO THE VICE PRESIDENCY

For a year leading up to the 1944 Democratic Party convention, Truman had been saying he wasn't interested in the vice presidency—he wanted to stay a senator.

Party insiders wanted Henry Wallace, Roosevelt's vice president since 1941, removed from the ticket because they considered him so liberal he would hurt Roosevelt in a close election.

Yet at the convention, Arthur Krock of the *New York Times* said the front-runners were Wallace, Senator Alben Barkley, presidential advisor Jimmy Byrnes, and Supreme Court Justice William O. Douglas. A poll done at the time found that 48 percent of Americans preferred Wallace; 22 percent preferred Byrnes; and 5 percent Truman.

But among Democratic insiders, Truman was seen as a default choice. He'd done well with the committee to investigate wartime production, refrained from racist comments, had a good record with labor, yet also seemed to appeal to conservatives. Truman himself came expecting to nominate Byrnes and privately thought Wallace would win a floor fight. He kept resisting the number two position. Finally, Roosevelt insiders called him into a hotel room so he could "overhear" a conversation between the president and Democratic Committee Chair Bob Hannegan.

"Bob," the president yelled, "have you got that fellow lined up yet?"

"No," replied Hannegan, "he is the contrariest goddamn mule from Missouri I ever dealt with."

"Well, you tell the senator that if he wants to break up the Democratic Party in the middle of the war, that's his responsibility." Then the president hung up. Reportedly, Truman's first words were, "Oh, shit."

Artillery Captain Harry S Truman in his "doughboy" uniform during World War I. "Doughboy" was a term given to American soldiers during the war. While the term's origins are uncertain, the explanation most often cited is that U.S. soldiers in the Mexican-American War would often get covered with a chalky dust from marching in northern Mexico, making them look like unbaked dough.

HARRY S TRUMAN

President Truman—Cold Warrior,
Frustrated Reformer

WEEK 26

PANIC—AND THEN PRESIDENT

On April 12, 1945, Harry S Truman arrived at a private hideaway in the Capitol for end-of-the-day "libations" with Speaker of the House Sam Rayburn. Truman had just mixed himself a drink when he was told that White House Press Secretary Stephen Early had left a message to call immediately. Truman dialed the number and said, "This is the VP."

Early told Truman to come to the White House as "quickly and as quietly" as he could. Truman later told his mother that he thought Roosevelt might want him to attend a funeral of an old friend, and said at another time, "I thought I was going down there to meet the president. I didn't allow myself to think anything else." But someone present said that Truman lost all his color as he put down the telephone. And as soon as he left Rayburn's office, he ran through the hallways of the Capitol.

He was driven to the White House, where two ushers took him up the elevator to the second floor, and brought him to a sitting room where Eleanor Roosevelt was waiting. She put her hand on Harry Truman's shoulder and said, "Harry, the president is dead."

Truman was silent for some time before he said, "Is there anything I can do for you?"

"Is there anything *we* can do for *you?*" the First Lady responded. "For you are the one in trouble now."

As the American people grieved over the loss of Roosevelt, they also worried about whether Harry Truman was up for the job. David Lilienthal, head of the Tennessee Valley Authority, felt physically ill when he thought of Truman as president. "The country and the world," he thought, "don't deserve to be left this way. . . ." The day after Roosevelt's death, Truman met a group of reporters after a lunch at the Capitol. "Boys, if you ever pray, pray for me now," he said in a moment of wheat-grain honesty. "I don't know whether you fellows ever had a load of hay fall on you, but when they told me yesterday what had happened, I felt like the moon, the stars, and all the planets had fallen on me."

THE TRUMAN DOCTRINE—
INTERVENING AGAINST COMMUNISM

In February 1947, the United States would respond to an international crisis in a way that would cement Harry Truman's reputation as a defender of democracy and, some would claim, launch the cold war. The crisis occurred when an exhausted Great Britain decided to pull troops and aid from Greece and Turkey. Would the faltering countries succumb to Communist takeovers if the United States didn't step in?

At the time, many American leaders were arguing for a return to a pre–World War II isolationist foreign policy. Truman advocated for an alternative that would become known as the Truman Doctrine, which he articulated in a short, somber speech before a joint session of Congress on March 12, 1947. During World War II, he said, the nations of Germany and Japan had tried "to impose their will, and their way of life, upon other countries." The fear now was that the Soviet Union would do the same.

Truman's idea was to push back—"containment" became the catchphrase—against the threat of Communist expansion. In Truman's view, countries around the world had two choices—one "based on the will of the majority . . . is distinguished by free institutions, representative government, free elections, guarantees of individual liberty, freedom of speech and religion, and freedom from political oppression." The other was based on the will of the minority and relied on "terror and oppression, a controlled press and radio, fixed elections, and the suppression of personal freedoms. . . ."

The United States should "support free peoples who are resisting attempted subjugation by armed minorities or by outside pressures. I believe that we must assist free peoples. . . . If we falter in our leadership, we may endanger the peace of the world, and we shall surely endanger the welfare of this nation."

The Truman Doctrine declared that the United States would police the globe, and Congress approved $400 million for military aid to Turkey and Greece. The journalist Walter Lippmann called the new containment policy a "strategic monstrosity" that would pull the United States into conflicts around the world. The next three decades would prove him right.

THE MARSHALL PLAN—ONE OF TRUMAN'S PROUDEST ACHIEVEMENTS

After World War II, a Europe devastated by war faced political instability, as it had after World War I. The Truman Administration feared France and Italy—where Communist parties refused to cooperate with existing governments—and other European nations were at risk of Communist takeovers. The former general and Secretary of State George Marshall declared, "The patient is sinking while the doctors deliberate."

By 1947, the United States already had given $3 billion in foreign relief to Europe, and the Republican Congress was steeled to cut taxes and expenditures. When Republican Senator Arthur Vandenberg read in the *New York Times* that $7 billion was being proposed for European aid, he called up journalist James Reston to tell him that he must be mistaken because Congress would never approve that much money to save anybody.

Truman invited House Minority Leader Sam Rayburn to the White House and told him the aid was needed to prevent the continent's economy from going "down the drain" in a depression, a spiral that would take the United States with it.

Clark Clifford, a Truman advisor, at one point suggested that the president put his name on the measure, but Truman understood that "[a]nything going up there bearing my name will quiver a couple of times, turn belly up, and die." In a few days he decided that the plan should have General George Marshall's name on it. "The worst Republican on the Hill can vote for it if we name it after the General," Truman told Clifford.

Truman was right. Many Republicans voted for the plan, especially after the Soviet Union and its satellite countries refused to participate, creating the impression that the aid would stave off the westward spread of Communism.

From 1947 until 1951, the United States gave $13 billion in aid to rebuild Europe. "I think it's one of the proudest moments in American history," said Clifford. "What happened during that period was that Harry Truman and the United States saved the free world."

TRUMAN FIRES GENERAL DOUGLAS MACARTHUR

On March 21, 1951, President Harry S Truman circulated a proposal with U.N. military leaders for a cease-fire with North Korea and China. Instead of deferring to Truman, General Douglas MacArthur, the American general leading U.N. forces, wrote the Chinese that their military was inferior and that the U.N. troops would drive the war into China unless they met with him and accepted unconditional surrender. Truman was furious that MacArthur had undermined his peace initiative. "I was ready to kick him into the North China Sea," he recalled later.

In his *Memoirs*, Truman wrote: "It was in open defiance of my orders as President and as Commander in Chief. This was a challenge to the President under the Constitution. It also flouted the policy of the United Nations. . . ." MacArthur's insubordination included being too aggressive, recommending the United States drop thirty to fifty atomic bombs on Chinese cities and separate Korea from Manchuria by laying down atomic waste along the Yalu River. Truman rejected such a devastating escalation of the war and decided he had to fire MacArthur.

Almost as soon as the president made the decision, a phone call came from a newspaperman that a "major resignation" had taken place in Tokyo. "He's not going to be allowed to quit on me," Truman supposedly said. "He's going to be fired!"

And fired he was. The headline that appeared all over the world on April 11 was a variation of TRUMAN FIRES MACARTHUR. Truman dismissed those who said firing such a popular general was a courageous decision. "Courage didn't have anything to do with it," Truman said. "General MacArthur was insubordinate and I fired him. That's all there was to it."

Afterward, MacArthur made an emotional address to a joint session of Congress (and to 30 million Americans via television) in which he promised "to fade away, an old soldier who tried to do his duty." Truman didn't view the address but he read it afterward, and pronounced it "a bunch of damn bullshit."

TRUMAN—A RACIST WHO SUPPORTED CIVIL RIGHTS?

When Harry S Truman grew up in Independence, Missouri, people waved their handkerchiefs when the song "Dixie" was played. Most storeowners refused to serve blacks, who were also barred from the town library, and were forced into inferior black schools and a ghetto. Truman was a bigot for much of his life. As a twenty-six-year-old he wrote: "I think one man is just as good as another so long as he's honest and decent and not a n——— or a Chinaman."

But in February 1948, President Harry Truman sent a message to Congress based on the Civil Rights Commission landmark report *To Secure These Rights*. Truman called on all levels of government to close "a serious gap between our ideals and our practices." He called for a federal law against lynching, and he wanted to strike down the poll taxes that kept blacks from voting in Southern states, and to end segregation on trains, buses, and airplanes.

"The Federal Government has a clear duty," he wrote in his address, "to see the Constitutional guarantees of individual liberties and of equal protection under the laws are not denied or abridged anywhere in the Union."

Before the 1948 election, a group of southern Democrats met with the president, suggesting he "soften" his racial message if he wanted their support (for more on the election of 1948, see page 346). Afterward, Truman wrote them a letter saying he grew up in a part of Missouri where "Jim Crowism" had thrived.

"But my stomach turned over," he wrote, "when I learned that Negro soldiers, just back from overseas, were being dumped out of army trucks in Mississippi and beaten. Whatever my inclinations as a native of Missouri might have been, as President I know this is bad. I shall fight to end evils like this." Most of his proposed civil rights legislation would be blocked by southern Democrats, but he would take whatever action possible, desegregating the armed forces by executive order in 1948.

"The wonderful, wonderful development in those years," said Clark Clifford, a Truman aide who pushed the president to support civil rights, "was Harry Truman's capacity to grow."

PLAINLY, TRUMAN SUMS UP HIS PRESIDENCY

After serving for eight years, Harry S Truman gave his farewell broadcast to the American people on January 15, 1953. The speech lacked any sparkling phrases, but was full of the plain-spun language typical of the man from Missouri.

He reminded listeners that his first decision was to move forward on the United Nations. Then, within four months, Germany surrendered, and he made the decision to use the atomic bomb against Japan "in the conviction it would save hundreds of thousands of lives—Japanese as well as American. . . ." (For more on Truman's decision to drop the atomic bomb, see page 376.)

His term had been dominated by the cold war, he noted, and he called his decision to rally U.N. troops and send them to Korea "the most important in my time as President. . . ." If Korea fell to the Communists, other countries would too, and "the courage and confidence of the free world would be ebbing away, just as it did in the 1930's. . . . [T]his time we met the test."

He was prescient about how the cold war would end. "As the free world grows stronger, more united, more attractive to men on both sides of the Iron Curtain—and as the Soviet hopes for easy expansion are blocked—then there will have to come a time of change in the Soviet world. Nobody can say for sure when that is going to be, or exactly how it will come about, whether by revolution, or trouble in the satellite states, or by a change inside the Kremlin. . . . I have a deep and abiding faith in the destiny of free men."

At home, Truman noted that employment was high and incomes had risen. He spoke of "a tremendous awakening of the American conscience on the great issues of civil rights. . . ."

"When Franklin Roosevelt died, I felt there must be a million men better qualified than I. . . . Through all of it . . . I have been well aware I did not really work alone—that you were working with me. . . . For that I shall be grateful, always."

HARRY S TRUMAN ADDRESSES THE NAACP

President Harry S Truman addressing the NAACP convention on the steps of the Lincoln Memorial in Washington, D.C., on June 29, 1947. A bigot for much of his life, Truman's message about race relations grew as president, and he even desegregated the armed forces in 1948.

All Like Ike—Dwight Eisenhower, the General as President

DWIGHT EISENHOWER—A BELATED RISE TO THE TOP

Dwight Eisenhower hardly had the résumé we expect of a future five-star general and U.S. president. Ike, his boyhood nickname, went to West Point for a free education as "one of the most promising backs in eastern football." But a knee injury ended his career, leaving him "almost despondent." His grades fell and he took up smoking. He graduated in the middle of his class academically, but in the top tier if measured by demerits. His peers best remembered him for his coaching skills.

He was greatly disappointed when he wasn't sent to Europe when World War I broke out. Instead, he was called upon to train cadets how to use tanks. In 1935, General Douglas MacArthur would take Eisenhower with him when he went to the Philippines to train Filipino troops, calling him "the best officer in the U.S. Army." But when Eisenhower returned home in 1939, he was still only a lieutenant colonel. He told his son that he didn't expect to make the rank of colonel until 1950, when he would be sixty, probably too old to become a general.

On December 12, 1941, five days after the Pearl Harbor attack, Eisenhower was called to Washington by Chief of Staff George Marshall to discuss the Philippines, under Japanese attack. The commander was impressed with Eisenhower's energy, poise, and his ability to make hard decisions, and was soon asking him not about the Philippines, but how he would fight a war in Europe.

"Are you satisfied with it?" Marshall asked Eisenhower about a proposed plan for invasion of Europe he was asked to devise. When Eisenhower said he thought the plan a good one, Marshall said, "Well, you better like it, because you're going to carry it out." Before the war was over, Eisenhower would lead the attack against Nazis in North Africa, the invasion of Sicily, and then Operation Overlord, the invasion of Europe onto the beaches of Normandy.

Eisenhower would return home a hero in June 1945. It wasn't long before Americans were drafting the general as the next president—an American tradition that had led to the election of George Washington, Andrew Jackson, Zachary Taylor, and Ulysses S. Grant—and in 1952, President Dwight D. Eisenhower.

EISENHOWER UNDERMINES JOSEPH MCCARTHY, BUT NEVER CONFRONTS HIM

The first chance Dwight D. Eisenhower had to take on Wisconsin's junior Republican Senator Joseph R. McCarthy and his charges that Communists had infiltrated the American government came on October 3, 1952, as Eisenhower's presidential campaign train whistled into Milwaukee. McCarthy, running for reelection as Wisconsin senator, had described Eisenhower's hero, General George C. Marshall, as a traitor for trying in 1946 to mediate peace in the Chinese civil war. Eisenhower had a prepared a defense of Marshall that he'd given in other stops, but he was asked to delete his criticism of McCarthy in Wisconsin for fear the Republicans would lose the state, as they had in 1948.

Eisenhower obliged, but the press found out. One *Washington Post* cartoon ran the headline ANYTHING TO WIN.

During his presidency, Eisenhower refused to speak out publicly against McCarthy, arguing that President Harry Truman's denunciations had only given him free press and prestige. For the first two years of his administration, Eisenhower seemed to give substance to McCarthy's charges by broadening statutes against espionage and sabotage, signing laws that stripped Fifth Amendment rights during investigations involving national security, and issuing an executive order permitting seven thousand federal employees to be fired as security risks.

But when McCarthy began his investigation of Communists in the U.S. Army in the spring of 1954, Eisenhower leaked information to McCarthy's committee members that the senator had sought special treatment for an aide drafted into the army. When McCarthy threatened to subpoena federal employees, Eisenhower claimed executive privilege, stopping him cold. During the hearings, McCarthy would overreach and self-destruct. On September 27, 1954, the Senate, quietly encouraged by Eisenhower, voted to censure McCarthy by a 75 to 12 vote.

Fred Greenstein, an Eisenhower biographer, argues that Eisenhower's "hidden-hand" tactics during McCarthy's hearings did a "perfect job of contributing to the downfall of Joe McCarthy." But political writer Robert Donovan has argued that Eisenhower provided no moral leadership. "What I hoped Eisenhower would do . . . was deliver one great speech about the evils of McCarthy and McCarthyism. . . . The speech would have had enormous impact."

HIGHWAYS—IKE'S PROUDEST DOMESTIC ACHIEVEMENT

Eisenhower's feats in World War II and his focus on foreign policy while president often overshadow his most transformative domestic initiative: the building of a national highway system.

When he came into office, a quarter of all America's roads were unfit for travel by car or truck, and those that were fit were slow going. Eisenhower had been concerned about America's roads since he traveled cross-country as a young soldier with the army in 1919. He spent sixty-one days crawling to San Francisco, as vehicles were stymied by mud or sand, and even crashed through wooden bridges.

Previous plans to build a highway network had been blocked by disputes over whether states or the federal government should pay for it. Eisenhower believed that the federal government should pay for most of the improvements, putting him in line with public works presidents such as John Quincy Adams and Franklin Roosevelt.

Eisenhower also saw the highways as a military measure. When he led Allied troops into Germany at the end of World War II, he was struck by Hitler's efficient autobahn system. An American highway system, Eisenhower believed, would provide quick escape routes from cities threatened with nuclear attack, and would facilitate the movement of military equipment around the country if war broke out.

In January 1956, Eisenhower signed the Interstate Highway Act, which would lead to the laying of more than forty thousand miles of four- to eight-lane highways, uniting the country as never before. Congress committed nearly $25 billion over a thirteen-year span, making it the largest public works project in American history. Despite long-term negative consequences—the destruction of urban neighborhoods by highways, a flight from cities to car-dependent suburbs, a national addiction to cheap oil, and increased air pollution—Eisenhower saw only the positives, and considered it his proudest domestic initiative. In his 1963 memoir, *Mandate for Change 1953–1956,* he explained why: "More than any single action by the government since the end of the war, this one would change the face of America. . . . Its impact on the American economy—the jobs it would produce in manufacturing and construction, the rural areas it would open up—was beyond calculation."

EISENHOWER ON CIVIL RIGHTS—DO HIS ACTIONS SPEAK LOUDER THAN WORDS?

The most important day in America during the 1950s might have been May 17, 1954, when the Supreme Court issued its *Brown v. Board of Education of Topeka* ruling, decreeing that "separate facilities are inherently unequal." The decision dismantled segregation, which had persisted for almost a century.

Publicly, Eisenhower said only that "the Supreme Court has spoken, and I am sworn to uphold the constitutional processes in this country; and I will obey." This legalistic response suggested to many that Eisenhower opposed the decision, and they were right. In private, he called the ruling "too sweeping" and "wrong," and told those in his inner circle that states, instead of federal courts or the federal government, should decide desegregation matters.

Some interpreted his silence as tacit approval for Southern resistance to desegregation. "With his wartime victor's laurels, with his high moral standing, his popularity . . . Dwight Eisenhower might well have swung most of the nation into acceptance," writes Tom Wicker in his biography of Eisenhower.

But David A. Nichols, author of *A Matter of Justice*, argues that we "must look closely at what he did, not just what he said, or we will miss much of what Eisenhower was about in civil rights."

Nichols credits Eisenhower with desegregating the District of Columbia in 1953 and doing the same with American combat units, implementing Truman's executive order from 1948. In 1957, Eisenhower supported civil rights legislation, the first since 1875, and did the same in 1960, winning Republicans to the cause. He also appointed a bevy of justices to lower and upper courts who would defend civil rights for a generation.

In 1957, when Arkansas's Governor Orval Faubus deployed National Guard troops in Little Rock to keep nine black students from entering the city's Central High School, Eisenhower sent in elite troops from the 101st Airborne, the first time since Reconstruction that federal troops were sent into the South to protect blacks—and the peace.

"A professional politician might have backed down," Senator Herman Talmadge, a segregationist Democrat from Georgia, wrote later, "but not Ike."

CURTAILING A RUNAWAY MILITARY BUDGET

Eisenhower left office warning about the dangers of a military-industrial complex, but he also fought waste and profligate spending in the military budget during his entire presidency. Early on, Eisenhower stated, "Every gun that is made, every warship launched, every rocket fired signifies, in the final sense, a theft from those who hunger and are not fed, those who are cold and are not clothed. The cost of one modern heavy bomber is this: a modern brick school in more than thirty cities."

Ever since the end of World War II, Eisenhower was appalled by the idea that the United States would have to endlessly spend "unconscionable sums" of money on defense. To do so, he believed, would damage the country economically by reducing productivity and exacerbating inflation.

But Eisenhower's struggle to curtail military spending was threatened on October 4, 1957, when the Soviets launched *Sputnik I*, the first unmanned earth satellite. Congress, the Joint Chiefs of Staff, and even private groups like the Ford Foundation and the Rockefeller Brothers Fund expressed a panic palpable across the nation, insisting that the country should spend on missiles, nuclear weapons, conventional forces, fallout shelters, and more.

A lesser president would have relented. But Eisenhower insisted that his defense budget was sufficient. "God help the nation when it has a President who doesn't know as much about the military as I do," he said. In a letter to a friend, he also wrote about the political implications he believed a permanent war footing would have. "Any person that doesn't clearly understand that . . . permanent maintenance of a crushing weight of military power would eventually produce dictatorship should not be entrusted with any kind of responsibility in our country." Eisenhower controlled the arms race; he came close to balancing the budget; he kept inflation under 1 percent.

"Eisenhower's calm, common-sense, deliberate response to *Sputnik*," writes Eisenhower biographer Stephen Ambrose, "may have been his finest gift to the nation, if only because he was the only man who could have given it."

THE U-2 DEBACLE DESTROYS POSSIBILITIES OF DÉTENTE

On February 11, 1960, President Dwight Eisenhower said he was willing to ban all nuclear tests—in the atmosphere, in the oceans, in outer space, and detectable underground ones. Eisenhower's proposal was bold, given that his top military advisors, powerful congressmen, and influential journalists almost all opposed it. Yet the Soviets responded positively, and a Paris summit was scheduled for May 19, 1960.

"May 1960 could become a very great May," the Communist Party newspaper *Pravda* wrote on May Day. "Men with great responsibility will meet in Paris. The fate of peoples will depend on what they decide." They weren't aware that Eisenhower had authorized a high-flying spy plane called a U-2 to determine Soviet missile strength, permitting the mission to fly no later than May first. On that day, pilot Francis Gary Powers flew his plane into Soviet airspace; thirteen hundred miles inside Russia he reported an engine flameout and then went silent.

On May 5, Khrushchev announced that an American plane had been shot down in its airspace. Believing the Soviets had no evidence (the CIA had told him the airplane would be obliterated if hit), Eisenhower announced that the plane was on a weather mission over Turkey but had strayed off course. The next day, Khrushchev revealed he had plane parts, a spool of spy film, and a pilot, "alive and kicking."

Eisenhower then said he hadn't authorized Powers to fly over Russia, and then said he had authorized the flights, but early in his administration. Eisenhower briefly considered resignation, and then came clean, disclosing that spying was "a distasteful but vital necessity." Columnist James Reston wrote: "Everything he was noted for—caution, patience, leadership, military skill, even good luck—suddenly eluded him precisely at the moment he needed them most."

In Paris, Khrushchev demanded an apology for the U-2 flights and wanted those responsible punished. Eisenhower refused. Khrushchev walked out and withdrew his invitation to visit Moscow. "The nuclear arms race and the Cold War," writes Tom Wicker in his biography of Eisenhower, "the vast expenditures to sustain both, with tensions only occasionally lessened and never removed, would continue for nearly thirty years, through seven more administrations, into the 1980s."

General Dwight Eisenhower giving orders to American paratroopers in England on June 6, 1944, D-day. As the men prepared for the assault, Eisenhower said, "I have full confidence in your courage, devotion to duty, and skill in battle. We will accept nothing less than full victory!"

The 1960s
(1960–1968)

JOHN F. KENNEDY

A Father's Ambition, a Son's Success

WEEK 28

JOSEPH KENNEDY'S AMBITIONS FOR HIS SON

John F. Kennedy would likely not have been president without the power, money, and prodding of his father, Joseph P. Kennedy, who made his money on Wall Street, producing Hollywood movies, and importing liquor. Joseph was an ambitious, cunning, third-generation Irish-Catholic immigrant who improved his political standing by marrying Rose E. Fitzgerald, daughter of John F. Fitzgerald, the Boston mayor.

Joseph taught his sons the "Kennedy standards," which meant not only excelling, but winning. "That's the only thing Jack gets really emotional about," his sister Eunice said, "when he loses."

Jack attended Harvard and wrote his senior thesis, *Why England Slept*, about the difficulties democracies faced dealing with totalitarian nations, based on England's response to Adolf Hitler. Joseph, ambassador to England under Franklin Roosevelt in the 1930s, shared ideas with his son and provided research materials. Joseph convinced *New York Times* journalist Arthur Krock to rewrite the text, Krock's agent found a publisher, and Time-Life publisher Henry Luce composed a foreword. When John helped save his shipmates after his PT boat 109 was rammed by a Japanese destroyer in August 1943, Joseph made sure that a positive *New Yorker* profile about Kennedy's actions got reprinted in *Reader's Digest*.

It was John's older brother, Joe Jr., who was groomed by his father to be the first Catholic president of the United States. But Joe Jr. was killed during a dangerous bombing mission in German-occupied France for which he volunteered. In 1957, when John was a U.S. senator, Joseph said, "I got Jack into politics. I was the one. I told him Joe was dead and that it was therefore his responsibility to run for Congress. He didn't want to. He felt he didn't have the ability and he still feels that way. But I told him he had to."

He ran for Congress in 1946 to represent Massachusetts's Eleventh District, which included Boston's North End and Charlestown. His father spent as much as $300,000, a staggering sum, on the campaign. "With what I'm spending," Joseph said, "I could elect my chauffeur."

THE IMAGE OF HEALTH HIDES A SICKLY JOHN KENNEDY

To many, John F. Kennedy was the picture of health, a vibrant man who liked to play football, golf, and tennis. But the truth was that he was sickly until the day he died.

In one two-year span, 1955 to 1957, he was hospitalized nine times for back problems, upper respiratory infections, irritable bowel syndrome, and chronic prostatitis, perhaps from a college sexual contact. After his death, Kennedy's mother, Rose, wrote in her memoirs that her son went on for years "trying to make others think—that he was a strong, robust, quite healthy person who just happened to be sick a good deal of the time." His father pulled strings to get Jack, with his bad back and gastrointestinal problems, past his navy physical. His bad back was reinjured when his boat was hit in the Pacific and aggravated further during an exploratory spinal surgery in 1944. It became so bad that by the mid-1950s he often walked with crutches.

He decided to undergo a risky double-fusion spinal operation in 1954 and was given last rites afterward. The pain never ended. To relieve the pain, he was prescribed procaine injections, exercise regimens, codeine, hot packs, ethyl chloride spray, and prednisone. While president, he sometimes wore a metal back brace, and one CBS journalist was shocked to see him being lowered from the back of a plane into a wheelchair.

In 1947, while Kennedy was abroad, he became so ill that a priest was called in to give him last rites. He was diagnosed with Addison's disease, a grave autoimmune illness that afflicts the adrenal glands, which are key in fighting infection and regulating body metabolism.

He told the public that Addison's was a recurrence of wartime malaria, but just before his presidential nomination in 1960, Nixon circulated rumors of his Addison's. Kennedy had two doctors issue a public letter stating that he was in excellent health. The Kennedy circle continued to lie about his health during his administration, and Robert Kennedy even went so far as to have some of his brother's medical records destroyed after his death.

A CATHOLIC PRESIDENT?

Throughout the presidential primaries in 1960, Kennedy was dogged by voter suspicions of his Catholicism, and the press held onto the issue like a lamprey. Before the Wisconsin presidential primary, the *Milwaukee Journal* listed each county under three headings: Democrats, Republicans, and Catholics. Photographers published pictures of Kennedy shaking hands with nuns. Bobby asked organizers in West Virginia, "Well, what are our problems?" One man shouted, "There's only one problem. He's a Catholic. That's our God-damned problem!"

The candidate finally told his aides, "I'm getting tired of these people who think I want to replace the gold at Fort Knox with a supply of holy water." (Jackie joked to a family friend that it was unfair to oppose her husband because of his Catholicism. "After all," she said, "he's such a poor Catholic.") Despite advice that he finesse the issue, Kennedy decided to make a live televised speech addressing his Catholicism before a group of Protestant ministers in Houston, Texas, on September 12, 1960.

Kennedy began by saying that although he was speaking about his Catholicism, he saw "far more critical issues in the 1960 election . . . for war and hunger and ignorance and despair know no religious barrier." Then he stated that he believed in "an America where the separation of church and state is absolute. . . . I believe in a President whose views on religion are his own private affair. . . . I am not the Catholic candidate for President. I am the Democratic Party's candidate for President, who happens also to be a Catholic. . . ."

A Catholic was targeted today, he said, but tomorrow it might be Jews, Quakers, Unitarians, or Baptists. If "forty million Americans lost their chance of being President on the day they were baptized, then it is the whole nation that will be the loser. . . ." Legendary House Speaker Sam Rayburn heard the speech on television. "By God, look at him—and listen to him!" said Rayburn. "He's eating them blood raw. The young feller will be a great President!"

ANATOMY OF AN ELECTION

In the 1960 presidential election, Republican Richard Nixon touted his governmental experience—his slogan was "Experience counts"—boasting that "after each of my foreign trips [as vice president] I have made recommendations which were adopted. . . ." Kennedy noted that he and Nixon came into Congress in 1946 and quipped, "Mr. Nixon is experienced, experienced in policies of retreat, defeat and weakness." He was referring to a claim that the United States was trailing the Soviet Union in defense, particularly a "missile gap."

Kennedy courted the liberal wing of his party, including Eleanor Roosevelt. She was suspicious of the Kennedys, yet after a meeting with Kennedy during the campaign, she wrote a friend, "I like him better than I ever had before because he seemed so little cock-sure, and I think he has a mind that is open to new ideas. . . ." When Martin Luther King, Jr., was jailed in Georgia for a trumped-up traffic violation while trying to desegregate Atlanta just weeks before the election, Kennedy made a call to Coretta Scott King—Nixon did not—and Bobby Kennedy secured King's release from jail. Blacks all over the country would vote overwhelmingly for Kennedy.

Meanwhile, Nixon's campaign faltered. He was ill during the first debate, watched by 70 million Americans, and it showed. Kennedy was more handsome, looked more relaxed, and impressed viewers with his command of details. Nixon pleaded with Eisenhower to stimulate the economy to help his candidacy, but Eisenhower refused, wanting to leave a balanced budget. Eisenhower did hit the campaign trail hard for Nixon, but when the candidate asked Eisenhower, who had a bad heart, to publicly draw attention to Kennedy's health problems, the president refused.

With over 68 million votes cast, Kennedy's edge was just 119,450 votes, the closest popular vote since Benjamin Harrison beat Grover Cleveland in 1888. Afterward, Kennedy asked his aide Kenny O'Donnell, "How did I manage to beat a guy like this by only a hundred thousand votes?"

JFK'S SOARING INAUGURAL

In preparation for his inaugural address, John F. Kennedy asked his favorite speechwriter, Ted Sorensen (for more on Sorensen, see page 340), to gather suggestions from the likes of Adlai Stevenson, the previous Democratic presidential candidate and a powerful orator, and Reverend Billy Graham, who sent biblical quotes. Kennedy set parameters—he wanted a crisp speech that wasn't partisan and emphasized foreign policy, Sorensen said. After Sorensen wrote a draft, Kennedy edited it, changing the *I*'s to *we*'s. Kennedy deleted the mention of domestic goals to shorten it. "I don't want people to think I'm a windbag," he said. His speech ran 1,355 words, half the 2,599-word average for the previous presidential inaugurals.

Kennedy rehearsed the speech wherever he went the day before his inauguration. Just before 1:00 P.M. on January 20, 1961, his breath a frosty white, he began as Jefferson did, emphasizing the similarities among Americans, saying, "We observe today not a victory of party but a celebration of freedom. . . ." He also emphasized renewal: "Let the word go forth from this time and place, to friend and foe alike, that the torch has been passed to a new generation of Americans. . . ."

Kennedy's speech also included one of the most enduring lines in inaugural history: "Now the trumpet summons us again—not as a call to bear arms, though arms we need—not as a call to battle, though embattled we are—but to bear the burden of a long twilight struggle, year in and year out 'rejoicing in hope, patient in tribulation'—a struggle against the common enemies of man: tyranny, poverty, disease, and war itself. . . . And so, my fellow Americans: ask not what your country can do for you—ask what you can do for your country."

THE TELEGENIC PRESIDENT

John F. Kennedy gained an edge—and probably the election—in the televised debates that showed him as more handsome, attractive, and cool than Richard M. Nixon. After he was elected, a debate emerged among his closest advisors: Should the president use live televised press conferences to reach the American people?

President Eisenhower had used televised press conferences since 1955, but they were often edited and broadcast later, sometimes "just before the national anthem, they got so dull," recalled one reporter. Kennedy's press secretary, Pierre Salinger, urged him to do press conferences live, although other aides feared a live broadcast would risk blunders. Kennedy liked the idea, thinking it was a way to bypass print journalists who often edited his message.

The president prepared carefully for his press conferences. The week before, Salinger would gather material on current issues from the major departments and aides assembled briefing books on foreign policy and economics. The president would study the material, like a student cramming for a test. The morning of the press conference, advisors would pepper Kennedy with questions. "I can handle that one—let's move on," the president might say. Once an aide suggested he evade a question. "I can evade questions without help," replied the president. "What I need is answers!"

Salinger came back with answers minutes before the 4:00 P.M. press conference, as the president came back from a nap. To guide the give-and-take, Salinger would tell some journalists that the president would have something to say about certain topics. Franklin Roosevelt's early press conferences had fewer than a hundred correspondents; Kennedy hosted twelve hundred journalists, mostly TV men. He stood on a platform and they surrounded him "like a college class about to hear a lecture."

The columnist James Reston marveled at Kennedy's performances. "How Kennedy knew the precise drop in milk consumption in 1960 . . . and the number of speeches cleared by the Defense Department is not quite clear, but anyway, he did. He either overwhelmed you with decimal points or disarmed you with a smile and a wisecrack."

JOHN F. KENNEDY SUFFERED FROM A BAD BACK AND MANY OTHER HEALTH PROBLEMS

John F. Kennedy fought through severe back pain and other health ailments for much of his life. Here Senator Kennedy is seen on crutches as he and wife Jacqueline enter a New York hospital in 1954.

JOHN F. KENNEDY

Responding to Crises—
Kennedy Grows in Office

KENNEDY STARES DOWN THE GENERALS
DURING THE CUBAN MISSILE CRISIS

In September 1962, the Soviet Union secretly sent nuclear missiles into Cuba, potentially doubling the number of nuclear weapons that could reach the continental United States and expanding their nuclear threat to the entire hemisphere. In the crisis that followed, which was probably the closest the world has come to nuclear holocaust, Kennedy is remembered as staring down the Russians. First, though, he had to stand up to his military advisors.

In the secret meetings during the thirteen days in October, the Joint Chiefs of Staff favored a massive air strike to debilitate the missiles. They added that follow-up bombings and perhaps an invasion might be necessary to ensure the missiles' destruction, actions that would lead to the death of thousands of soldiers as well as Cuban civilians. Kennedy also feared a military response might push the Soviets to invade West Berlin and trigger an escalation into World War III. "If we listen to [the military advisors], and do what they want us to do," Kennedy said, "none of us will be alive later to tell them that they were wrong."

Kennedy began to lean toward action that "lessens the chances of a nuclear exchange, which obviously is the final failure." On the evening of October 22, the president spoke to 100 million people, the largest television audience yet for a presidential address. He announced that a blockade of Cuba had been established, and warned that "should these offensive military preparations continue . . . further action will be justified."

The country and the world waited. Fortunately, both sides desperately sought a peaceful resolution. Khrushchev ordered Soviet ships to turn back from the blockade; Kennedy promised publicly not to invade Cuba and agreed secretly to remove American missiles from Turkey. Afterward, Curtis LeMay, Chief of Staff of the U.S. Air Force, called the agreement "the greatest defeat in our history." Yet Kennedy's ability to "resist pressure from military chiefs" and his faith in "patient diplomacy and measured pressure," writes historian Robert Dallek, "were essential contributions to the peaceful outcome of the crisis."

KENNEDY'S PEACE SPEECH

Although John F. Kennedy entered office as a hawk, he was transformed by how the United States and the Soviet Union almost stumbled into nuclear war during the Cuban missile crisis. The change became clear during his June 10, 1963, commencement address to American University graduates. He told the students he would speak of "a topic on which ignorance too often abounds . . . yet it is the most important topic on earth: world peace." Kennedy said, "Too many of us think it is impossible. . . . But that . . . leads to the conclusion that . . . mankind is doomed. . . . Our problems are manmade—therefore, they can be solved by man. . . ."

He argued that the two superpowers had the most to gain from détente. In a war, "all we have built, all we have worked for, would be destroyed in the first 24 hours . . . we are both devoting massive sums of money to weapons that could be better devoted to combating ignorance, poverty, and disease. . . ."

While many Americans found Soviet Communism "profoundly repugnant," he said, "we can still hail the Russian people for their many achievements—in science and space, in economic and industrial growth, in culture and in acts of courage." He asked Americans to recognize that during World War II "at least 20 million [Russians] lost their lives. . . . A third of the nation's territory . . . was turned into a wasteland. . . ."

Kennedy urged Americans to see the similarities they shared with the Soviet people. "[O]ur most basic common link is that we all inhabit this small planet. We all breathe the same air. We all cherish our children's future. And we are all mortal."

Kennedy's speech "received barely a mention in the press," writes historian Lawrence Freedman. But it was noticed by Soviet premier Nikita Khrushchev, who went so far as to call it the "best speech by any President since [Franklin] Roosevelt." Ten weeks later the two nations would sign the Nuclear Test Ban Treaty, the first of its kind in the nuclear era (for more on the treaty, see page 371).

EVENTS CONVINCE KENNEDY TO ADDRESS CIVIL RIGHTS

The Kennedy administration backed away from any major civil rights legislation in its first two years for fear of alienating white southern Democrats. Though the president named the first blacks to serve on U.S. district courts, he also promoted a handful of segregationist judges to the federal bench in the South. In 1963, Martin Luther King pronounced that while Kennedy's tenure was slightly better than Eisenhower's regarding civil rights, "the plight of the vast majority of Negroes remains the same."

But the civil rights movement forced Kennedy to act. In 1961, he sent federal marshals into Alabama to protect the freedom riders, who were working to destroy segregated transportation. In late 1962, the president sent federal troops to restore order at the University of Mississippi, where blacks were trying to enroll.

Beginning in May 1963, Martin Luther King and other civil rights activists launched a series of demonstrations to draw attention to segregated schools, restaurants, drinking fountains, and bathrooms in Birmingham, which had suffered so many racial bombings that many African Americans referred to it as "Bombingham."

The activists staged pray-ins and sit-ins at lunch counters and department stores, and when they marched, local police officers jailed hundreds, including schoolchildren. Over the next few days, Eugene "Bull" Connor, the city's police commissioner, used snarling dogs and policemen with clubs, cattle prods, and high-pressure water hoses to stop the marchers, stunning Americans—including the president—who watched on the evening news.

The crisis continued when, on June 11, two black students, Vivian Malone and James Hood, tried to register at the University of Alabama, the last state university without black students. Alabama Governor George Wallace kept his promise to block them at the door, and then Kennedy sent federalized National Guardsmen to escort them in. Kennedy had reserved airtime on national TV in case the standoff turned violent. When it didn't, his top advisors urged him to cancel the address, but his brother Bobby urged him to go ahead, and it turned out to be one of the most memorable speeches of his life.

KENNEDY'S PLEA FOR RACIAL EQUALITY

Ted Sorensen had six hours to craft Kennedy's civil rights speech on June 11, 1963, and he handed it to the president five minutes before airtime. "This is not a sectional issue," Kennedy said in the televised address.

> This is not even a legal or legislative issue alone. . . . We are confronted primarily with a moral issue. It is as old as the Scriptures and as clear as the American Constitution. The heart of the question is whether all Americans are to be afforded equal rights and equal opportunities. . . . One hundred years of delay have passed since President Lincoln freed the slaves, yet . . . their grandsons, are not fully free. . . . And this Nation, for all its hopes and all its boasts, will not be fully free until all its citizens are free. We preach freedom around the world, and we mean it, and we cherish our freedom here at home, but are we to say to the world, and . . . to each other that this is the land of the free except for the Negroes . . . ? The fires of frustration and discord are burning in every city. . . . [O]ur task, our obligation, is to make that revolution, that change, peaceful and constructive. . . . Today there are Negroes, unemployed . . . with inadequate education . . . without hope. . . . It seems to me that these are matters which concern us all. . . .

A week later, on June 19, Kennedy sent Congress a strong civil rights bill prohibiting segregation in public places, banning discrimination when federal money was received, and advancing school integration, but southern Democrats would cork it up in committee. Later, Martin Luther King, Jr., called the speech the "most eloquent, passionate, and unequivocal plea for civil rights . . . ever made by any President."

ASSASSINATION

In November 1963, the last month of his life, John F. Kennedy, forty-six years old, was looking to his reelection campaign. He wondered which Republican would face him in the 1964 election. Would it be Nelson Rockefeller, the liberal New Yorker? Or the former president of General Motors, Mitch Romney, whom he feared most? Or doctrinaire conservative Barry Goldwater, whom he thought he could beat easily? Meanwhile, he would take a political tour through eleven states, most in the West, which he hoped to swing Democrat come the election.

Just before noon on Friday, November 22, Air Force One touched down at Dallas's Love Field, and the official welcoming party handed Jacqueline a bouquet of red roses. A motorcade was planned, and the protective bubble was ordered taken off his blue Lincoln limousine. As they drove through a large crowd, Mrs. Connelly, wife of Texas Governor John Connelly, seated in the front of the car, turned to say, "You can't say that Dallas isn't friendly to you today." The president's reply was cut off by gunshots. The second shot tore through the president's throat, but the third shot hit the lower portion of Kennedy's brain. The limousine sped to Parkland Memorial Hospital, where doctors desperately tried to revive the president. White House Press Secretary Malcolm Kilduff, his voice shaky, then read a statement: "President John F. Kennedy died at approximately 1:00 P.M., central standard time, today here in Dallas."

The enduring image from the funeral that followed was John Jr., almost three years old, standing at the bottom of the steps of St. Matthew's Cathedral as his father's coffin was brought out. His mother then leaned over and whispered, "John, you can salute Daddy now and say good-bye to him." John tucked in his chin. He tightened his left arm to his side, then cocked his right arm in a child's salute. And the nation wept.

WHAT IS KENNEDY'S LEGACY?

Was the Kennedy legacy the stuff of legend, a modern-day Camelot that transformed a nation? Or was he a president whose image dazzled Americans, distracting the public from a presidency that stumbled often and had no major achievements?

Kennedy fans believe his idealism inspired the nation, especially the nation's youth. They claim that he unleashed an era of sacrifice, commitment, and vision expressed in programs such as the Peace Corps. He asked the nation to literally reach for the moon, and the nation took up the challenge.

They say that during his presidency Americans felt hope, a nearly utopian interlude that followed the uninspired Eisenhower years and preceded urban race riots, the Vietnam War, and the Watergate scandal. To those who loved him, he was a wise student of history, who remained calm during the Cuban Missile Crisis and encouraged détente with the Soviet Union. He was also a man of courage, taking on the civil rights issue at his own political peril in the spring of 1963.

His death killed the promise. "It was as if . . . Lincoln had been killed six months after Gettysburg," his aide Arthur Schlesinger, Jr., noted, "or Franklin Roosevelt at the end of 1935 or Truman before the Marshall Plan." While he failed to pass major legislation on civil rights or the elimination of poverty, his supporters maintain that he launched those efforts, and deserves some credit for their eventual passage.

Others maintain he was more myth than man: a president who was aided by soaring prose he did not write, a handsome face, and able handlers; a president who stumbled horribly at the Bay of Pigs (for more on the Bay of Pigs, see page 378); began the escalation of the war in Vietnam, and failed to pass major legislation on civil rights, Medicare, tax reform, education, or programs to alleviate poverty. To these critics, he was a philanderer who risked blackmail.

Still, when Americans were asked in 1996 to pick any past president to guide them, whom did they choose? John F. Kennedy.

PRESIDENT JOHN F. KENNEDY DELIVERS
HIS INAUGURAL ADDRESS

President Kennedy delivers his inaugural speech on January 20, 1961.
Seated nearby are his wife, Jacqueline Kennedy, and former President
Dwight D. Eisenhower. The address took a total of fourteen minutes from
beginning to end, making it one of the shortest yet most memorable inaugural
addresses in American history.

LYNDON B. JOHNSON

A Powerful Politician Pursues
the Great Society

WEEK 30

THE JOHNSON TREATMENT—MYTH OR REALITY?

Senate leader Lyndon B. Johnson, perhaps the most successful Senate leader in American history, managed to produce significant legislation under a Republican president—Dwight Eisenhower. He succeeded despite the fact that the "only real power available to the leader is the power of persuasion," as Johnson explained in 1960. What, then, was his secret?

Some said his success depended on how he used his body—he was a bulky 6 feet 3 inches tall—and his larger-than-life personality to persuade senators one-on-one. At the time, journalists Rowland Evans and Robert Novak described Johnson's mix of bluster and persuasion as "the Treatment," which included "supplication, accusation, cajolery, exuberance, scorn, tears, complaint, the hint of threat. . . . He moved in close, his face a scant millimeter from his target, his eyes widening and narrowing, his eyebrows rising and falling. From his pockets poured clippings, memos, statistics. The Treatment (was) an almost hypnotic experience and rendered the target stunned and helpless."

Johnson called such portrayals "nonsense" passed among "intellectuals." The portrayal conjured up a "back-alley job . . . holding the guy by the collar, twisting his arm behind his back, dangling a carrot in front of his nose, and holding a club over his head. . . . I'd have to be some sort of acrobatic genius to carry it off, and the Senator in question, well, he'd have to be pretty weak and pretty meek to be simply standing there like a paralyzed idiot."

Johnson and others credited his success to his diligent preparation. He'd always master the details of a bill, listen to senators about how to tweak it, and was acutely attuned how to best progress it through the Senate. He worked day and night to persuade senators individually. "He understood fully . . . the philosophy, the ideologies, of the senators," said Senator Henry Jackson. "He was keenly aware of what would fly with them and what would not." In his office, he would act the liberal with New Yorkers and the oil man with Texans. Johnson put it another way: "I know those senators from eyeball to asshole."

JOHNSON—ONE OF THE MOST IMPORTANT
VP SELECTIONS EVER

Jack Kennedy made one of the most crucial decisions of his presidency before he was elected—the selection of Texas senator Lyndon B. Johnson as vice president, the man who would turn Kennedy's lofty idealism into life-changing legislation.

Labor and civil rights leaders almost snuffed Kennedy's selection of Johnson, thinking the Southerner would do nothing to further their cause. But Kennedy went ahead and asked the Texan anyway, convinced he needed to balance his liberal reputation with someone from the South, where the election would be hotly contested.

Not everyone expected Johnson to accept the offer, wondering why the majority leader would give up his post for the position that John Adams once described as "the most insignificant office that ever the invention of man contrived or his imagination conceived." But Johnson believed his power in the Senate had been dependent on Eisenhower's passivity—a presidential style he didn't expect from Kennedy or Richard Nixon. As far as the job being inconsequential, Johnson told one friend, "Power is where power goes." He saw the position as a parking spot outside the big garage he'd long coveted—the presidency. Seven vice presidents had ascended to America's highest office—one in five, fairly good odds. The vice presidency would give Johnson eight years, if lucky, to grow into a national figure before a presidential run in 1968.

It was an awkward pairing. Johnson, master of the Senate, had to hold the music for a colleague who had been eight years his junior and a mediocre senator. "He never said a word of importance in the Senate and he never did a thing," Johnson said of Kennedy. Kennedy said privately, "I spent years of my life when I could not get consideration for a bill until I went around and begged Lyndon Johnson to let it go ahead."

But the alliance was politically successful, and Theodore Sorensen, Kennedy's advisor, gave Johnson credit for winning the election, helping Kennedy "salvage several Southern states the Republicans had counted on capturing, with an intensive campaign mixture of carrots and sticks. . . ."

JOHNSON'S VISION OF THE GREAT SOCIETY

On May 22, 1964, just four months after he had assumed the presidency, Lyndon Johnson spoke at the commencement of the University of Michigan, giving voice to his vision for the country:

> For a century we labored to settle and to subdue a continent. For half a century we called upon unbounded invention and untiring industry to create an order of plenty for all of our people. The challenge of the next half century is whether we have the wisdom to use that wealth to enrich and elevate our national life, and to advance the quality of our American civilization. . . . For in your time we have the opportunity to move not only toward the rich society and the powerful society, but upward to the Great Society. . . . [W]here men are more concerned with the quality of their goals than the quantity of their goods.

Johnson said Americans needed to build the Great Society "in our cities, in our countryside, and in our classrooms." He also called on Americans to stop environmental degradation. "We have always prided ourselves on being not only America the strong and America the free, but America the beautiful. Today that beauty is in danger. The water we drink, the food we eat, the very air that we breathe, are threatened with pollution. . . . And once man can no longer walk with beauty or wonder at nature his spirit will wither and his sustenance be wasted."

The Great Society was "a place where every child can find knowledge to enrich his mind and to enlarge his talents" and needed to be built in the "classrooms of America" where "your children's lives will be shaped. . . ." He pointed out that nearly 54 million Americans more than one quarter of the population—had not finished high school. "Poverty must not be a bar to learning," he said, "and learning must offer an escape from poverty." It was as idealistic as any speech made by any president, and it would be followed by heroic successes, and Shakespearean tragedy.

A DIZZYING MOUNTAIN OF LEGISLATION— THE GREAT SOCIETY

Lyndon B. Johnson wanted to win the election in 1964 in a landslide, and he did, destroying Barry Goldwater by 16 million votes, receiving 61 percent of the popular vote. His hopes for his presidency were equally grand: He wanted to be one of the greatest, with domestic achievements rivaling those of his political hero, Franklin Delano Roosevelt.

Johnson's dizzying successes were born from numerous factors: JFK's assassination, which created sympathy for his progressive agenda; Johnson's own mastery of the legislative process; a postwar populace that had grown hungry for racial equality; a 2 to 1 Democratic majority in the House and the Senate; and the president's unstoppable energy. He began by passing initiatives that had stalled under Kennedy, including a tax-reduction bill and civil rights measures in 1964 and 1965 that did more for blacks than any president since Abraham Lincoln, ending segregation and persistent obstacles to black voting.

In his 1964 State of the Union message, he announced an "unconditional war on poverty in America." Through Medicaid and Medicare, he provided health care to the poor and the elderly, the largest extension of direct government benefits since Roosevelt's Social Security Act. By 1976, the programs paid for the medical costs of one in five Americans. He provided help to underprivileged preschoolers in Head Start programs, and his Elementary and Secondary Education Act for the first time siphoned federal dollars to local schools. Today, many college students receive aid from programs spawned in pursuit of the Great Society.

He provided legal aid and urban housing to the indigent. He established the National Endowment for the Arts and Humanities, and public television and radio. His administration also championed conservation, including funding for clean air and clean rivers, highway beautification, and the addition of millions of acres to the country's protected wilderness. He passed consumer protection bills that required truth in labeling and packaging and automobile safety. The sheer magnitude of his legislation would eclipse Roosevelt's, but like Roosevelt, he and his administration would increasingly be distracted by war.

JOHNSON CHANGES THE NATION'S PROFILE—
IMMIGRATION REFORM

On October 3, 1965, in the shadow of the Statue of Liberty in New York Harbor, President Lyndon Johnson signed the Immigration and Nationality Act of 1965. "This bill we sign today is not a revolutionary bill," Johnson said. "It does not affect the lives of millions. It will not restructure the shape of our daily lives, or really add importantly to either our wealth or our power."

But the bill *was* revolutionary, and it would affect the lives of millions, launching one of the greatest immigration tides in U.S. history. Since its passage, 18 million legal immigrants have entered the country (millions more illegally), triple the number who came during the previous thirty years. It reshaped our daily lives, changing the foods we eat, the languages we speak, and who labors within our borders.

Johnson's bill struck down the immigration law established in 1924, which admitted immigrants based on their country of origin. This quota system explicitly favored northern Europeans, particularly the Irish, English, and Germans over Asians.

Johnson thought these policies were "alien to the American Dream," and told House Speaker John McCormack, "There is no piece of legislation . . . that in terms of decency and equity is more demanding of passage than the immigration bill." Nearly all politicians and immigration experts thought the bill would only marginally affect the influx of immigrants.

But they were wrong. Foreign-born Americans have quadrupled from nearly 10 million in 1970 to about 38 million in 2007. The largest influx would come from the elimination of quotas for family members of U.S. citizens and refugees. Asians and Latin Americans, far more eager to immigrate to the United States than Europeans, have dominated the flow of immigrants since 1965. Mexicans, Indians, Filipinos, and Chinese now dominate the American immigrant groups. In the year before Johnson's bill was passed, only 25,000 Asians and 105,000 Central and South Americans immigrated. Now, roughly a million immigrants come from those regions. Northern European languages are now only occasionally heard in the United States; the country's second language is unequivocally Spanish.

GOVERNOR GEORGE WALLACE GETS
THE JOHNSON TREATMENT

After Lyndon Johnson passed the Civil Rights Act of 1964, which barred discrimination in public places and employment, he planned to put off any more civil rights legislation in 1965, but events interfered. Martin Luther King, Jr., determined to force politicians to establish voting rights for blacks, held a voter registration march in Selma, Alabama, on March 7, 1965. Alabama Governor George Wallace sent in the state police, who billy clubbed protesters in attacks that were broadcast on national TV.

Civil rights advocates pressured Johnson to send in the National Guard. Instead, Johnson waited. Wallace, who feared violence would ruin his national political ambitions, requested a meeting with Johnson. The president accepted.

He settled Wallace on a couch in the Oval Office and took a higher seat in a rocking chair. He appealed to Wallace's ambition, saying he could build a national reputation as the first southern governor who supported racial harmony and social reform. When he called on Wallace to persuade Alabama registrars to give blacks the vote, Wallace said he didn't have the power to change their minds. "Don't shit me about your persuasive power, George," Johnson replied. "I saw you . . . attacking me [on television]. And you know what? You were so damn persuasive that I had to turn off the set before you had me changing my mind."

Johnson finally appealed to Wallace's concern for his legacy. "You got a lot of poor people down there in Alabama, a lot of ignorant people. You can do a lot for them, George. . . . What do you want left after you when you die? Do you want a Great . . . Big . . . Marble monument that reads GEORGE WALLACE—HE BUILT? . . . Or do you want a little piece of scrawny pine board lying across that harsh, caliche soil that reads GEORGE WALLACE—HE HATED?" After the meeting, Wallace said, "If I hadn't left when I did, he'd have had me coming out *for* civil rights."

This photo, taken on July 2, 1964, shows President Lyndon Johnson shaking the hand of the Reverend Martin Luther King, Jr., during the signing of Johnson's Civil Rights Act. The landmark legislation outlawed the major forms of discrimination against African Americans that had been in place for almost a century.

LYNDON B. JOHNSON

The Vietnam War Undermines
the Great Society

WEEK 31

THE VOTING RIGHTS ACT—
SOUTHERN BLACKS GET THE VOTE

Two days after meeting with Alabama Governor George Wallace in March 1965, President Lyndon Johnson sent troops to Selma, Alabama, to protect determined marchers calling for black voting rights. On March 15, amid public outrage at attacks on marchers in Selma, Johnson presented the Voting Rights Act to Congress.

"At times history and fate meet at a single time in a single place to shape a turning point in man's unending search for freedom . . . ," he said, "so it was a century ago at Appomattox. So it was last week in Selma, Alabama. . . . Our mission is at once the oldest and the most basic of this country—to right wrong, to do justice, to serve man. . . . There is no moral issue. It is wrong . . . to deny any of your fellow Americans the right to vote. . . . [I]t is not just Negroes, but really it is all of us who must overcome the crippling legacy of bigotry and injustice." Then Johnson paused, raised his hands, and repeated the words from the old Baptist hymn that had become the clarion call of the civil rights movement: "And . . . we . . . *shall* . . . overcome."

In Birmingham, Martin Luther King, Jr., wept at the words.

One hundred years after the end of America's Civil War, Johnson quickly shepherded through Congress the Voting Rights Act of 1965, banning poll taxes and literacy tests and other barriers that had kept blacks from voting. Johnson called it "a triumph for freedom as huge as any victory that has ever been won on any battlefield." By 1968, the number of blacks registered in the eleven former Confederate states had jumped to an average of 62 percent. The few hundred African-American national officeholders in 1965 grew to six thousand by 1989. But the law did something else, as well: It began the reintegration of the South, both black and white, into the political fabric of the nation.

WATTS RIOTING UNDERMINES JOHNSON'S GREAT SOCIETY

Just five days after Johnson signed the Voting Rights Act on August 6, 1965, the optimism for racial justice in America went up in flames in a black section of Los Angeles called Watts. For generations, the country had neglected urban areas like Watts, leaving them with inadequate housing, deficient public schools, ferocious crime, and dismal prospects for the young. In such places, the talk of love, brotherhood, and nonviolence turned to talk of white oppression, black power, and violent retribution.

In Watts, rioting and the police response over five days led to the death of thirty-four people and the destruction of $35 million worth of property, much of it burned. The political climate, as Johnson well understood, immediately shifted. Sympathy for blacks turned to fear and the number of guns bought by white suburbanites spiked. The stock of a conservative actor turned California politician named Ronald Reagan rose too. Fear of black violence seemed to replace hope for a more just and integrated society.

Joseph Califano, Johnson's principal domestic advisor, wrote in his book *Triumph and Tragedy of Lyndon Johnson: The White House Years,* "how acutely Johnson feared that the reforms to which he had dedicated his presidency were in mortal danger, not only from those who opposed [them], but from those he was trying to help."

The next summer, riots roiled in thirty-eight cities, most of them northern. Television images of young black rioters screaming, "Burn, baby, burn," would further inflame the fears of white Americans. In 1964, 34 percent of Americans thought blacks were moving too fast in their call for racial and economic justice; by 1966, the number had jumped to 85 percent. Johnson's dream of building a Great Society through legislative means had been badly singed. Some said Johnson had raised expectations for a just society too high, too fast; others said America had waited too long to provide blacks with justice.

GULF OF TONKIN RESOLUTION
BEGINS THE ESCALATION IN VIETNAM

In the spring of 1964, Lyndon Johnson would have been happy to put the issue of how to proceed in Vietnam in the cupboard until after the election. But South Vietnam was faltering badly, and if the Communist North Vietnamese won the war before election day, Johnson's Republican opponent, Barry Goldwater, a major general in the air force reserve, would inevitably blame the defeat on Johnson, hurting the president's election chances.

This was the backdrop when on August 2, three North Vietnamese torpedo boats attacked the USS *Maddox*, a U.S. destroyer in the Gulf of Tonkin along the coast of North Vietnam. The *Maddox* struck back, sinking one torpedo boat and damaging another. On August 4, reports came in that the *Maddox* had been attacked again; later that afternoon, word came from the ship that the torpedo attacks might have been imagined. While history still debates what happened in those waters, Johnson told Americans that night on television that he'd ordered a retaliatory bombing in North Vietnam. He also said the attacks had been unprovoked, although U.S. forces had been involved in raids on the North for months.

Johnson asked for the power to expand the war in Vietnam without further authorization from Congress. After just two days of hearings and a debate that lasted forty minutes, the House voted 416 to 0 to pass a resolution and just two senators voted against it, giving him that power. Johnson thought the bombing let the North Vietnamese know he was serious about defending South Vietnam.

Many also saw the American response as a way for Johnson to improve the chances for his election. By responding militarily, he showed, as Doris Kearns Goodwin has written, that the president who called himself a "man of peace" was "not a man of weakness or timidity." The nuanced political position would help him destroy Goldwater in the fall election.

But the open-ended resolution was also like a giant noose, giving Johnson the latitude to escalate a war that the American people had neither debated nor decided to fight, an escalation that would eventually destroy his Great Society and his presidency (for more on the consequences of the Vietnam War, see page 379).

JOHNSON TRIES SECRETLY TO ESCALATE THE WAR

Johnson had made a campaign promise in 1964 not to send young Americans to fight in Vietnam, but as he entered his first full term, there was steady pressure to prevent South Vietnam from falling to the Communist North Vietnamese. Johnson's top advisors all agreed that a line in the jungle had to be drawn across Vietnam.

First they told him bombing would do the trick. When that failed to weaken North Vietnamese leader Ho Chi Minh or bring him to the negotiating table, they recommended more bombing sorties. When that failed, military leaders said troops were needed on the ground. On March 10, 1965, fifteen hundred troops were brought in to protect an air base near Da Nang. Then, two weeks later, more troops were called for—to protect the men originally sent. By the end of April, fifty thousand more American soldiers were on the ground. That same month, troops received permission to engage in combat if nearby South Vietnamese troops were in trouble. By June, they received permission to act on their own. By July 1965, Johnson and his top advisors decided that over two hundred thousand American soldiers were needed. War was being waged—but what to tell the American people?

Most of his advisors recommended that he call a state of emergency, ask Congress to increase taxes to pay for the war, and call up 235,000 reservists. But Johnson hesitated at such a bald call to action, fearing it would kill all funding for his Great Society programs. He decided to go to war quietly, telling the American people as little as he could, as absurd as that sounds, and hoping the war might be won quickly.

Americans soon saw through Johnson's evasions and half-truths. "How do you know when Lyndon Johnson is telling the truth?" began a joke that circulated at the time. "When he pulls his earlobe, or scratches his chin, he's telling the truth. When he begins to move his lips, you know he's lying."

JOHNSON'S PREDICAMENT IN VIETNAM— IN HIS OWN WORDS

In 1970, Johnson explained his fateful decision to escalate the war to the writer Doris Kearns Goodwin. "I knew from the start," he told her, "that I was bound to be crucified either way I moved. . . ."

> History provided too many cases where the sound of the bugle put an immediate end to the hopes and dreams for the best reformers; the Spanish-American War drowned the populist spirit; World War I ended Woodrow Wilson's New Freedom; World War II brought the New Deal to a close. Once the war began, then all those conservatives in the Congress would use it as a weapon against the Great Society . . . not because they were against the poor . . . but because the war had to come first. . . .
>
> Yet everything I knew about history told me that if I got out of Vietnam and let Ho Chi Minh run through the streets of Saigon, then I'd be doing exactly what Chamberlain did in World War II. I'd be giving a big fat reward to aggression. . . . [T]here would follow in the country . . . a mean and destructive debate . . . that would shatter my Presidency, kill my administration, and damage our democracy. . . .
>
> For this time there would be Robert Kennedy out in front leading the fight against me, telling everyone that I had betrayed John Kennedy's commitment to South Vietnam. That I had let a democracy fall into the hands of the Communists. That I was a coward. . . . But there was more. You see, I was as sure as any man could be that once we showed how weak we were, Moscow and Peking would move in a flash to exploit our weakness. . . . And so would begin World War III. So you see, I was bound to be crucified either way I moved.

VIETNAM ENDS JOHNSON'S PRESIDENCY

The Vietcong's Tet Offensive, launched in late January 1968 against more than a hundred South Vietnamese cities and military targets, changed the political fortunes of Lyndon Johnson as much as any event in his career. Johnson had been telling the American people for months that the enemy was on the verge of collapse. The fierceness of the Tet Offensive showed that the enemy was stronger than anyone had suspected.

Forty percent of Americans had approved of Johnson's handling of the war at the end of January 1968; six weeks later, 28 percent did. CBS's Walter Cronkite said on air that "we are mired in stalemate." Johnson noted, "If I've lost Cronkite, I've lost Middle America." Even Johnson's top foreign policy advisors, who had urged him to fight on, saw the Tet Offensive as proof that the war in Vietnam could not be won.

The unpopularity of Johnson and the war became apparent in the New Hampshire primary on March 12, 1968, when Minnesota Senator Eugene McCarthy, an antiwar candidate who was not taken seriously by the media, won a stunning 42 percent of the vote to Johnson's 49 percent. Johnson's nemesis, Robert Kennedy, jumped into the Democratic primaries next, posing a credible threat to Johnson in the Wisconsin, Oregon, Indiana, and California primaries.

On March 31, 1968, Lyndon Johnson addressed a nationwide TV audience from the White House. He talked about the war in Vietnam and of a bombing halt "to de-escalate the conflict." Many thought they were hearing nothing new, when the president said, "I shall not seek, and will not accept, the nomination of my party for another term as your president."

Johnson would leave office on January 20, 1969. At age twenty-three, during the Great Depression, he'd come to Washington to serve as a legislative assistant. Over three decades, he served as a congressman, senator, vice president, and finally president. Now he returned home to the Hill Country of Texas where, as his father had once said, "The people know when you're sick and care when you die."

While the call to take American troops out of Vietnam swelled in 1968 after the Tet Offensive, protesters came out against the war much earlier in the conflict. Pictured here are members of the Students for a Democratic Society, picketing outside the White House in 1965.

The
CONSERVATIVE ERA
(1968–2008)

Corruption and Its Aftermath—
Richard Nixon, Gerald Ford,
and Jimmy Carter

NIXON AND VIETNAM: THE "MADMAN" THEORY APPLIED

Richard Nixon inherited the Vietnam War when he took office in 1969. Although many expected he'd end the war quickly, it continued for four more years. During that time, U.S. troops invaded Cambodia and Laos, and the U.S. Air Force dropped more than twice as many tons of bombs as were dropped during World War II. American bombs and soldiers killed up to a million more Vietnamese, mostly civilians, and 20,553 more American soldiers died.

Nixon maintained that he wanted an "honorable peace," one that would not undermine U.S. credibility. He worried that "if we fail to meet this crisis, all other nations will be on notice that . . . the United States, when a real crisis comes, will be found wanting."

To force the North Vietnamese to accept a settlement that would allow the United States to claim it had not been defeated, Nixon steadily ratcheted up the devastation throughout Indochina. He was putting into practice what he called his "madman" theory. "I want the North Vietnamese to believe I've reached the point where I might do *anything* to stop the war. We'll just slip them the word that, 'for God's sake, you know Nixon is obsessed about Communism. We can't constrain him when he's angry—and he has his hand on the nuclear button'—and Ho Chi Minh himself will be in Paris in two days begging for peace."

Nixon didn't press the "nuclear button," but he sought, in his words, to "bomb the bastards off the earth." The bombing reached a crescendo in December 1972 when, infuriated by North Vietnamese intransigence, Nixon ordered an all-out air assault; for twelve days, B-52s pulverized Hanoi and Haiphong. The *New York Times* described it as "terrorism on an unprecedented scale," and columnist James Reston called it "war by tantrum."

One month later, Nixon ended America's involvement in the war. Twenty-seven months after that, the North Vietnamese, riding triumphantly into Saigon, got their victory and a unified Vietnam.

BEIJING SURPRISE

"This was the week that changed the world." Thus did Richard Nixon describe his dramatic 1972 visit to China. Ever since Mao's Communist Party had seized power in 1949, the United States had sought to contain and isolate China, viewing it as an archenemy. Nixon wanted to end the cold war between the two countries in order to gain Chinese help in countering the Soviet Union and in extricating the United States from Vietnam. A poker player in his younger days, Nixon gambled that his personal diplomacy could break down the great wall of hostility between China and the United States.

The prevailing anti-Communist sentiment in the United States made it electoral suicide for any politician to even suggest a rapprochement with China. Nixon believed his impeccable anti-Communist credentials would give him the political cover needed to reverse course. However, he also knew that if his initial overtures to China became known before the Chinese agreed to host him, opponents would have time to thwart his plans. Nixon therefore went to extreme lengths to conceal his request for an invitation to visit China, keeping his own State Department in the dark and confiding only in Henry Kissinger, his national security advisor.

Through the Pakistani dictator Yahya Khan, Nixon contacted Chou En-lai, the Chinese premier, and the two of them began exchanging a series of typed, unsigned notes. Nixon then had Kissinger, while on a visit to Pakistan, fake a sudden illness to elude the press and fly secretly to China. Only when Kissinger had returned with the desired invitation did Nixon reveal the news to a thunderstruck nation. The *New York Post*'s Max Lerner summed up public reaction: "[T]he politics of surprise leads through the Gates of Astonishment into the Kingdom of Hope."

Eight months later, Nixon landed in Beijing, having practiced eating with chopsticks on the flight. He shook hands with Mao, toasted his hosts in the Great Hall of the People—and conducted intense negotiations that would lead, in 1978, to the establishment of full diplomatic relations with China. Today, China is America's number two trading partner and leading creditor. Nixon's visit was momentous indeed.

NIXON RESIGNS AMIDST THE WATERGATE SCANDAL

JULY 31, 1974: 3:50 A.M.—President Nixon agonizes over his only two options: Resign, or be tried in the Senate for a scandal that reveals years of illegal activity against his enemies and a bungled attempt by the White House to cover it up.

He has had a nightmarish ten days. The House Judiciary Committee impeached him for obstruction of justice, abuse of power, and defiance of congressional subpoenas. A week earlier, the Supreme Court unanimously ordered him to release taped conversations relating to the Watergate scandal.

Nixon's top aides worry that not only is his presidency collapsing, but that he is too. Ed Cox, Nixon's son-in-law, panics. "The president was up walking the halls last night," Cox notifies a confidante, "talking to pictures of former presidents." Cox also fears that Nixon may commit suicide. Months earlier, dreading the same thing, Al Haig, Nixon's chief of staff, asked Nixon's doctor to stop his medications.

Nixon writes in his diary, *"End career as a fighter."* But for days, he continues an anguished wavering.

AUGUST 1: Nixon confides to Haig that he will resign. Four days later, he tells him he'll "fight to the finish."

AUGUST 6: Only seven senators now support Nixon. Announcing to Haig and his press secretary that he will resign, Nixon declares, "Well, I screwed it up good, real good, didn't I?" Two speeches are prepared: a resignation and a nonresignation.

AUGUST 7: Nixon meets with Secretary of State Kissinger late that night. "[T]he agony and the loss of what was about to happen became most acute for me during that conversation," Nixon wrote later. "I asked him to pray with me, . . . and we knelt." Profoundly shaken, Kissinger reports that as they knelt, Nixon sobbed, beating the carpet, "What have I done? What has happened?"

AUGUST 8: 9:00 P.M.—Nixon gives his resignation address from the Oval Office.

AUGUST 9, 1974: 11:35 A.M.—Richard Nixon becomes the only president to resign. Determined throughout his political life to get back at his "enemies," Nixon sums up his own tragedy in his final words to his White House staff: "[A]lways remember, others may hate you, but those who hate you don't win unless you hate them, and then you destroy yourself."

WATERGATE EPILOGUE: FORD PARDONS NIXON

After escorting the Nixons to their helicopter on August 9, 1974, Gerald Ford, the House minority leader before being chosen by Nixon eight months earlier to serve as vice president, went into the White House and took the oath of office.

"My fellow Americans," he said in his acceptance speech, "our long national nightmare is over." Known for his decency, Ford worried that the line was too harsh, but his speechwriter Robert Hartmann insisted it stay and was "what everybody needs to hear . . . like FDR saying 'all we have to fear is fear itself.'" Afterward, Senate Majority Leader Mike Mansfield, speaking for many Americans, said, "The sun is shining again."

But the goodwill the nation expressed toward Ford dissolved on September 8 when Ford pardoned Nixon for any illegal activities he may have committed during his five years in office. The *New York Times* editorialized: "This blundering intervention is a body blow to the President's own credibility and to the public's reviving confidence in the integrity of Government."

When Ford had been asked at his vice presidential confirmation hearings about a pardon for the embattled Nixon, he'd said, "I don't think the country would stand for it." But he'd changed his mind. "We had to close the wound," he said later. "We had to let the healing that is inherent in the American people take over. But I didn't explain that well enough." Ford's popularity fell twenty-two points overnight. On September 17, nine days after Ford addressed the country, Nixon called Ford and offered to reject the pardon. Ford turned down the offer.

People wondered: Had Ford made a deal—his pardon in exchange for Nixon's resignation? "There was no deal, period, under no circumstances," Ford insisted. A House investigation, led by the majority Democrats, cleared Ford of any impropriety, and history, too—citing his lifelong integrity—has absolved him. The pardon dogged Ford throughout his presidency, undoubtedly tipping the election to Jimmy Carter in the extremely close 1976 presidential race. As writer Barry Werth put it, Jerry Ford had indeed "smother[ed] a grenade" for his old friend Richard Nixon (for more on the Watergate scandal, see page 354).

THE HUMAN RIGHTS PRESIDENT?

"[O]ur commitment to human rights must be absolute." Thus did Jimmy Carter, in his inaugural address on January 20, 1977, proclaim a new touchstone for U.S. foreign policy. Following through on his pledge, Carter cut aid to at least eight human rights violators, including Argentina and Uruguay. But Carter could not, or would not, significantly alter the prevailing practice whereby ideological loyalty and economic self-interest gained precedence over human rights in U.S. foreign policy (for Carter's human rights stance during his postpresidency, see page 387).

The problem Carter faced was succinctly summarized in a report by his administration to Congress in 1977. It stated: "[A] number of countries with deplorable records of human rights observances are also countries where we have important security and foreign policy interests."

Iran was a prime example. The shah, a brutal dictator put into power by the CIA in 1954, relied upon his secret police and torture to suppress widespread opposition to his rule. Amnesty International reported in 1976 that "[n]o country in the world has a worse record of human rights than Iran."

But Iran also exported massive amounts of oil, purchased billions of dollars worth of U.S.-made weaponry, and served as America's proxy in policing the Middle East. So when Iranians took to the streets in 1978 to demand the shah's overthrow, the Carter administration sought to prop up his regime with arms and diplomatic support. Carter's efforts failed, however, and Ayatollah Khomeini's self-styled Islamic revolution swept the shah from power, as chants of "death to America" reverberated in the streets of Tehran and images of burning American flags appeared on the nightly news.

Carter now did disregard U.S. geopolitical interests for humanitarian reasons: He allowed the critically ill shah to enter the United States for medical treatment. Furious Iranians stormed the U.S. embassy in Tehran, seizing fifty-two hostages. Carter's inability to secure their release for the remaining 444 days of his presidency guaranteed that he would not have another term in which to try to reconcile human rights and realpolitik.

JIMMY CARTER AND ENERGY: AN UNWELCOME MESSAGE

Carter's presidency focused, and foundered, on the issue of energy. Boldly departing from the national consensus that the American way of life should, and could, continue to be premised on the consumption of vast amounts of cheap petroleum, Carter asked Americans to use less oil, pay more for it, and develop alternative energy sources.

Two weeks after taking office, Carter, wearing a sweater and sitting by an open fire, told a nationwide TV audience that his energy program would "emphasize conservation"—then asked people to lower their thermostats. Ten weeks later, Carter returned to the airwaves for an—in his words—"unpleasant talk." He described the United States as "the most wasteful nation on earth," proclaimed the effort to reduce petroleum consumption "the moral equivalent of war," and called for "sacrifices" to win that war.

Carter asked Congress for legislation that would achieve these conservation goals. But the Senate, reluctant to enlist in Carter's "war," took eighteen months to pass a drastically weakened version of what Carter sought.

Sharply rising oil prices in 1979 prompted Carter to try again, telling Americans that he would raise oil prices by decontrolling them, and proposing a windfall profits tax on oil companies to offset the impact of higher fuel prices on low-income families, promote conservation, and encourage the development of alternative energy sources.

Republicans, led by Ronald Reagan, pounced on Carter: "They tell us that we must learn to live with less, . . . that . . . America . . . will be a place where—because of our past excesses—it will be impossible to dream and make those dreams come true. I don't believe that," Reagan proclaimed. "And I don't believe [the American people] do, either."

The 1980 presidential election proved Reagan right. Voters vastly preferred the optimism and license of Ronald Reagan's "morning in America" to the self-restraint of Carter's "war." In 1986, Reagan removed the solar panels that Carter had had installed on the White House roof. They have yet to be reinstalled.

Richard Nixon is shown climbing aboard a helicopter on the South Lawn of the White House after his resignation on August 9, 1974. The helicopter took Nixon to Andrews Air Force Base, where he boarded Air Force One, which took him to his home in San Clemente, California.

RONALD REAGAN

A Struggling Actor Becomes
a Successful Politician

WEEK 33

A LIFEGUARD, A RESCUER

In his retirement, one of the places Ronald Reagan often spoke of was a beach in Dixon, a small town in northwestern Illinois, where his family moved when he was nine. In that small town, he went to his mother's church and played on the football team.

At sixteen, he applied to be a lifeguard at a beach on the treacherous Rock River. Park officials worried that the sixteen-year-old was too slight to handle the job, but Jack, Ronald's father, assured them that his son had taken lifesaving at the local YMCA. "Dutch," as he was known, would work there for six summers. Reagan started each day at the beach picking up food and chopping a three-hundred-pound block of ice into one-hundred-pound blocks for three coolers. He worked twelve-hour days, seven days a week, supplementing his $15 weekly wage with private swimming lessons for the children of the affluent. All his earnings went to pay for college.

As a lifeguard, Reagan played the role that he would often inhabit in his political career: rescuer. The nearsighted Dutch would toss off his thick horn-rimmed glasses if he spotted somebody struggling in the current. On August 3, 1928, he made the front page of the *Dixon Daily Telegraph* by saving a drowning man after another rescuer had given up. After he was elected president, one radio announcer said, "The Rock River flows for you tonight, Mr. President." Edmund Morris, one of Reagan's biographers, says that Reagan's "subsequent political career . . . was devoted to the general theme of rescue," whether from Hollywood Communists, student protesters, liberal spenders, or what he called the "evil empire"—the Soviet Union.

Through his six summers as lifeguard, Reagan put a notch in a log for every person he saved. Late in life, he would show visitors a picture in his office of the Rock River beach. "You see, that's where I used to be a lifeguard. I saved seventy-seven lives there."

FIRST, AN ACTOR

Some might say Ronald Reagan's first career—as an actor—prepared him for his career as a politician. "There have been times in this office," Reagan told TV reporter David Brinkley in 1988, as he was about to leave office, "when I've wondered how you could do the job if you hadn't been an actor." As an actor, he was diligent and reliable and always prepared, a valuable commodity in Warner's B film division, where, "the studio didn't want movies good," as Reagan put it. "It wanted them Thursday."

He acted in more than fifty films, most of them B movies, although some, such as *Knute Rockne—All American* (1940), leaned toward the A-list. In that movie, he played the Notre Dame halfback George Gipp. The film had a scene where Gipp, dying, tells Rockne, "One day when things are tough, maybe you can ask the boys to get in there and win just one for the Gipper." Forty years later, during his presidential runs, reporters referred to him as "the Gipper." He gained critical praise for his role in the 1942 film *King's Row*, a story about a small town with a dark side. After Reagan's character romances the daughter of a sadistic surgeon, the surgeon amputates his legs. Reagan's character wakes up and says, "Where's the rest of me?" which became the title of his first autobiography, a reference to Reagan's attempt to express more of himself through politics.

When World War II broke out, Reagan joined the army, but his bad eyesight kept him out of combat. Instead, he made training films and some war propaganda movies. After the war, Reagan sought more serious roles, but Warner Brothers preferred him for comedic roles. In nearly every one of his films, he played a good guy, and writer Garry Wills later wrote that he won over his audiences by playing "the heartwarming role of himself." Reagan's film career faded through the 1950s, but he would slowly find a second act in politics, where he would eventually win over a far larger audience: voters.

REAGAN GOES CORPORATE—AND CONSERVATIVE

In 1954, his film career sputtering, Ronald Reagan was hired to host the TV series *General Electric Theater,* which aired every Sunday morning. It was steady work for the father of three young children, paying $125,000 a year.

It also required Reagan to plug GE products and give speeches to GE employees.

During these years, Reagan, who was a Democrat earlier in his life, shifted rightward politically. He absorbed GE's concerns that government was too big and wasteful and that taxes were too high. But in 1962, some GE officials, having grown wary of their spokesman after he supported Richard Nixon in 1960, asked him to avoid politics. Reagan refused—and his contract wasn't renewed.

But he had become a popular conservative speaker, and the Barry Goldwater campaign gave him a spot on national television on October 27, 1964, to support Goldwater's run against Lyndon Johnson. Reagan delivered "The Speech," as it was remembered by Reaganauts, called "A Time for Choosing." "All of the catchphrases that he'd found worked well," notes Edmund Morris, "all the ideology that he'd polished during his years as a GE corporate spokesman and emerging political orator, it all came together at this moment." In the highlight of the speech, Reagan borrowed phrases from Franklin Roosevelt and Abraham Lincoln.

"You and I have a rendezvous with destiny. We can preserve for our children this, the last best hope of man on earth, or we can sentence them to take the first step into a thousand years of darkness. If we fail, at least let our children and our children's children say of us we justified our brief moment here. We did all that could be done."

Reagan's speech brought in $1 million, more than any political speech had raised before, and political columnist David S. Broder called it "the most successful political debut since William Jennings Bryan electrified the 1896 Democratic convention with his 'Cross of Gold' speech." Goldwater got trounced, but Reagan was now a politician.

UNDERESTIMATED—AND THEN *GOVERNOR* REAGAN

Barry Goldwater's dismal failure in his presidential run in 1964 was a blessing to Ronald Reagan's career. Compared to the dour Goldwater, Reagan was upbeat and popular. While Reagan never publicly criticized Goldwater, he told his wife, Nancy, that he thought the problem with Goldwater's campaign hadn't been the message but the messenger. And while some predicted that the defeat of Goldwater was the end of the Republican Party, the optimistic Reagan saw his run as a starting point for its renewal.

Reagan now scanned the horizon for what to do next, and was encouraged when his friend, song-and-dance actor George Murphy, beat former John F. Kennedy press secretary Pierre Salinger for U.S. senator from California in 1964. The next best local opportunity, up in 1966, was the state's governorship. California Governor Pat Brown, the two-term Democratic incumbent, thought Reagan would be vulnerable because he was on the far right and had never been elected to public office. But the Brown camp was blind to Reagan's strengths.

He spoke better than most politicians because of his work on radio and in the movies. He was a hard worker and more competitive than he seemed. Californians also saw him as a friendly figure—he was the hero in almost every one of his movies. Those gifts led him to unite a fractured Republican Party after the primaries, adopting the so-called Eleventh Commandment of Republican Chairman Gaylord Parkinson: "Thou shall not speak ill of any fellow Republican."

He also came down on the side of law and order when student violence broke out on the Berkeley campus at the University of California. He told the press that he respected the right to peaceful protest, but would tell demonstrators to "obey the rules or get out."

Reagan would win the election against Brown by a million votes, in large part because of the four hundred thousand defections he received from conservative working-class Democratic voters in Southern California. These Reagan supporters would become known as Reagan Democrats, and they would buoy his political fortunes for the rest of his career.

REAGANOMICS ARRIVES

When Reagan came into office, inflation was in double digits and the budget deficit was swelling. The president immediately addressed the American people, saying that the United States was in the "worst economic mess since the Depression," and promised tough remedies. "We are threatened with an economic calamity of tremendous proportions and the old business-as-usual treatment can't save it."

Reagan's solution was as simple as it was controversial: Drastically reduce the size of the federal government, which he felt hampered economic vitality, and stimulate the economy through deep tax cuts. Reagan believed that if people were allowed to work unfettered by government regulation they would work harder and produce more, that cutting taxes and limiting government interference would lower inflation and unemployment, and boost economic growth. This booming economy would create additional personal income and corporate profits, which would mean more tax revenue, which he predicted would balance the federal budget by 1984. But many held that this economic theory was wishful thinking, and George Bush, Reagan's Republican challenger in 1980, called it "voodoo economics." The press dismissed it as "Reaganomics."

Most controversial were the proposed budget cuts, many of which fell on programs that helped the poor. "I'm trying to undo LBJ's Great Society," Reagan wrote in his diary. "It was his war on poverty that led us to this mess."

But how would Reagan get such a conservative economic agenda passed while Democrats held a fifty-one-vote majority in the House of Representatives, led by Speaker Thomas P. (Tip) O'Neill of Massachusetts? Reagan refused to compromise, and he followed Chief of Staff James Baker's suggestion that he agree not to campaign against any of the so-called Boll Weevils—conservative southern Democrats—who voted for his plan. In the first hundred days of his administration, President Reagan met with 467 legislators; in a single night, Reagan phoned twenty-nine members of Congress. But Reagan's economic plan was still expected to die in Congress—until a deranged young man tried to kill the president.

A BULLET TO THE CHEST—AND A QUICK RECOVERY

On March 30, 1981, two months and ten days into his first term, President Ronald Reagan was leaving an appearance at the Washington Hilton Hotel through a side entrance and paused at a reporter's question. Then what sounded like firecrackers popped to Reagan's left. "What the hell's that?" he asked.

It turned out to be six bullets shot by John Hinckley, Jr., a twenty-five-year-old who said he was trying to impress actress Jodie Foster. A Secret Service detail threw Reagan into the presidential limousine. Reagan at first thought he'd broken a rib, but as he straightened up, he coughed up blood. The car sped to George Washington Hospital; the president had been hit by a bullet that had settled within an inch of his heart. When Nancy got to the hospital, the president, borrowing a line from the boxer Jack Dempsey after he lost the heavyweight title to Gene Tunney, told her, "Honey, I forgot to duck."

When Reagan was wheeled into the operating room, he told the surgeon that he hoped he was a Republican. "Today, Mr. President," the surgeon replied, "we're all Republican."

Many considered it providence that Reagan had survived the assassination attempt, and his approval rating shot to 70 percent. His aides wanted to capitalize on the goodwill, and a month after he was shot they asked him to appear before Congress to push for his economic program, which proposed deep budget and tax cuts. Like the nation, the gathered senators and congressmen were moved to see the president, who had clearly lost weight, and gave him a hero's welcome.

On August 13, Reagan signed a budget and tax cut, which led to a 25-percent reduction in taxes, delivered in stages over three years, and big increases in defense spending. It passed when sixty-three Democrats, many conservative Southerners that Reagan had promised not to campaign against if they supported the bill, joined the Republicans. Speaker "Tip" O'Neill, gracious in defeat, noted that "the will of the people is to go along with the President."

Ronald Reagan, the newly elected governor of California, on horseback in December 1966. Reagan would serve as governor from 1967 until 1975. He would then set his sights on the presidency, losing a close primary fight to Gerald Ford in 1976 before being elected in 1980.

RONALD REAGAN

President Reagan—Reaganomics at Home, Cold Warrior Abroad

PROSPERITY—BUT NOT FOR ALL

Reagan has often been credited with reviving a moribund economy and launching one of the greatest peacetime periods of economic growth in the nation's history. When he came into office, unemployment was at 7.2 percent, the annual inflation rate was at 12 percent, and interest rates had topped 20 percent. Eight years later, unemployment was at 5.5 percent, inflation at 4.4 percent, and the interest rate at 9.3 percent. Eighteen million new jobs were filled and the gross domestic product doubled.

But Sean Wilentz, author of *The Age of Reagan*, has noted that these economic returns were not shared equally. "The new prosperity was heavily skewed to the top," writes Wilentz, "while average hourly wages and middle-class real hourly incomes stagnated during the 1980s, and while the average family real income for the bottom fifth of Americans fell by 7 percent, the share of the nation's wealth held by the top 1 percent of the population grew from 22 percent in 1979 to 39 percent in 1989. . . . The so-called Reagan boom brought inequalities of living standards reminiscent of the nineteenth century robber barons' Gilded Age."

Reagan—with his optimism, his rhetoric, and his determination—was able to transform what were once right-wing economic assumptions into mainstream ones. High taxes on the rich were seen not as a responsibility they should bear but as a hindrance to the economy. Reagan's assumption that government spending was wasteful and a drag on the economy, regardless of where or how wisely it was spent, also became the norm. In this sense, Reagan oversaw an ideological revolution, one that Wilentz notes lasted from 1980 through George W. Bush's term in 2008, making it "longer than the ages of Jefferson and Jackson, longer than the Gilded Age or the Progressive era; and virtually as long as the combined era of the New Deal, Fair Deal, New Frontier, and the Great Society."

A HISTORIC DEFICIT

When Ronald Reagan came into office, he replaced a portrait of Thomas Jefferson in the White House cabinet room with one of Calvin Coolidge. "[I]f you go back, I don't know if the country has ever had a higher level of prosperity than it did under Coolidge," Reagan said just as he entered office. "And he actually reduced the national debt, he cut taxes several times across the board." Reagan believed he could do the same.

Reaganomics was similar to the economic policies put forward by Andrew Mellon, Calvin Coolidge's secretary of the treasury. Both believed in cutting taxes, especially for big business. After two terms, Reagan had reduced the corporate share of taxes paid as a proportion of the total from 25 percent under President Dwight Eisenhower to 8 percent. The idea was that with lower taxes, corporations and the wealthy would make more money and invest it to create more jobs, benefiting the lower and middle classes, a theory called "trickle-down." An expanding economy would produce more tax revenue for the government, even with lower tax rates. But this economic boom never happened, and Reagan biographer Lou Cannon points out that private wealth grew only by 8 percent during the Reagan years, as compared to 31 percent from 1975 to 1980.

The largest peacetime expansion of the military budget in American history also swelled the deficit. In six years under Reagan, military spending jumped 50 percent in constant dollars. The largest debtor presidents—including George Washington, Abraham Lincoln, Woodrow Wilson, Franklin Roosevelt, and George W. Bush—presided over wars that increased American debt. Reagan's peacetime military buildup cost more in adjusted dollars than the Vietnam War under Lyndon Johnson.

The debt was also exploded because Reagan and Congress were unable to shrink the size of government. The number of government workers increased at a faster rate under Reagan than under Jimmy Carter.

For all these reasons, from 1980 to 1989 the federal debt tripled from $994 billion to $2.8 trillion. Having proposed eight budgets that weren't balanced, Reagan, upon leaving office, could only refer to his inability to eliminate the debt as one of his "regrets."

THE GREAT COMMUNICATOR

What made Ronald Reagan the Great Communicator? Some say his skills as an actor gave him an edge over other politicians. While Reagan relied on speechwriters, he also wrote, rewrote, and rehearsed his speeches. In his autobiography, *An American Life*, Reagan said that when preparing for a speech, he would picture the kind of people he grew up with, such as those gathered in a bar or barbershop, and imagine he was speaking directly to them. That gave his speeches a conversational feel.

He didn't try to impress his audiences with statistics, and when he did cite figures off-the-cuff in press conferences, he often got them wrong. He preferred to speak in stories, throwing in humor and one-liners, such as "There you go again" (against Jimmy Carter in a debate), or the line he borrowed from Clint Eastwood—"Go ahead—make my day" (when Congress considered a boost in taxes).

What most Americans sensed when he spoke was a sincere man with strong convictions, however soft he was on the details of his policies. "Reagan was not believable because he was the Great Communicator," Reagan chronicler Lou Cannon has written. "He was the Great Communicator because he was believable." His longtime aide, Michael Deaver, said, "He's the only person I've ever met who doesn't have to weigh things—his ideas seem to come from the depth of the man. He's resolved something, his being or what he is, a long time ago."

"I never thought it was my style or the words that I used that made a difference; it was the content," Reagan said during his farewell address. "I wasn't a great communicator, but I communicated great things, and they didn't spring full bloom from my brow, they came from the heart of a great nation—from our experience, our wisdom, and our belief in the principles that have guided us for two centuries. They called it the Reagan Revolution. . . . [B]ut for me it always seemed more like the great rediscovery, a rediscovery of our values and our common sense."

RONALD REAGAN, PEACEMAKER

Ronald Reagan is usually remembered as a lifelong anti-Communist who increased defense spending 50 percent in his first five years in office, called the Soviet Union an "evil empire," and so famously pronounced in Berlin in 1987: "Mr. Gorbachev: tear down this wall." What's usually forgotten is Reagan's quiet passion for nuclear disarmament and his willingness to negotiate and compromise with the Soviets, traits that were just as crucial in reaching historic disarmament accords with the Soviet Union.

Reagan's antinuclear sympathies were evident when the TV movie *The Day After*, about the fate of the people in Lawrence, Kansas, after a nuclear exchange, was watched by 100 million Americans. The movie aired in November 1983, shortly after troop exercises by NATO in Western Europe triggered the highest alert by the Soviet military leaders, who feared it might be a prelude to a U.S. attack. At the time, the Reagan Administration also was pushing a plan to install intermediate-range nuclear Pershing II missiles in Europe, which many Europeans resisted, believing it could lead to a nuclear war on their continent.

U.S. peace activists, who had brought out a million people to New York City's antinuke protest in Central Park in June 1982, watched the political movie in living rooms all over the country. Little did they know that Reagan watched it as well.

"It's powerfully done, all $7 million worth," Reagan wrote in his diary. "It's very effective and left me greatly depressed."

In public, Reagan converted his worries about an apocalyptic war into a pacifistic-sounding version of his "Morning in America" vision. "My dream," Reagan said in January 1984, "is to see the day when nuclear weapons will be banished from the face of the Earth." He actively pursued the dream when the Soviet Union's Communist Party replaced a string of aged conservative leaders with a charismatic reformer, Mikhail Gorbachev. The first meeting between Reagan and Gorbachev, in Iceland, would be one of the most remarkable in the Cold War era, and would lead to Ronald Reagan's most impressive foreign policy achievement.

REYKJAVIK—THE COLD WAR SHIFTS

One historian has called what transpired in Reykjavik, Iceland, over a weekend in October 1986 "one of the strangest episodes in the annals of nuclear diplomacy." Beforehand, the White House downplayed the superpower summit as a "planning session for the full-dress summit in Washington," but Soviet leader Mikhail Gorbachev, wanting to stop the arms race, startled the American negotiators by offering "a bold, unorthodox" plan to cut strategic nuclear missiles by 50 percent. Gorbachev even offered to scale back the Warsaw Pact's huge superiority in conventional weapons over NATO.

The United States had long sought such reductions; Secretary of State George Shultz said the Soviet leader "was laying gifts at our feet." At the Sunday session, Reagan upped the ante, offering to eliminate all nuclear missiles. "We can do that," Gorbachev said. "Let's eliminate them."

But the men stalled over Reagan's Strategic Defense Initiative, known as the "Star Wars" program, which he imagined could create a shield protecting the United States from nuclear missiles. Gorbachev, fearing it would tilt the nuclear balance, insisted it remain in the laboratory; Reagan refused, saying he'd promised it to the American people.

As Reagan headed to his car to leave, Gorbachev told him, "You have missed the unique chance of going down in history as a great president who paved the way for nuclear disarmament." Reagan responded, "That applies to both of us." When the Reykjavik discussions leaked, military hawks condemned Reagan for foolishly flirting with huge reductions in nuclear weapons; liberals castigated him for squandering a historic disarmament agreement because of his obsession with the "Star Wars" defense.

But the summit bore fruit. Fourteen months later, Reagan and Gorbachev agreed to take SS-20 and Pershing missiles out of Europe. The president who Americans feared might start a nuclear war agreed with Gorbachev to cut back nuclear stockpiles for the first time ever. After the Intermediate-Range Nuclear Forces Treaty was signed in 1987, Reagan sent a telegram to Nicholas Meyer, the director of the movie *The Day After*, the depiction of nuclear war that had so moved Reagan. "Don't think your movie didn't have any part of this," wrote Reagan, "because it did."

THE IRAN-CONTRA AFFAIR

Two days before the 1986 midterm elections, a Lebanese magazine reported that the Reagan administration had sent arms to Iran in exchange for the release of seven American hostages in Beirut, defying Reagan's repeated pledge never to deal with terrorists. Outgoing Republican senator Barry Goldwater called the deal "probably one of the major mistakes the United Stated had ever made in foreign policy."

But there was more. It was soon revealed that the money the Iranians had paid for the weapons had been secretly diverted to pay for arms for the Contras, a right-wing opposition force that was fighting the leftist Sandinista government in Nicaragua. That funding violated the Boland amendments, laws passed by Congress that banned any U.S. agency from funding the Contras in Nicaragua, an attempt by Congress to prevent another Vietnam-like war.

Reagan had either approved of the two major foreign policy decisions or was uninformed about them, which would have given credence to those who believed the president was too out of touch to govern.

In one month, the president's approval rating dropped twenty points, the steepest one-month decline since 1936. One third of all Americans thought he should resign. Then, and to this day, people have asked what the president knew, and when, about the hostage deal and the diversion of funds to the Contras. Finally, in a February 1987 press conference, Reagan gave his version of what he'd done.

"A few months ago, I told the American people I did not trade arms for hostages," he said. "My heart and my best intentions still tell me that's true, but the facts and evidence tell me it is not. . . ." He again denied knowledge of the diversion of funds to the Contras, "but as president, I cannot escape responsibility."

Americans, perhaps reluctant to see another failed presidency, forgave Reagan. Talk of impeachment fizzled. Reagan's successor, President George H. W. Bush, pardoned six of eleven convicted participants, and no one went to jail. Reagan's presidency was tarnished, but he still left office with the highest approval rating of any president since Franklin Roosevelt.

President Ronald Reagan says good-bye to Soviet General Secretary Mikhail Gorbachev after their last meeting at Hofdi House, in Reykjavik, Iceland, in 1986. While the two men discussed serious arms reductions, including the elimination of all nuclear missiles, the talks eventually broke down over disagreement over Reagan's Strategic Defense Initiative (SDI). Their disappointment is visible in this photograph.

George H. W. Bush Tempers
the Reagan Revolution

WEEK 35

DID REAGAN END THE COLD WAR?

By the time the hawkish Ronald Reagan left office, the cold war was largely over. How much credit does he deserve for its demise?

Some political analysts say the cold war ended because of large political forces—the inability of the Soviet economy to create wealth, resistance movements in Eastern European countries such as Poland, the costly failed war in Afghanistan, the Chernobyl nuclear accident, or the policy of containment supported by every U.S. President since Harry Truman. But Alexander Bessmertnykh, a Soviet official involved in the Reykjavik negotiations, says the cold war was "ended by human beings, by people who were dedicated to eradicating this part of history."

Much of the credit is given to Soviet leader Mikhail Gorbachev, whom *Time* magazine chose as its Man of the Decade in 1990. Gorbachev took the initiative on disarmament, calling for "radical solutions," including a ban on all nuclear weapons when the leaders met in Reykjavik, Iceland, in 1986. Ten years after the Berlin Wall came down, Gorbachev said he could have preserved it, but only by "shooting ordinary people," which was against "my moral principles."

But historians have acknowledged that Reagan played an important role in the process, pointing out that his unprecedented U.S. military buildup might have forced Soviet leaders to the bargaining table to curtail a military arms race they couldn't afford. Reagan's unswerving support for the Solidarity movement in Poland and his continual pro-democracy rhetoric—"Mr. Gorbachev, tear down this wall," said in 1987 in Berlin—inspired many even inside Communist countries.

"I am not sure what happened would have happened," Gorbachev told the History Channel in 2002, "had [Reagan] not been there." Writer Sean Wilentz, no conservative, has granted that "[Reagan's] success in helping finally to end the cold war is . . . arguably the greatest single presidential achievement since 1945."

If nothing else, Reagan responded to Gorbachev's overtures. While walking through Red Square on a visit to Moscow late in his second term, Reagan was asked, "You still think you are in an evil empire, Mr. President?"

"No," he responded. "I was talking about another time. Another era."

A GRACEFUL RECOGNITION OF ALZHEIMER'S DISEASE

On November 5, 1994, former President Ronald Reagan wrote a hand-written letter to inform the American people that he had Alzheimer's disease. Biographer Edmund Morris called it a "masterly piece of writing," which had the "simplicity of a fundamentally religious nature accepting the inevitable." It began, "My fellow Americans,"

I have recently been told that I am one of the millions of Americans who will be afflicted with Alzheimer's disease. . . .

In the past, Nancy suffered from breast cancer and I had cancer surgeries. We found through our open disclosures we were able to raise public awareness. We were happy that as a result many more people underwent testing. They were treated in early stages and able to return to normal, healthy lives.

So now we feel it is important to share it with you. In opening our hearts, we hope this might promote greater awareness of this condition. . . .

At the moment, I feel just fine. I intend to live the remainder of the years God gives me on this earth doing the things I have always done. . . . Unfortunately, as Alzheimer's disease progresses, the family often bears a heavy burden. I only wish there was some way I could spare Nancy from this painful experience. . . .

In closing, let me thank you, the American people, for giving me the great honor of allowing me to serve as your president. When the Lord calls me home, whenever that may be, I will leave the greatest love for this country of ours and eternal optimism for its future.

I now begin the journey that will lead me into the sunset of my life. I know that for America there will always be a bright dawn ahead.

Thank you, my friends.

Sincerely,
Ronald Reagan

BUSH'S ROLE IN THE END OF THE COLD WAR

The cold war ended symbolically on November 10, 1989, when the people of Berlin began to knock down a wall that had divided East and West Berlin since 1961. Unsure what to do, border guards waited for instructions that never arrived.

As Marlin Fitzwater, George H. W. Bush's press secretary, saw the wire reports, he went into the study next to the Oval Office where President Bush was watching people climb over the wall on CNN. Fitzwater later recorded the conversation that transpired:

"Do you want to make a statement?"

"Why?" the president said. . . .

"Why?" I repeated. "This is an incredibly historic day. People will want to know what it means. They need some presidential assurance that the world is OK." The president just looked at me. He understood the historic point, of course, but his vision was taking him into a future of German reunification, diminished communism, and a new world order to be established. "Listen, Marlin," he said, "I'm not going to dance on the Berlin Wall. The last thing I want to do is brag about winning the cold war, or bringing the wall down."

Fitzwater convinced the president to allow the press corps into the Oval Office. When one reporter noted, "You don't seem elated," Bush responded, "I'm elated. I'm just not an emotional kind of guy." Bush later said that as he answered reporters' questions, his mind "kept racing over a possible Soviet crackdown, turning all the happiness to tragedy." That's what had happened in 1968, when tanks rolled into Czechoslovakia to crush the political liberalization of the Prague Spring.

But the crackdown didn't happen this time. Instead, over the next two years came the collapse of Communist governments in Eastern Europe, the crumbling of the Warsaw Pact, and Germany's reunification and its membership in NATO. Bush oversaw it all with careful diplomacy that one historian called "one of the greatest moments in the history of American statecraft."

THE FIRST IRAQ WAR—
IRAQI FORCES REMOVED FROM KUWAIT

On August 1, 1990, a year and a half into his term, George H. W. Bush was told by an advisor that Iraq, with the fourth largest military in the world, had rolled into neighboring Kuwait after a dispute over oil fields. Bush, a World War II veteran, saw Saddam Hussein as a military bully intent on grabbing up territory. Bush made it clear that he wasn't going to accept the takeover of Kuwait as a fait accompli.

"This will not stand," he told the press.

Hussein threatened to put Western hostages, including children, in harm's way if Iraq was attacked. Israel braced for a chemical attack, as Hussein had used chemical weapons in Iraq's eight-year war against Iran and against opposition in his own country. Many worried that a U.S. attack would provoke a Mideast war.

Bush worked methodically to win U.N. support, as President Harry Truman had done after the North Koreans invaded South Korea. The Soviet Union quickly condemned Iraq's invasion, marking the first time the two superpowers had agreed on the response to an international crisis since the cold war began. U.S. leaders persuaded the U.N. Security Council to condemn the Iraqi attack and endorse an embargo on trade with Iraq. On November 29, Bush won U.N. support for a plan that called for the United States to use "all necessary means" to evict Iraqi forces from Kuwait if it didn't withdraw by January 15, 1991. After that deadline passed, a twenty-eight-nation coalition that included five hundred thousand soldiers attacked Iraq in an invasion called Operation Desert Storm. Sophisticated airplanes, missiles, and tanks quickly defeated the Iraqi forces, which fled Kuwait.

But Hussein remained in power, and he turned his military against minorities whom Bush had encouraged to rise up during the war.

"Some people said, 'Why didn't you guys take care of Saddam when you had the chance?'" Bush's Secretary of State James Baker noted after the second Iraq War had gone awry under George W. Bush. "Well, guess what. . . . Nobody asks me that question anymore."

CLEANING UP THE DEFICIT—AND BREAKING A PROMISE

Many considered George H. W. Bush's acceptance speech at the Republican convention in 1988 the best speech he ever delivered. In it, he spoke of a "kinder, gentler nation" buoyed by volunteers and communities, which he called "a thousand points of light." But the section that drew the most raucous applause regarded taxes, and was delivered with a string of dramatic pauses and a line from a Clint Eastwood movie.

"The Congress will push me to raise taxes, and I'll say no," Bush said. ". . . All I can say to them is: 'Read my lips. No new taxes.'" Richard Darman, a Bush budget advisor, had crossed the line out, aware that the promise would put the administration in a bind. But the speechwriter, Peggy Noonan, had fought for it as the best sound bite in the speech.

The perfect sound bite and the convention helped cut Democrat Michael Dukakis's lead in half, but the tax promise would become a political noose around Bush's neck (for more on the election of 1988, see page 347). He'd inherited a budget deficit of $2.7 trillion from Ronald Reagan, as well as having to bail out the nation's savings and loans, financial institutions so mismanaged under Reagan that they were expected to add another $125 billion to the debt over three years. The General Accounting Office said higher taxes were part of any "credible" plan to curtail the deficit.

Bush called in Democratic leaders, who agreed to cut government spending if Bush raised taxes. Bush knew that breaking his ballyhooed campaign promise "could mean a one-term Presidency," as he wrote in his diary, "but it's that important for the country." Bush signed a budget that increased taxes on the wealthy from a 28-percent to a 31.5-percent tax rate, cutting $500 billion from the deficit over five years.

Many condemned Bush for violating a tenet of the Reagan revolution. But if Bush had not reversed himself, "Ronald Reagan would be associated with an economic collapse," Bush biographer Timothy Naftali has said. "Instead, because George Bush was willing to give Americans strong medicine, Bush gave Reagan a different legacy."

GEORGE BUSH—TOO MODERATE FOR
THE REPUBLICAN PARTY?

After American-led forces pushed the Iraqi army from Kuwait, George H. W. Bush's approval ratings soared to 89 percent, the highest recorded in presidential polling to that point.

But on domestic matters, Bush was not so popular among the conservatives in his party. The first act of his presidency was to sweep Reaganites from appointed positions, alienating conservative Republicans. He'd reversed his "read my lips" promise to not raise taxes—a cardinal sin among the far right. And in an interview on *20/20*, Bush said he believed there should be no "litmus test" that would prevent gays from serving in his cabinet, infuriating many social conservatives, including his own vice president, Dan Quayle.

Many Republicans also disapproved of his two most successful domestic initiatives, the Americans with Disabilities Act in 1990, which forbade discrimination against 43 million Americans with disabilities, and the Clean Air Act Amendments of 1990. The latter established stricter standards for many pollutants and tackled ozone depletion and acid rain. The Bush administration also joined with 150 other countries in signing the Rio Treaty, which set voluntary guideposts for reducing greenhouse emissions. The president of The Conservation Fund maintained that "no president since Teddy Roosevelt has done more to protect the wild heritage of America than George Bush."

But for right-wing voters, these achievements were liabilities, seen as new bureaucratic intrusions into the free market. In 1992, Patrick Buchanan, a fiery former Nixon speechwriter, campaigned against "King George" and claimed 37 percent of the vote in the New Hampshire primary. An even bigger threat was conservative Texas billionaire H. Ross Perot, who would take 19 percent of the votes in the 1992 election, drawing two voters away from Bush for every one he drew from Clinton.

"[Bush] let the right be hijacked . . . ," John Robert Greene, a Bush biographer, has said. "It was that lack of prescience; it was that lack of understanding, the power of the political right in 1992, that cost George Bush the election."

GEORGE H. W. BUSH TAKES THE PRESIDENTIAL OATH OF OFFICE

George H. W. Bush served eight years as vice president before he took the oath of office on January 20, 1989, from Chief Justice William Rehnquist. Vice President Dan Quayle and First Lady Barbara Bush look on.

A Democrat Moves to the Center—
Bill Clinton

HEALTH-CARE REFORM: AN OBITUARY

When Bill Clinton took office in 1993, 37 million Americans had no health-care coverage. Pledging to achieve affordable health care for all, he put First Lady Hillary Clinton in charge (for more on Hillary Clinton, see page 332). Cabinet members, White House officials, and 511 experts worked feverishly under her direction to hash out a bill. "[W]e were betting the farm on health care," stated chief domestic policy advisor Bruce Reed. They lost.

What went wrong?

Many point to powerful interests that had blocked health-care reform for decades.

"We were on the front lines of an increasingly hostile ideological conflict," Hillary later wrote. "We soon learned that nothing was off-limits in this war." Opponents, including drug and insurance companies, "successfully characterized the plan as the government taking over health care," noted Roger Altman, deputy treasury secretary. The Clintons were viciously demonized, even threatened, forcing the first lady to wear a bulletproof vest at rallies.

Others blame Hillary. She rejected much advice and waited too long to activate grassroots support. "I find [Hillary] to be among the most self-righteous people I've ever known in my life," said Bob Boorstein, media deputy for Clinton's health-care task force. "[I]t's her great flaw, it's what killed health care." Pamela Bailey, assistant health secretary, felt Hillary "galvanized every single sector of health care against her." Others believe that antireform forces would have killed any meaningful bill regardless of who led the reform effort.

Allies urged compromise, but the Clintons were adamant. Senators Patrick Moynihan and Robert Dole sent signals that a deal could be made. "They dropped the ball," remarked Dole, "and we didn't help them pick it up."

In a meeting on June 22, 1994, advisors talked deal making. "As long as I am President," Clinton shouted, "I plan to keep fighting for serious reform. I did not get elected to compromise on this issue." At that, one meeting participant noted, "At 10:22 P.M. tonight, health care died."

Its death spelled doom for the Democrats. That fall, ultraconservatives swept to victory in both houses, undermining Clinton's progressive social agenda for his final six years in office.

BILL CLINTON—OVERLOOKING GENOCIDE

The genocide started on April 6, 1994. Over the next eight weeks, Hutu extremists slaughtered upward of 800,000 Tutsis in Rwanda. Throughout, Bill Clinton took no meaningful action to stop the killing.

Anthony Lake, Clinton's national security advisor, would later say that the failure to intervene had been a "sin of omission—of never considering" it. Others saw a sin of commission, with Human Rights Watch accusing the Clinton administration of being the "main stumbling block to international actions to stop the massacres." Even as the death toll mounted, the United States successfully lobbied to slash the U.N. peacekeeping force in Rwanda from 2,100 to 270 troops, and then to block reinforcements.

Afterward, Clinton acknowledged that he "did not immediately call these crimes by their rightful name, genocide." Had he done so, the pressure to intervene would have increased. As a Defense Department document, "Secret Discussion Paper: Rwanda," put it: "Be Careful. . . . Genocide finding could commit [the U.S. government] to actually 'do something.' "

Four years after the genocide, Clinton went to Rwanda to meet with some of the survivors. One, Venuste Karasira, told him, "We died because we were left by the United Nations soldiers." Appearing visibly moved, Clinton responded by admitting that "[w]e in the United States and the world community did not do as much as we could have and should have to try to limit what occurred in Rwanda in 1994." Clinton would later tell a friend that his encounter with the victims of a genocide he had not tried to stop was "the most emotionally searing point" of his presidency.

In his memoirs, Clinton said that he did not intervene because he was "so preoccupied with [the crisis] in Bosnia, the memory of [the recent deaths of eighteen U.S. peacekeeping troops in] Somalia, and with opposition in Congress to military deployments in faraway places not vital to our national interests." He called his "failure to try to stop Rwanda's tragedies . . . one of the greatest regrets of my presidency."

CLINTON STANDS UP—
AND THE GOVERNMENT SHUTS DOWN

The 1994 midterm elections devastated the Democrats: Republicans won majorities in both Houses for the first time in four decades. Led by U.S. Representative Newt Gingrich, they promised to reduce the size of government and cut taxes.

"Gingrich's Revolutionaries" wanted to balance the budget in seven years. They urged major cuts, including $270 billion in Medicare, the popular federal health plan for older Americans. They also wanted a $240 billion tax cut, although that would further unbalance the budget. Clinton swore to protect key social programs.

The stalemate intensified throughout 1995. Both parties were sure Clinton would give in to Gingrich. A top Clinton advisor joked that aides wanted to disable Clinton's phones "to keep him from calling Newt and trading away the store."

In a meeting on November 13, House Majority Leader Dick Armey said that if Clinton didn't back down, his presidency would be dead. Clinton raged back that he would never agree to their cuts "even if I drop to 5 percent in the polls. If you want your budget, you'll have to get someone else to sit in this chair!"

At noon the following day, eight hundred thousand nonessential federal workers were furloughed—40 percent of the nation's nondefense workforce. Unable to receive Social Security checks and other benefits, Americans grew angry—but not at Clinton. "The shutdown was devastating . . . on how it branded . . . the Republican Party as meanspirited and out of touch," bemoaned Scott Reed, a Republican campaign manager. Senator Robert Dole called Gingrich's decision to shut down the government "dumb, dumb, dumb."

The shutdown ended after six days. Although it was renewed for three weeks, the Gingrich forces had lost the public's trust. "We made a mistake," Gingrich told Clinton. "We thought you would cave."

Clinton's decision to risk his presidency for what he believed earned him bipartisan respect. "To make the decision that he might have to do something that would cost him that office," said Leon Panetta, Clinton's chief of staff, "was a very important Rubicon for Bill Clinton."

CLINTON PURSUES A BALANCED BUDGET

At the beginning of 1995, shortly after their sweeping midterm election victory, Republicans announced their intention to balance the federal budget in seven years. They aimed to reduce funding for entitlement programs and reduce taxes, particularly for the wealthiest. Clinton had initially denounced their plan but had not offered one of his own.

But he soon grew to feel it was "indefensible" not to offer a Democratic budget-balancing plan. In response to an aide who wanted him to hold off on a Democratic plan, he snapped, "That's fine. When people say, 'Where's your plan?' I'll say, 'Oh, I'm just the President of the United States. You want me to have a plan?'" In May 1995, the president seized the initiative by countering the Republican plan with one that balanced the budget, but in ten years. He also urged Democrats to scale back their progressive agenda because it would cost the government too much.

Reaction was swift. The plan was "a quantum leap backward for social policy," fumed Donald Payne, chair of the Congressional Black Caucus. "This isn't leadership. It's bullsh-t." Senator Moynihan declared, "He doesn't understand that he's conceding the principles."

Republicans pushed for passage of their leaner plan instead of Clinton's far more moderate one. Five months later, there was a showdown. Clinton vetoed the Republicans' budget, and the federal government shut down. Republicans were blamed for the folly. Clinton's more modest plan eventually passed and he was given much of the credit for the economic boom that followed. Despite later scandals, Clinton remained popular—for good reason. His policies (along with years of relative peace and the high-tech boom) helped create 20 million new jobs. Unemployment fell to a twenty-year low, inflation to a thirty-year low. By the end of his second term, an annual *deficit* of $29 billion had become an annual *surplus* of $160 billion.

Clinton left office with the highest approval rating in history and a projected *surplus* of $5 trillion for 2006–2015. Five years later, under George W. Bush, a *deficit* of $3.47 trillion was projected for the same period.

ENDING WELFARE AS WE KNOW IT

Running for the White House in 1992, Bill Clinton promised to "end welfare as we know it." By all accounts, Clinton, who grew up on the outskirts of poverty, cared about the plight of the poor and genuinely believed that they would benefit from "a more empowering, work-oriented approach to helping poor people." As governor of Arkansas, he initiated Project Success, which aimed to transition people from welfare to work by providing them with schooling and job training.

But once elected, Clinton reluctantly shelved welfare reform to focus on deficit reduction and health care. The Republicans then seized the initiative, twice passing bills that Clinton subsequently vetoed because he felt they would punish the poor rather than help them out of poverty. Seeking to corner Clinton politically, the Republicans proposed another watered-down bill in July 1996.

The new bill incorporated some of Clinton's ideas about moving welfare recipients into jobs. But it ended the New Deal's guarantee of welfare assistance to needy mothers and children, and contained provisions that Clinton thought particularly nasty, especially one prohibiting assistance to legal immigrants. Clinton called it "a decent welfare bill wrapped in a sack of sh-t."

Clinton now faced a major dilemma. He wanted welfare reform, but not a mean-spirited variety. If he signed the bill, he would alienate his liberal constituency. If he vetoed it, he might never get another crack at welfare reform—and Dick Morris, his top political advisor, was telling him that "a veto would be a political disaster" in the upcoming election.

In the end, Clinton reluctantly signed the bill, promising to fight to repeal its more punitive provisions. Summing up his liberal supporters' reaction, Marion Wright Edelman, head of the Children's Defense Fund—and Clinton's close friend and ally—said the bill would leave "a moral blot on his presidency and our nation." But the voters apparently approved, reelecting him in a landslide that November.

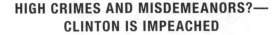

HIGH CRIMES AND MISDEMEANORS?—
CLINTON IS IMPEACHED

In November 1995, Democratic President Bill Clinton had outfoxed Republicans by maneuvering them into shutting down the government, angering the public. The showdown led to Clinton's political renaissance and a second term in the White House. But that same November, Clinton had started a sexual relationship with Monica Lewinsky, a White House intern, that would threaten his presidency. Ten times between November 1995 and March 1997 President Clinton had "inappropriate sexual contact" with Lewinsky. A year and a half later, he was impeached on charges relating to his concealment of this affair.

The *Washington Post* broke the first credible story on January 21, 1998. Clinton hotly denied all allegations, as did Lewinsky, but supporters were badly shaken. "Oh, my God, an intern," thought Bob Kerrey, a Democratic senator. "He's toast." In his autobiography, Clinton wrote, "I was deeply ashamed of it and didn't want it to come out." Conservatives demanded Clinton's resignation.

Ken Starr, the special prosecutor, doggedly pursued the story, as Clinton and Lewinsky had lied under oath about their affair. In September 1998, Starr published his report. The public cringed at hearing the graphic details of Clinton's trysts (for more on Clinton's sexual scandals, see page 355). But Starr felt that people needed to know the particulars in order to understand what Clinton had done.

That November, the Democrats did well in the off-year elections. The election results worried many Republicans, but they launched the second presidential impeachment trial in U.S. history on January 7, 1999. Polls indicated that 62 percent of Americans opposed impeachment. Clinton was impeached in the House but acquitted in the Senate. Detractors thought Clinton deserved the public scolding; supporters thought of the impeachment proceedings as a sexual, and politically based, witch hunt. Yet one thing was certain—Clinton's indiscretion and the reaction to it ended chances of his passing major domestic or international policy initiatives. His presidency had survived, but his reputation and political effectiveness had been severely damaged.

Bill Clinton and Hillary Rodham met while the two attended Yale Law School.
They are pictured here on campus in New Haven, Connecticut, in January, 1972.
The two married on October 11, 1975.

A Republican Moves to the Right—
George W. Bush

A LATE CONVERSION AND A CALL TO DUTY

In his 2000 campaign memoir, *A Charge to Keep: My Journey to the White House*, George W. Bush recounts a 1985 encounter he had with the esteemed Reverend Billy Graham. Graham had been invited up to Kennebunkport, Maine, and one evening he sat around with the Bush family and spoke about faith. George W., forty years old at the time, listened deeply.

Bush said later, "Something was missing in my life, and Billy Graham stimulated my heart—I would like to say planted the mustard seed which grew, and started me on a journey, a walk, to recommit myself to Jesus Christ."

Bush's second key religious encounter took place in January 1999 while he was the popular governor of Texas. He was attending a private service at a Methodist church in Austin when Pastor Mark Craig spoke of Moses' reluctance to lead his people. Craig explained that Moses had told God that he spoke poorly, was deeply flawed, he was busy tending sheep, and had family obligations—but still he was chosen. As Bush writes it, Craig talked about "the need for honesty in government; he warned that leaders who cheat on their wives will cheat on their country" an obvious reference to Bill Clinton—and said people were "starved for leaders who have ethical and moral courage."

Afterward, George's mother, Barbara, told him that Craig was speaking to him. "Pastor Craig had prodded me out of my comfortable life . . . toward a national campaign," George Bush wrote. Soon after, Bush would attend a men's community Bible study group at a Presbyterian church in Midland once a week, and as part of his transformation, he gave up drinking, which was undermining his marriage to Laura.

Bush would startle many during the presidential campaign when he said Jesus Christ was his favorite philosopher. Faith also guided him during his presidency. When *Washington Post* reporter Bob Woodward asked him whether he sought advice from his father, George H. W. Bush, in the lead-up to the second Gulf War, George W. said, "There's a higher Father I appeal to." His faith impressed and comforted many supporters, yet frightened detractors, who feared it fed an assumption "that he knows the truth."

SEPTEMBER 11, 2001, DEFINES THE BUSH PRESIDENCY

As of the morning of September 11, 2001, George Bush's approval rating had sunk to a tepid 51 percent. Yet the president had passed a significant tax cut earlier in the year and was pushing to pass his education package, which had brought him to the Emma T. Booker Elementary School in Sarasota, Florida, for a photo op.

Before he entered the classroom that Tuesday morning, he was informed an airplane had crashed into one of the World Trade Center towers in New York City. As Bush listened to a reading of the book *The Pet Goat*, an aide whispered that a second plane had hit the second tower. "They had declared war on us," Bush thought, "and I made up my mind at that moment that we were going to war."

Bush would tell reporters crowded into the Oval Office on Thursday, September 13, "Understand, this is now the focus of my administration." But what people would remember is that Friday afternoon, when George Bush came to the World Trade Center site and stepped onto the towers' debris. When somebody called out, "We can't hear you," Bush wrapped an arm around a firefighter, grabbed a bullhorn, and called out, "I can hear you! The rest of the world hears you. And the people who knocked these buildings down will hear all of us soon!" They were the words of a president who had suddenly found his voice as America's commander in chief.

"We will not waver," Bush said in a national address. "We will not tire, we will not falter, and we will not fail."

In a month, the United States overthrew the Taliban government in Afghanistan, which had supported al-Qaeda, the group responsible for the attack. Bush would lead a Republican takeover of Congress in 2002, a war to overthrow Iraq's Saddam Hussein in the spring of 2003, and a successful reelection bid in 2004. In May 2003, a poll by the Pew Research Center asked the public to give one or two words to describe Bush, and nearly all were positive, such as *honest, good, leader, great*, and *courageous*.

WHY DID WE INVADE IRAQ?

The day after the September 11, 2001, attacks, Richard Clarke, the National Security Council's counterterrorism expert, said that George Bush pulled him aside and asked, "See if you can find evidence of an Iraqi connection here." Clarke paused.

"But Mr. President, Iraq didn't do this," Clarke replied. "Al-Qaeda did." Clarke knew that al-Qaeda, a little-known terrorist group, was based in Afghanistan, and had no credible links to Iraq. It would soon be revealed that none of the attackers were Iraqi; most came from Saudi Arabia.

All this has led Clarke and many Americans to ask: Why did Bush launch a war against Iraq?

The administration initially said the invasion was to rid the country of weapons of mass destruction and to depose its leader, Saddam Hussein, who might use them. "I could only imagine the destruction possible if an enemy dictator passed his WMD to terrorists," Bush wrote in his autobiography. Secretary of State Condoleezza Rice expressed the fear as, "[W]e don't want the smoking gun to be a mushroom cloud."

But after the U.S. occupation, no WMDs were found. "No one was more shocked or angry than I was when we didn't find the weapons," Bush wrote in his autobiography. "I had a sickening feeling every time I thought about it. I still do."

The administration then fell back on the argument that the overthrow of Saddam Hussein would inspire a bloom of democracies elsewhere in the Middle East. Many in the United States assumed the U.S. invasion of Iraq was a war for oil, which was difficult to prove. Others felt Bush wanted this war to demonstrate U.S. power around the world or to bolster Israel. Another theory held that Bush wanted to outdo his father in Iraq or to avenge an assassination attempt Hussein is alleged to have made against George H. W. Bush.

Perhaps the reasons were many. "For bureaucratic reasons," Paul Wolfowitz, one of the administration proponents of the invasion, said in an interview afterward, "we settled on one issue, weapons of mass destruction, because it was the one reason everyone could agree on."

EVERYTHING GOES WRONG IN IRAQ

On May 1, 2003, the administration of George Bush organized a photo op in which the president, wearing the uniform of an air force combat pilot, landed with fanfare on the aircraft carrier *Abraham Lincoln* off San Diego, stepping under a banner that read MISSION ACCOMPLISHED.

But in the six weeks it had taken for American soldiers to roll to Baghdad, the occupation had already stumbled. In the days after Saddam Hussein's statue had been toppled, looters had ransacked antiquities from the National Museum of Iraq. Secretary of Defense Donald Rumsfeld responded, "Stuff happens." U.S. Administrator Paul Bremer banned Saddam Hussein's Ba'ath Party from serving in the government, and everyday services, like mail delivery, came to a halt. Bremer also disbanded the Iraqi army, putting four hundred thousand soldiers on the street, many of whom joined a fast-growing insurgency. Rumsfeld also prevailed in deploying a "light footprint" of troops in the country, which would prove inadequate to keep the peace.

As a power vacuum opened, insurgent nationalists employed suicide bombers and improvised explosive devices (IEDs) on roads to blow up American vehicles, and a "low-key, guerrilla-type war" evolved. American bureaucrats retreated to the barricaded Baghdad area called the Green Zone. American support for the war plummeted after graphic photos were released in April 2004 of American soldiers humiliating and torturing Iraqi prisoners in Baghdad's Abu Ghraib prison.

In February 2006, the bombing of the Askariya Mosque in Samarra, a revered Shiite shrine, set off a wave of violence that amounted to a civil war between Sunni and Shia Muslims. As the violence in Iraq continued, Democrats swept the 2006 elections, and Bush's approval ratings sank to the low twenties. Rumsfeld was let go. In 2007, Bush sent a "surge" of forty thousand troops to Iraq, which many believed helped stabilize the shaky, Shiite-controlled Iraqi government.

"As they stand up, we will stand down," Bush repeated.

An estimated 1.5 million people fled Iraq during the war. As of 2010, 4,404 American soldiers had been killed and 31,827 wounded. The estimates of the number of Iraqis who died during the war varies wildly, from 150,000 to over 1 million. By the time Bush left office, order had been largely restored. While he admitted that some of the intelligence on the war was "wrong," he insisted that overthrowing Hussein had been "the right thing to do."

FROM A HISTORIC SURPLUS
TO HISTORIC DEFICIT IN EIGHT YEARS

In 2000, President Bill Clinton left President George W. Bush a surplus estimated at almost $5 trillion through 2010. By the time Bush left office, he'd left a debt of $10 trillion, or $35,000 for every man, woman, and child. What happened?

A recession that hit just after Bush came into office ate into the surplus. Bush also passed his first major tax cut in June 2001, believing the surplus was "the people's money." It was the first major tax cut since Ronald Reagan, and it reduced federal tax revenues by $1.35 trillion over ten years. In 2002, Bush proposed another major tax cut at the same time he campaigned for an invasion of Iraq. Secretary of the Treasury Paul O'Neill protested cutting taxes while going to war, but Bush ignored O'Neill's advice, and then fired him. Vice President Dick Cheney cast the deciding vote on this second tax cut in May 2003, two months after the U.S. invasion of Iraq.

The administration estimated the war would cost $50 to $60 billion, but when the combat mission ended in 2010, experts placed the cost between $1 and $3 trillion.

Conservative economist Bruce Bartlett denounced Bush as a "pretend conservative" who cut taxes, but allowed the deficit to grow because he made little effort to rein in government expenditures. After the September 11 attacks, Bush agreed to bail out airlines and established a Department of Homeland Security, expanding the government bureaucracy. In January 2006, Bush would make one more contribution to the deficit: Medicare Part D, a prescription drug benefit. It reduced out of pocket expenses for seniors, yet many considered it a boondoggle to the pharmaceutical companies. Medicare Part D alone cost the country $60 billion a year.

Why did the Bush administration run up the debt? Was it to "starve the beast," using huge deficits to force eventual cutbacks in government spending? Was it lack of fiscal discipline? Or was it because Bush prioritized a "war on terror" no matter what the cost? In the end, these are questions for historians.

THE NATION LOSES FAITH IN ITS LEADER—KATRINA

In his autobiography, George W. Bush tells the story of then-President Lyndon Johnson, who flew from Washington, D.C., to New Orleans on the night Hurricane Betsy devastated the city in 1965. When Johnson was guided to a dark, overcrowded shelter in the Ninth Ward, he yelled, "This is your president! I'm here to help you!"

"Unfortunately," wrote Bush, "I did not follow his example."

Hurricane Katrina hit New Orleans on Monday morning, August 29, 2005, breaching the levees and quickly flooding much of the city.

That day, Bush was on a speaking tour through the West. Aides pressed him to get back to Washington, but he stopped for two nights and a day at his family ranch in Crawford, Texas, heading back to Washington on Wednesday morning. On the way, the plane flew low over New Orleans. Press photographers were let into the cabin of Air Force One. "The photo of me hovering over the damage suggested I was detached from the suffering on the ground," Bush wrote in his autobiography. "That wasn't how I felt."

On television, the world watched as people, mostly African Americans, were stranded on their roofs; 1,836 people had drowned. The roughly thirty thousand people who had gathered at the city's Superdome were running out of food and water.

Finally, on Friday, five days after the hurricane had hit, Bush flew to Mobile, Alabama, encouraging Michael Brown, the director of the Federal Emergency Management Agency (FEMA), which had become a nest for Bush cronies. "Brownie, you're doing a heck of a job," the President said, but he was one of the few who thought so.

Bush's reputation would never recover. Six months after Katrina, a CBS News poll found that two of three Americans did not think Bush responded adequately to the needs of Katrina victims. In 2008, most respondents to a Pew Research Center poll chose the word "incompetent" to describe Bush; his approval rating fell to 24 percent by the time he left office, as low as Harry Truman's when he left office. Bush acknowledged that the hurricane's impact "eroded citizens' trust in their government. It exacerbated divisions in our society and politics. And it cast a cloud over my second term."

President George W. Bush addresses a crowd at the World Trade Center site on September 11, 2001. In response to a rescue worker who yelled, "I can't hear you!" Bush responded, "I can hear you! I can hear you! The rest of the world hears you! And the people who knocked these buildings down will hear all of us soon!"

A New Era?—
Barack Obama

WEEK 38

MORE THAN THE FIRST BLACK PRESIDENT

In the history books, Barack Obama will be listed as the first African-American U.S. president, but his identity is much richer and more complicated. "I am the son of a black man from Kenya and a white woman from Kansas," he said in his "More Perfect Union" speech, delivered on March 18, 2008. His father, Barack Hussein Obama, Sr., was a Kenyan academic; his mother, Stanley Anne, could trace her father's family back to the small Irish town of Moneygall.

Obama's parents met in 1960 in a Russian class at the University of Hawaii. In his memoir, *Dreams from My Father*, Obama said that Stanley Anne's parents were uneasy about the prospects of a black son-in-law, and his father's Kenyan family didn't want their blood "sullied by a white woman."

Barack was born in Hawaii, in a country where many African Americans couldn't vote. When his father left, his mother next married an Indonesian, and the couple went to Jakarta, where Obama attended St. Francis elementary school in the most populous Muslim nation in the world. The boy was called Barry Soetoro, after his stepfather's family name.

When that marriage fractured, Obama's mother returned to Hawaii, and Barack attended Punahou, an elite Honolulu prep school. Few blacks enrolled, and the young Obama sometimes hid himself behind closed doors to read African-American writers such as Richard Wright, James Baldwin, and Malcolm X, "trying to reconcile the world as I'd found it with the terms of my birth."

He married Michelle Robinson, a woman who "carries within her the blood of slaves and slaveowners," Obama would say. The couple settled in Hyde Park, an integrated neighborhood on Chicago's South Side. Obama came to national prominence after an electrifying speech at the 2004 Democratic convention.

In 2006, Obama holed himself up in a Chicago conference room with his key political advisors to decide whether he should run for president. "You need to ask yourself, Why do you want to do this?" Michelle asked pointedly. "This I know," Obama said. "When I raise my hand and take that oath of office, I think the world will look at us differently. And millions of kids across this country will look at themselves differently."

OBAMA SPEAKS ABOUT RACE—AND WINS THE ELECTION

On March 13, 2008, nine days after Hillary Clinton had beaten Barack Obama in the Texas and Ohio Democratic primaries, ABC aired video excerpts of speeches given by Obama's pastor, Reverend Jeremiah Wright, including statements such as: "Not God bless America! God *damn* America"; that the United States had invented the AIDS virus "as a means of genocide against people of color"; and that the September 11 attacks were payback for U.S. acts such as supporting Israel.

Wright's inflammatory views led many Americans to question Obama's position on race. Clinton said of Wright: "He would not have been my pastor." Aware that his historic campaign was threatened with collapse, Obama delivered a speech five days later near Philadelphia's Independence Hall, where America's founders signed the Constitution.

As most politicians would have done, Obama condemned the aired "snippets" of Wright's speeches in "unequivocal terms." Yet Obama also admitted that Wright "was like family to me. . . . I can no more disown him than I can disown the black community [or] my white grandmother—a woman who helped raise me . . . and who on more than one occasion has uttered racial or ethnic stereotypes that made me cringe. These people are a part of me. And they are a part of America, this country that I love."

Obama accepted black frustration with racial injustice, but he also recognized white working class anger regarding race, his larger point being "that working together we can move beyond some of our old racial wounds, and that in fact we have no choice if we are to continue on the path of a more perfect union." Obama called for racial healing and cooperation.

A former Clinton speechwriter called the speech "brave, thoughtful, honest—how often are any of these adjectives applied to a speech by a politician, let alone in the heat of a campaign?" In a CBS poll, 71 percent of respondents said he'd effectively explained his relationship with Wright. Hendrik Hertzberg, a *New Yorker* columnist, might have put it best: "The speech helped elect Obama as the President of the United States."

A STIMULUS PACKAGE—SUCCESS OR FAILURE?

Barack Obama entered office facing the worst economic collapse since the one Franklin Roosevelt had faced in 1932. The stock market had buckled. Virtually no credit was available. Major banks, investment houses, and American car companies collapsed. The unemployment rate jumped toward double digits, a benchmark the nation hadn't seen since 1982. The country was hemorrhaging 750,000 jobs a month and the economy was shrinking at a projected annual rate of 6 percent.

Attempting to prevent a worldwide depression, Obama and a Democratic Congress passed a $787 billion stimulus package—the equivalent of five years of spending in the Iraq and Afghanistan wars—in Obama's first month in office. The Recovery and Reinvestment Act had three parts: a third of the money went to state and local governments to keep employees such as teachers and firefighters from being laid off; another third became a $400 middle-class tax credit, one of the largest short-term tax cuts in American history; and the last third was spent on infrastructure improvements such as the repair of bridges and tunnels, the largest infusion of infrastructure money since the Interstate Highway Act in the 1950s. The bill also spent record amounts on education and clean energy.

Republican Representative Eric Cantor called the bill "full of pork-barrel spending, government waste, and massive borrowing cleverly called 'stimulus.'" Republicans, preferring a larger reliance on tax cuts, predicted it would swell the deficit. Only three Republican senators voted for the bill.

Most economists say the stimulus helped prevent a global economic meltdown and kept U.S. unemployment from jumping as high as twenty percent, Depression territory. But these were what Obama called "counterfactuals," which were impossible to prove, and many Americans considered the stimulus a failure. Two years after the stimulus passed, unemployment still lingered around nine percent.

In the summer of 2011, House Speaker John Boehner said the weak job market "is more evidence that the misguided 'stimulus' spending binge, excessive regulations and an overwhelming national debt continue to hold back private-sector job creation in our country." Obama's first major act as president had been bold and controversial; his second one would be even more so.

OBAMA'S HISTORIC HEALTH-CARE REFORM

On election night in November 2008, when it became clear Barack Obama would be elected president, he asked himself what single achievement would help most Americans. His answer was health-care reform.

Presidents Franklin Roosevelt, Harry Truman, and Bill Clinton had all seen their national health-care bills undermined by doctors, insurance companies, and opponents of big government. Most of Obama's aides believed he should focus his first year on digging the country out of the recession and ending two wars.

But Obama pushed it, believing his first year in office would provide the best chance for passage. The bill moved like molasses through both Houses, as the White House courted Republican support. Then in August 2009, people shouted down public officials and the health-care bill at town hall meetings, expressing the fear of many Americans that the bill would increase their health-care costs, raise their taxes, interfere with their choice of doctors, and hurt the quality of their care. Republican officials, suspicious of government solutions and the price of the plan, smelled blood. "If we're able to stop Obama on this," South Carolina Senator Jim DeMint said, "it will be his Waterloo."

Then, in January 2010, Scott Brown, a Republican and an opponent of the bill, was elected to Ted Kennedy's Senate seat after Kennedy died from brain cancer. The 60-vote majority Democrats needed for passage in the Senate was gone. Republicans wanted to restart the debate; some Democrats urged Obama to take a piecemeal approach to reform. Obama pushed for the bill's passage.

Congress narrowly passed the Affordable Care Act in March 2010, providing insurance for 31 million more Americans. It also outlawed the denial of coverage to people with pre-existing medical conditions, subsidized private coverage, and more closely regulated private insurers. The Congressional Budget Office said the bill would cut $138 billion from the deficit over a decade.

The reform was Obama's most impressive achievement in his first two years, and his most controversial. Not one Republican voted for the bill, and many congressional Republicans were elected in 2010 on a promise to overturn it.

A "SHELLACKING" IN THE MIDTERM ELECTIONS

Barack Obama rose to the presidency in 2008 on the engines of hope and change. But in the 2010 midterm elections, the Democratic Party received what Obama called a "shellacking," losing six Senate seats, ten governorships, and sixty House seats, the biggest swing there since 1948.

What happened? Nearly nine in ten voters were worried about how the economy would fare over the next year, and 40 percent said their financial situation had deteriorated since Obama became president. "If right now we had 5 percent unemployment instead of 9.6 percent unemployment," Obama said in a post-election press conference, "then people would have more confidence in [my] policy choices."

Republicans interpreted the election as a rebuke of the Obama administration's big government solutions, including the stimulus package and the health-care bill, which they argued had only ballooned the debt and caused economic stagnation. "The American people have sent an unmistakable message to [Obama] tonight," said John Boehner, the new House Republican Speaker, "and that message is 'change course!'"

Many pundits suggested Obama had been too liberal and needed to tack toward the center, as Clinton had done after his party's midterm losses in 1994. But critics on the left argued that Obama had been too conservative, and one progressive asserted the election had been lost by "corporate Democrats who refused to stand up and fight for real change." In their eyes, an economic recovery had been held back by conservative Democrats who pushed for too small a stimulus, undermined a true government-run health-care system, and put Wall Street's interests before Main Street's.

Many argued Obama had not properly explained or publicized his achievements, such as the health-care bill, Wall Street reform, or the middle-class tax break embedded in the stimulus. "[A] couple of great communicators, Ronald Reagan and Bill Clinton, were standing at this podium two years into their presidency," Obama replied, "[because] the economy wasn't working the way it needed to be." Yet Obama's fate in 2012 most likely rested with how the economy would fare, as the last president to get re-elected with as high an unemployment rate was Franklin Delano Roosevelt during the Great Depression.

OBAMA WITHDRAWS FROM TWO WARS

Barack Obama inherited two wars from the administration of George Bush—one in Afghanistan, started seven years earlier to remove the Taliban government and destroy al-Qaeda; and another in Iraq, launched five years earlier. Obama, keeping a campaign promise, began to withdraw American combat troops from Iraq in June 2009, but in Afghanistan—by then, the longest military engagement in American history—Obama rejected immediate withdrawal, fearful that if the Taliban came back into power the country would again become a safe haven for al-Qaeda.

An administration debate was launched. General Stanley McChrystal urged a surge of eighty thousand troops and called for an open-ended commitment. Vice President Joseph Biden wanted to draw down troops and to rely instead on U.S. Predator missiles and special forces to disrupt the Taliban. Obama would split the difference, calling for a surge of forty thousand more troops in late 2009, bringing the total in the country to about one hundred thousand. The left accused the president of continuing the war unnecessarily.

On June 21, 2011, President Obama said that a drawdown of thirty thousand troops would take place over the next year. The right now said he was abandoning the fight against al-Qaeda. Obama also noted that one hundred thousand troops had been withdrawn from Iraq, noting that after the deaths of six thousand American soldiers in Iraq and Afghanistan, "the tide of war is receding."

"Over the last decade, we have spent a trillion dollars on war, at a time of rising debt and hard economic times," President Obama said. "Now, we must invest in America's greatest resource: our people."

But as 2012 approached, Obama faced a host of challenges at home. All efforts at bipartisanship had failed. The government was not only divided, but polarized, as Republicans, pushed rightward by their Tea Party members, and Democrats moved away from each other. Americans were increasingly holding Obama, rather than George W. Bush, responsible for the stagnant economy. Little had been done to avert the looming climate catastrophe. Many who had voted for Obama hoping he would bring change to Washington had become disillusioned. Howard Dean, the former presidential candidate, said the problem wasn't with Obama or Republican leaders, but with the American people. "Politicians follow," he said. "They don't lead. We lead, collectively, all of us."

Newly sworn-in President Barack Obama and First Lady Michelle Obama watch the inaugural parade in front of the White House on January 20, 2009.

PART II

The Best, *the* Worst, *and* *the* Most Interesting Presidents

Most Influential—
and Interesting—First Ladies

WEEK 39

ABIGAIL ADAMS—THE FIRST INFLUENTIAL FIRST LADY

Abigail Adams was the first of many influential First Ladies, swaying John Adams's politics with her charm, wit, and intelligence. Those qualities shine through the articulate letters she wrote to her husband, who was often away from home. "My pen is always freer than my tongue," she admitted in one letter. "I have wrote many things to you that I suppose I never could have talk'd." He called her "my best, dearest, worthiest wisest friend in the World."

In the letters, Abigail is opinionated and fearless. In the leadup to the Revolution, she encouraged John to establish an independent country, and later called on her husband to create a country that respected women:

> In the new Code of Laws . . . I desire you would remember the ladies, and be more generous and favorable to them than your ancestors. Do not put such unlimited power into the hands of the husbands. Remember all men would be tyrants if they could. If particular care and attention is not paid to the ladies we are determined to foment a rebellion, and will not hold ourselves bound by any laws in which we have no voice or representation.

She also favored better treatment of African Americans. Just before her husband was inaugurated president in 1796, she wrote him of an incident involving James Prince, a free black boy she had taught to read in Quincy. With her approval James began attending classes at a new school for apprentices. But soon word came that the other boys intended to leave rather than attend with a black boy.

"The Boy is a Freeman as much as any of the young men," she wrote John, "and merely because his Face is Black is he to be denied instruction? How is he to be qualified to procure a livelihood? Is this the Christian principle of doing unto others as we would have others do to us?" In this case Abigail did more than write: She called the schoolboys in and convinced them to stay.

DOLLEY MADISON—THE *FIRST* FIRST LADY

Dolley Madison's first political success might have been getting her husband James—socially awkward, some said rude—elected president. Dolley deftly campaigned for her husband, her second, at dinner parties and soirees in the months leading up to the nomination. She was the first president's wife to do so: Martha Washington hated the limelight and had not needed to campaign for her famous husband; Abigail Adams exerted her influence on John behind the scenes; and Jefferson was long widowed by the time he ran for the presidency.

Dolley gladly campaigned in social settings for the man who would be her companion for forty years, and her charm was a powerful asset. When Charles Pinckney lost the presidency to James Madison in 1808, he commented bitterly, "I might have had a better chance had I faced Mr. Madison alone. I was beaten by Mr. and *Mrs.* Madison."

Dolley's biggest contribution to American politics might have been the civility she brought to Washington. At the time, politics was a rambunctious affair, with politicians often resorting to fisticuffs and duels to settle political disagreements. Dolley provided a social place for political enemies to meet, and, as historian Catherine Allgor says, to "work out things—they can compromise, they can talk, they can make deals." That place was the White House, which she turned from a private residence into a public space with public rooms decorated with American furniture. She opened the doors to parties every Wednesday, with crowds so dense they were called "squeezes." The nastiness of politics was smoothed over by port wine and ice cream and Mrs. Madison's graciousness.

Dolley also understood the importance of political symbols. She managed to rescue the Gilbert Stuart portrait of George Washington just before the British burned the White House to the ground in 1814. Many wanted to abandon Washington and make Philadelphia the new capital; Dolley believed the capital was an important American symbol, and by way of argument, she moved back to the city and started holding parties again. By nine votes, Congress decided to rebuild Washington.

DID EDITH RUN THE GOVERNMENT AFTER WOODROW'S STROKE?

At 8:50 A.M. on October 2, 1919, Edith Wilson, President Woodrow Wilson's wife, picked up a private phone, circumventing the White House switchboard. She urgently asked the White House usher to call the president's doctor. Ten minutes after Dr. Cary Grayson entered Wilson's bedroom, he came out and exclaimed, "My God, the President is paralyzed." Wilson had suffered a stroke and was seriously incapacitated for at least six of his last eighteen months as president.

Edith and her husband's doctors decided to issue only "general statements" about Wilson's health. Dr. Grayson made a note that "Mrs. Wilson . . . was absolutely opposed to any other course." Accordingly, Grayson wrote bulletins about Wilson's "nervous exhaustion"—never mentioning the word *stroke*.

For weeks Edith refused to allow even the vice president into Wilson's room. She handled all correspondence, suspending urgent matters of state by explaining that "the Drs insist all business shall be kept from him." According to Edith, "I, myself, never made a single decision regarding the disposition of public affairs." Due to the nature of Wilson's illness, however, Edith's claim has been strongly contested. Labor strife, marine deployments, treaty ratification—no one knew who was deciding White House policy. Wilson's confidential secretary eventually quit: "I got awfully tired of doing nothing . . . Mrs. Wilson apparently ran the whole show." People began to say that the United States had a "government by petticoat."

Did this limbo period, during which the Senate rejected the Paris peace treaty that settled World War I, make World War II more likely? If Vice President Marshall had taken the reins, a modified treaty would likely have been ratified, with U.S. participation in the League of Nations (for more on the failed League of Nations, see page 370). Hitler's military buildup—thus World War II—might have been prevented.

Wilson slowly improved. He served out his term, dying three years later. The Twenty-fifth Amendment, ratified in 1967 after Kennedy's assassination, now provides a mechanism to transfer power to the vice president if a disagreement arises about whether the president is able "to discharge his powers and duties."

ELEANOR ROOSEVELT:
THE CONSCIENCE OF AN ADMINISTRATION

Orphaned at age ten, Eleanor Roosevelt lived a quiet life with a cold grandmother until she was sent to boarding school in London at age sixteen. There, under the careful tutoring of Marie Souvestre, a Parisian teacher, Eleanor blossomed. "She gave me an intellectual curiosity and a standard of living which have never left me," she later wrote. Yet throughout her youth and early marriage, Eleanor was awkward in social situations, intimidated by public speaking, and ignorant about government. At first, she occupied her time as a mother: From 1906 to 1916, she gave birth to six children.

In her early thirties, Eleanor helped run canteens for servicemen during World War I, and visited the wounded and sick. "I loved it," she wrote later. "I simply ate it up." The League of Women Voters exposed her to feminist politics.

After Franklin was stricken with polio in 1921, Eleanor stepped up her campaigning for him. She even took speech lessons to lower the range of her voice and get comfortable with public speaking. Ultimately, she became the conscience of the Roosevelt administration, visiting coal miners, sharecroppers, and the unemployed. She pushed hard to give visas to European Jews seeking asylum and protested the internment of Japanese-Americans—both fights she lost.

In 1939, she publicly resigned from the Daughters of the American Revolution because it had refused to let the African-American singer, Marian Anderson, perform at Constitution Hall. She worked ceaselessly on civil rights issues, fighting to get more blacks hired in government jobs, enact antilynching laws, and end racial discrimination in the armed forces, industry, and public housing. When asked if her left-leaning views might hurt him among conservative voters, Franklin said, "Well, that's my wife, and I can't be expected to do anything about her."

Eleanor was sixty-one when Franklin died in 1945. She'd spend another seventeen years fighting for causes she believed in. She was largely responsible for one of the most important documents of the twentieth century, the Universal Declaration of Human Rights, and President Harry S Truman gave her the title First Lady of the World.

BETTY FORD—BEING "SOMEBODY"

As a political widow marooned with young children in a Virginia suburb in 1965, Betty Ford had a nervous breakdown that required psychiatric treatment. She would later describe the emotional pain she felt at that time: "I was convinced that the more important [my husband] became, the less important I became. . . . Hadn't I once been somebody in this world?"

Betty Ford was adamant that "being First Lady should [not] prevent me from expressing my views." And express them she did, regardless of whom she embarrassed, shocked, or offended. She applauded abortion rights, called for monetary compensation for housewives (including First Ladies), defended the civil liberties of gays, suggested that she would have tried marijuana in her youth if given the opportunity, publicly contemplated the idea that her own daughter might be having premarital sex, and noted that she planned to sleep with the president "as often as possible." She campaigned energetically but unsuccessfully for the equal rights amendment, which would have made discrimination on the basis of sex unconstitutional.

Ford used her platform as First Lady to educate the public about breast cancer when she had a mastectomy in 1974. At the time, breast cancer was a taboo subject, and mastectomies were anathema in the prevailing "bosom-oriented culture." Breaking with convention, Ford spoke candidly about her own battle with breast cancer, her "worry about disfigurement," and her feelings about having "lost a breast."

With her husband's defeat in 1976, Betty Ford lost her bully pulpit and with it her purpose in life. Her substance abuse problem, which she'd battled since 1965, worsened. Finally, her family forced her into a residential detoxification clinic. When she came out, she resolved to help other substance abusers. In 1982, she opened the now-renowned Betty Ford Center for substance abuse treatment. As a role model and activist in the fight against substance abuse, Betty Ford became "somebody in this world" in her own right. As one beneficiary of her clinic observed: "That woman is going to be long remembered—and not as the wife of a president."

HILLARY RODHAM CLINTON:
GROUNDBREAKING FIRST LADY

Four-year-old Hillary came home crying. She wanted to play with Suzy O'Callahan and her seven brothers, but Suzy wouldn't let her. "Go back out there," Dorothy Rodham told her daughter, "and if Suzy hits you, you have my permission to hit her back. You have to stand up for yourself. There's no room in this house for cowards." Later Hillary ran home again: "I can play with the boys now!"

Born October 26, 1947, Hillary Rodham grew up in a middle-class Chicago suburb. Hugh, her strict father, was a small businessman and staunch Republican. Her mother, a housewife and closet Democrat, believed in social justice. Her daughter absorbed that belief and determined "to measure my choices not against the moment, but against eternal values."

But gender often stymied her choices. After Hillary lost an election in high school, her opponent told her she was "really stupid if [she] thought a girl could be elected president." At age fourteen, she wrote a letter to NASA asking if she might be an astronaut, but was told they did not take girls.

Even by 1992, when her husband, Bill, was elected president, the country didn't want its First Lady to play with the boys. Although 58 percent of Americans then had a favorable impression of Hillary, 80 percent felt that she should not have a major administration role. A close advisor warned her husband: "The more she seems strong, the more you will inevitably seem weak." She seemed as much an issue as the health-care reform she unsuccessfully oversaw in 1993.

Hillary, as journalist Carl Bernstein wrote, "inflame[ed] the politics of gender in a way not seen since the first days of radical feminism in America." A vicious anti-Hillary campaign was unleashed. "I think," stated her former youth minister, "the United States would tolerate a woman president better than a professional, intellectual, uppity First Lady." "It's not me, personally," Hillary said. "It's the changes I represent."

In 2000, Hillary Rodham Clinton—while First Lady—was elected senator from New York. In 2008, she made a near-successful bid for the Democratic presidential nomination, and President Obama appointed her secretary of state in 2009.

First Lady Eleanor Roosevelt presents the NAACP's Springarn Medal to Marian Anderson in 1939 for "that American Negro who has made the highest achievement in any honorable field of endeavor." Roosevelt publicly resigned from the Daughters of the American Revolution the same year to protest the organization's refusal to let Anderson perform at Constitution Hall.

Best Writers— and Speakers

WEEK 40

JEFFERSON—A GREAT WRITER, A POOR SPEAKER

The American people generally expect their presidents to speak often in public. But Thomas Jefferson rarely spoke or appeared at public functions. While John Adams and George Washington gave many public addresses, Jefferson gave only two speeches during his presidency, as far as we know: his two inaugural addresses.

His preferred form of political dialogue with everyone—friends, politicians, cabinet members, and the American people—was the written word. He described his administrative duties as "a steady and uniform course. It keeps me from 10 to 12 and 13 hours a day at my writing table, giving me an interval of 4 hours for riding, dining and a little unbending." He began his day around 5:00 A.M. and worked alone, writing until 9:00 A.M. He visited with cabinet officers and congressmen the rest of the morning, went riding in the afternoon, and had dinner at 3:30 P.M., which was often a social or political event. He returned to his desk at about 6:00 or 7:00 P.M. to write again until 10:00 P.M.

His first year in office he wrote 677 letters—about two a day—not including internal correspondences with his cabinet. Over his life, he wrote roughly nineteen thousand letters and received twenty-six thousand more.

But Jefferson might have been making a virtue out of his weaknesses. He was a notoriously poor speaker and often preferred being alone to the hubbub of public politics. (John Adams reported that "the whole Time I sat with him in Congress, I never heard him utter three sentences together.")

In his biography of Jefferson, *American Sphinx*, Joseph Ellis calls Jefferson one of the "most secluded and publicly invisible presidents in American history." Yet Jefferson's writing left Americans with a treasure trove of documents: a written, public, and accurate record of what he thought politically and personally throughout his lifetime.

LINCOLN EDITS BEAUTIFULLY—
THE INAUGURAL'S LAST PARAGRAPH

Lincoln's writing could sometimes be lawyerly, but in his best writing—his Gettysburg Address, his second inaugural, and at the end of his first inaugural—he often cut to the core of an issue and mixed the plainspoken with poetry.

When Lincoln asked William Seward, his secretary of state, to review his first inaugural, Seward found the draft too provocative, fearing it could provoke both Virginia and Maryland to secede, leaving the capital surrounded by Confederate states. He struck Lincoln's bellicose ending—"With you, and not with me, is the solemn question of 'Shall it be peace, or a sword?'"—and instead suggested that Lincoln use words "of affection—some of calm and cheerful confidence." Lincoln chiseled Seward's flowery last paragraph into a shorter, sharper coda.

SEWARD'S DRAFT	LINCOLN'S DELIVERED VERSION
I close	I am loath to close.
We are not, we must not be, aliens or enemies, but fellow-countrymen and brethren.	We are not enemies, but friends. We must not be enemies.
Although passion has strained our bonds of affection too hardly, they must not, I am sure they will not, be broken.	Though passion may have strained, it must not break our bonds of affection.
The mystic chords which proceeding from so many battle fields and so many patriot graves	The mystic chords of memory, stretching from every battle-field, and patriot grave,
pass through all the hearts and all the hearths in this broad continent of ours will yet again harmonize in their ancient music when breathed upon by the guardian angel of the nation.	to every living heart and hearth-stone, all over this broad land, will yet swell the chords of the Union, when again touched, as surely they will be, by the better angels of our nature.

ANDREW JOHNSON'S DRUNKEN PERFORMANCE— THE WORST (VICE-) PRESIDENTIAL SPEECH IN AMERICAN HISTORY?

Andrew Johnson had a reputation as a fine speaker. "He held his crowd spellbound," said one early political rival of an earlier effort. "There was always in his speeches more or less wit, humor, and anecdote, which relieved them from tedium and heaviness."

That's why his legendarily bad performance at the second inauguration of Abraham Lincoln in 1865 came as a shock. Some biographers have claimed that Johnson was sick before the 1865 inaugural—typhoid is sometimes mentioned—which may be true. What is certain is that he was drunk. Johnson had a few glasses of whiskey with the outgoing vice president, Hannibal Hamlin, at the Capitol before the inauguration kicked off. "Perhaps [Hamlin], having been dumped by Lincoln, in favor of Johnson, was attempting to exact revenge," writes author Annette Gordon-Reed in her biography.

By the time Johnson got to the podium, he was unsteadily drunk. According to one newspaper account, he told the gathered politicians they owed everything they were to "the people," and then addressed Lincoln's cabinet members.

"And I will say to you, Mr. Secretary Seward, and to you, Mr. Secretary Stanton, and to you, Mr. Secretary—(to a gentleman nearby, sotto voce, 'Who is the Secretary of the Navy?' the person addressed replied in a whisper, 'Mr. Welles')—and to you Mr. Secretary Welles. . . ."

Hamlin finally convinced Johnson to close, and Johnson slurred to a finish. When he took the oath of office, he put his hand on the Bible, raised it high in the air, and said in a grandiloquent voice: "I kiss this Book in the face of my nation of the United States." Observer Zachariah Chandler wrote to his wife: "I was never so mortified in my life, had I been able to find a hole I would have dropped through it out of sight."

Johnson's attempt seemed even more pathetic given what followed: Lincoln's speech, which Frederick Douglass described as "more like a sermon than a state paper." He was referring to Lincoln's second inaugural address, considered among the greatest political speeches in American history.

THE PERSONAL MEMOIRS OF U.S. GRANT

When ex-President Ulysses S. Grant thought he'd become a millionaire in the stock market, he turned down an offer from *Century* magazine to write accounts of his wartime experience. But after losing all his money in a Wall Street scam in 1884, an impoverished Grant wrote the editors to see if they were still interested.

They were. Grant wrote four articles, and was about to sign a contract to publish his memoirs as well when his old friend Samuel Clemens stopped by and examined the agreement. "I didn't know whether to laugh or cry," Clemens wrote of the offer, which was the kind "they would have offered to any unknown Comanche Indian whose book they thought might sell 3,000 or 4,000 copies." As Clemens figured it, *Century* had paid Grant only $500 for each of the articles, a series that Clemens estimated had earned *Century* $100,000 from additional subscribers and advertisers.

Clemens told Grant he was establishing his own publishing house and would like to release Grant's memoirs after he published a book of his own—*The Adventures of Huckleberry Finn*. Grant started his memoirs knowing he had throat cancer. He worked daily, although he was often in pain or dulled by medication, getting down 275,000 words in less than a year.

The prose was as clear and direct as Grant's military orders. On Lee's surrender at Appomattox, he wrote: "I felt like anything rather than rejoicing at the downfall of a foe who had fought so long and so valiantly, and had suffered so much for a cause, though that cause was, I believe, one of the worst for which a people ever fought." The book has been praised as one of the finest memoirs in American political history.

Grant finished the book just a few weeks before he died. In the few months after his death, 250,000 copies of the two-volume set were sold. The only financial success of Grant's life would come posthumously, earning $450,000 for Grant's impoverished family.

HARRY TRUMAN—FROM A BAD READER
TO A SPONTANEOUS HELL-RAISER

Harry Truman is generally considered one of the worst presidential speakers of the twentieth century—until the 1948 presidential election. For most of his political life, Truman read scripts—not altogether scintillating ones—in a voice as flat as a Missouri prairie. He'd elevate his pitch when the crowd got larger and read a little faster when he found a section particularly boring. His one oratorical flourish was to saw his arms stiffly through the air, his fingers pressed tightly together, like chopping wood, only far less exciting.

But when he got on the campaign train in 1948, trailing Thomas Dewey by a large margin, he tried a new approach. One day he gave a dry prepared speech on the radio, but when he got off the air, he spoke without text, letting his feisty style come through. His press secretary, Charlie Ross, noted that the audience "went wild."

For the rest of the campaign, usually from the back of a train while on a thirty-two-thousand-mile tour across the country, Truman spoke spontaneously, giving about 350 speeches, many showcasing his humor, usually at a Republican's expense. At a plowing contest, he said, "We plowed under a lot of Republicans out there," and at another stop he said that the GOP stood for Grand Old Platitudes. At another stop he riffed on the topic of Herbert Hoover, the last Republican president: "You remember the Hoover cart . . . the remains of the old tin Lizzie being pulled by a mule, because you couldn't afford to buy a new car, you couldn't afford to buy gas for the old one. . . . By the way, I asked the Department of Agriculture at Washington about this Hoover cart. They said it is the only automobile in the world that eats oats."

The dull campaigner was now dynamic. In Seattle, Washington, a man yelled from a gallery, "Give 'em hell, Harry!" and Harry called back that he never gave anybody hell, just "told the truth on the Republicans and they thought it was hell." It became a call and response at every stop.

JOHN F. KENNEDY'S BEHIND-THE-SCENES WRITER:
THEODORE SORENSEN

John F. Kennedy's inaugural address is one of the most memorable of the twentieth century, and Martin Luther King, Jr., called another Kennedy speech the "most eloquent, passionate, and unequivocal plea for civil rights . . . ever made by any President." Kennedy is also the only president to win a Pulitzer Prize, for *Profiles in Courage*. But in each of these endeavors, Kennedy had help from a key aide: Theodore Sorensen.

After graduating first in his law school class, Sorensen came to Washington to find a job, and newly elected Senator Kennedy hired him after two five-minute interviews.

Sorensen became a key aide, and was soon writing articles with Kennedy for the *New York Times Magazine, Atlantic Monthly,* and the *New Republic.* Sorensen traveled with Kennedy as he stumped for the 1960 Democratic nomination. "Day after day . . . he's up there on the platform speaking and I'm in the audience listening . . . learning what worked, what he liked, what he used. . . . His style and my style, his standard, and my standard, merged." Such overlap created doubts over who wrote what, and there was controversy over Kennedy's authorship of *Profiles in Courage.* Sorensen signed an affidavit that the book was Kennedy's, although he later admitted he played "an important role" in its authorship.

Sorensen strove for short sentences and simple words, and he was also fond of inverted parallelisms, such as "Ask not what your country can do for you, ask what you can do for your country," which he penned for Kennedy's inaugural address in 1961.

But Sorensen believed his most important piece of writing was done for an audience of one. On Saturday, October 27, 1962, Kennedy chose Sorensen to write a key letter to Nikita Khrushchev outlining a diplomatic solution to the Cuban Missile Crisis. He had forty-five minutes. "I knew that any mistakes in my letter—anything that angered or soured Khrushchev," Sorensen said later, "could result in the end of America, maybe the end of the world." The letter pushed for a peaceful solution; Khrushchev responded positively and nuclear war was avoided.

Thomas Jefferson was one of the best writers to hold the office of president.
This 1825 lithograph shows Jefferson at his writing table, with Benjamin Franklin
looking on.

Most Controversial Elections

WEEK 41

PRESIDENT BURR? HOW JEFFERSON BEAT ADAMS BUT ALMOST LOST TO AARON BURR

The first great slanderous presidential campaign was the second contest between Republican Thomas Jefferson and Federalist John Adams in 1800. One Federalist described Jefferson as a "mean-spirited, low-lived fellow, the son of a half-breed Indian squaw, sired by a Virginia mulatto father. . . ." At one point, the Federalists came up with another strategy for winning over voters: They suggested Jefferson had died.

For their part, the Republicans spread rumors that Adams planned to have a son marry one of George III's daughters, thereby starting an American monarchy reuniting England and the United States. They also accused him of sending his running mate, Thomas Pinckney, to England to fetch two pretty girls as mistresses for Adams and two more for himself. "[I]f this be true," joked Adams, "General Pinckney has kept them all for himself and cheated me out of my two."

Adams received just eight fewer electoral votes than Jefferson, but the result devolved into chaos because electors couldn't distinguish between the president and vice president on their ballots, and both Jefferson and his running mate Aaron Burr had received seventy-three electoral votes.

All except for Burr assumed that Jefferson was the president, and that sent the election into the House of Representatives, controlled by the losing Federalists. In thirty-five separate votes, Jefferson couldn't get the nine states he needed to win the election. Some Federalists threatened a new election, and Jefferson's allies advised Republican states to have their militia ready to march into Washington "for the purpose, not of promoting, but of preventing, revolution. . . ."

The deciding figure was Alexander Hamilton, who disliked Jefferson but loathed Burr, whom he called "the most unfit man in the United States for the office of President." With Hamilton's support, Jefferson won on the thirty-sixth ballot. The new Congress passed the Twelfth Amendment, which separated votes for the president and vice president. Three years later, Burr and Hamilton dueled again with pistols, and this time Burr won their rivalry with a bullet that killed Hamilton.

THE CORRUPT BARGAIN—AND THE 1828 REMATCH
BETWEEN JOHN QUINCY ADAMS AND ANDREW JACKSON

The rematch election in 1828 between John Quincy Adams and Andrew Jackson might have been the nastiest presidential campaign in American history.

The attacks from the Jackson camp were relatively mild. Jackson's men accused Adams of bringing gambling instruments—a billiards table—into the White House. They also claimed that Adams had procured American women for the czar while he was a U.S. minister in Russia. The one accusation that drew political blood was that Adams had struck what Jackson called a "corrupt bargain" with Henry Clay in the 1824 presidential election, buying Clay's crucial support in the House of Representatives with an appointment to secretary of state.

Adams's supporters circulated rumors that Thomas Jefferson said "the Republic would not last long" with Jackson as president. They also reprinted old letters written to show that Jackson couldn't spell—blasphemy to those who preferred more educated presidents, such as Jefferson, Madison, Monroe, and the Adamses.

They also recounted Jackson's dueling escapades, making him sound treacherous, and portrayed him as a slave trader (although slave ownership was nearly a prerequisite for the presidency at the time). Adams's men even went after the war hero's military record, accusing him of executing soldiers during the War of 1812. They accused his wife, Rachel, of taking up with Jackson while she was still married; newspapers called her a philanderer and a whore.

Jackson put up with the attacks, knowing they were meant to provoke him into unpresidential responses. But one day, while reading a newspaper, he broke down sobbing. Rachel asked what was wrong. "Myself I can defend," Jackson said, jabbing at the newspaper. "You I can defend; but now they have assailed even the memory of my mother."

"General Jackson's mother was a COMMON PROSTITUTE," said the article, "brought to this country by the British soldiers! She afterward married a MULATTO MAN, with whom she had several children, of which . . . General JACKSON IS ONE!!!"

THE BULL MOOSE AS THIRD PARTY—
ROOSEVELT HELPS ELECT WILSON

The election of 1912 was decided by the entrance of a third party: the indefatigable Theodore Roosevelt. In 1908, after nearly eight years in office, Roosevelt, respecting the unwritten rule that presidents would serve just two terms, handpicked his dutiful lieutenant, William Howard Taft, to succeed him. Taft won, but lacked the vitality of his predecessor, proving himself more cautious and conservative than Roosevelt.

Roosevelt denounced his former protégé as a "flubdub with a streak of the second rate and the common in him." Roosevelt jumped into the primaries, labeling Taft a "fathead" and a "puzzlewit." Someone suggested that both men withdraw and pick a compromise candidate. "I'll name the compromise candidate," Roosevelt responded. "He'll be me. I'll name the compromise platform. It will be our platform." Taft took the blows for a bit, and then reacted. "I am in this fight to perform a great public duty . . . of keeping Theodore Roosevelt out of the White House."

With the support of the party's base, Roosevelt won the popular vote in nine of twelve state primaries; Taft took just one. But the Republican state conventions elected delegates loyal to Taft and he won the party's nomination on the first ballot. Teddy and his followers—reformers, feminists, social workers, laborers—walked out of the convention and formed their own party, the Progressive Party, which called for better factory conditions, women's suffrage, the popular election of senators, a federal income tax, and the conservation of natural resources. "I'm feeling like a Bull Moose," Roosevelt told reporters, which is how the party got its nickname: the Bull Moose Party.

With the Republicans bitterly divided, all the Democrats had to do to win was choose their candidate carefully. They picked the progressive ex-president of Princeton University, Woodrow Wilson.

Wilson took forty of the forty-eight states, Roosevelt six, and Taft two. "We are beaten," said Roosevelt. "There is only one thing to do and that is to go back to the Republican Party. You can't hold a party like the Progressive Party together. . . . There are no loaves and fishes."

DEWEY DEFEATS TRUMAN
UNTIL TRUMAN DEFEATS DEWEY

At the 1948 Democratic convention, a flock of doves was set free from a fake liberty bell, and they swirled the hall as Sam Rayburn, Speaker of the House, was introducing President Harry Truman. One dove crashed into a balcony and came tumbling down, and a prognosticating reporter quipped, "There lies Harry S Truman." Truman would have none of it, coming onto the dais and trumpeting, "Senator Barkley and I are going to win this election and make those Republicans like it— don't you forget that."

When politicians need a story about the ability of an underdog to win, of the importance of fighting until the end, they cite the presidential campaign of 1948. The Democratic Party had fractured into three parts—Henry Wallace, the former Roosevelt vice president, on the left, Dixiecrat Strom Thurmond on the right, and Truman standing weakly between the two sides. All the polls picked Dewey, the Republican candidate, to win.

Everyone except Truman seemed to expect Truman to lose. "I was not brought up to run from a fight," he declared. In campaign stops, he broke from prepared speeches and charmed crowds with his friendliness, humor, and frankness. He also decided to run not against Thomas Dewey, but against the Republican Congress, saying they were interested only in "the welfare of the better classes." Truman called Congress back into session in July, and made them vote on legislation on education, national health care, civil rights, and inexpensive electricity. After nothing was passed, Truman ran against what he called "the do-nothing Congress" and conducted an exhausting campaign that covered twenty-two thousand miles by train, delivering 275 speeches.

"I'm going to fight hard," he told his vice presidential running mate. "I'm going to give them hell."

In the days leading up to the election, Dewey planned his inauguration. The election wasn't even that close. Truman won by 5 percent, making the pollsters wrong by more than 10 percent. He carried twenty-eight states to Dewey's sixteen. Truman couldn't resist holding up a *Chicago Tribune* newspaper with the headline DEWEY DEFEATS TRUMAN.

GEORGE BUSH GOES NEGATIVE

In 1988, some advised Republican presidential candidate George Bush to distance himself from outgoing President Ronald Reagan. Former President Richard Nixon suggested that Bush announce he would replace the entire Reagan cabinet if elected, showing "you *are* a tough, no-nonsense administrator who isn't afraid to take bold actions. . . ."

But Lee Atwater, a hard-hitting Bush campaign aide, recommended instead that they attack Democratic candidate Michael Dukakis. Nixon cautioned against it. "Don't do it. Anyone who tries to show strength by a strong voice and strong gestures conveys the opposite impression. . . ."

Dukakis led the campaign by ten percentage points in May 1988. Bush reluctantly attacked, saying Dukakis's foreign policy had been "born in Harvard Yard's boutique" and that he was a "card-carrying member of the ACLU," echoing McCarthyesque charges made during the 1950s against "card carrying members of the Communist Party."

Then, after Labor Day, a group supporting George Bush ran a national ad that featured Willie Horton, a convicted murderer who had knifed a man and raped his wife while on furlough from a Massachusetts prison. The ad blamed Dukakis for the furlough program. Many saw the ad as racist—Horton was African American and looked menacing. The ad ran for twenty-eight days before the Bush campaign asked the group to take it off the air. Then the Bush campaign aired its own ad attacking the furlough program.

"One of the ironies of George Bush's life is that a fundamentally decent man presided over a moment when politics got meaner and rougher," says author Evan Thomas. "'88 was the year of the handler, of bringing in political consultants who played very hard and very tough. . . . 1988 was kind of a rough, trivial campaign. Lee Atwater and these henchmen . . . not really staying on the high road and talking about the great issues of the day, but rather sniping at their opponent to find some weakness in him. And Bush put up with that."

BUSH V. GORE—THE SUPREME COURT,
NOT THE PEOPLE, DECIDE

As Election Day 2000 drifted into evening, it was clear that while Democratic candidate Al Gore would win the popular vote by more than half a million votes, he or Republican George W. Bush would need Florida to gain the 270 electoral votes necessary to win. Although CBS anchorman Dan Rather predicted that Gore would take Florida, poll watchers picked Bush as the winner, and Gore called Bush to concede. But as Bush's lead diminished through the night, Gore withdrew his concession.

Florida law required a recount in such a close vote, and two days later, the recount ended with Bush declared the winner by three hundred votes. But the Gore camp found major irregularities in the voting and demanded a hand recount in three counties. When Katharine Harris, Florida's secretary of state and a Bush campaign worker, refused, Democrats won a Florida Supreme Court decision requiring her to extend the deadline to complete hand recounts.

"It's a sad day for America and the Constitution," James A. Baker III, Bush's chief lawyer, complained after the decision, "when a court decides the outcome of an election."

But officials in Dade County, which included Miami, said they couldn't finish their counting in time, and Harris quickly stepped in and declared Bush the winner. The Democrats went back to the Florida Supreme Court, which voted to extend the deadline in Dade County and in all Florida counties for hand recounts. The Republicans appealed the decision to the Supreme Court. On December 12, the court, in a 5 to 4 decision along political lines, made one of its most controversial decisions ever, halting the recount, and in effect declaring Bush the winner.

"Although we may never know with complete certainty the identity of the winner of this year's presidential election, the identity of the loser is perfectly clear," wrote Justice John Paul Stevens in his stinging dissent. "It is the nation's confidence in the judge as an impartial guardian of the rule of law."

"In this democracy of 200 million citizens, the people have spoken," said comedian Mark Russell, "all five of them."

HARRY TRUMAN'S HISTORIC UPSET

In one of the most famous photos in presidential election history, President
Harry Truman holds up a *Chicago Tribune* with the headline DEWEY DEFEATS
TRUMAN. Most preelection polls had Republican New York Governor Thomas
E. Dewey beating Truman, but Truman ended up defeating Dewey soundly,
carrying twenty-eight states to Dewey's sixteen.

Scandals, Dressed and Undressed

WEEK 42

THOMAS JEFFERSON'S SLAVE CHILDREN—
HOW THE VERDICT HAS CHANGED

In 1802, a disgruntled journalist charged that Thomas Jefferson fathered children by his slave Sally Hemings. For decades, the Jeffersons scoffed at the allegation, as did historians.

But in 1873, Madison Hemings, Sally's second-to-last son, published a memoir claiming that his mother, Sally, had "become Mr. Jefferson's concubine" while a teenager in Paris, about half a dozen years after Jefferson's wife, Martha, had died. He said that he and his siblings "were the only children of [Jefferson's] by a slave woman." Madison said his mother balked at coming back to Virginia as a slave after the freedoms she enjoyed in France, but "he promised her extraordinary privileges, and made a solemn pledge that her children should be freed at the age of twenty-one years." According to Madison, "It was her duty . . . to take care of his chamber and wardrobe, look after us children and do such light work as sewing." Significantly, in his *Farm Book*, Jefferson records the fathers of slave children born at Monticello—except for Sally's.

Then, in 1998, geneticists did DNA testing of five men in the Jefferson and Hemings line, and concluded that someone in the Jefferson line fathered Sally's youngest son, Eston Hemings, most likely Thomas Jefferson. In 2000, an archaeologist at the Thomas Jefferson Memorial Foundation, looking at the DNA testing and the whereabouts of other Jeffersons nine months prior to each of Sally's births, concluded that the odds someone besides Thomas Jefferson fathered Hemings's children were ten thousand to one. Now nearly all Jefferson scholars assume he fathered at least Eston, and probably all Sally's children.

But mysteries remain: Were the sexual relations coerced or consensual? Did Jefferson even consider Sally black, given she had a biracial mother and a white father? Was the relationship just physical, or was it loving? "It is difficult, if not impossible, to answer these questions," writes Jefferson scholar R. B. Bernstein, "because there is so little evidence."

ULYSSES S. GRANT—GUILTY BY ASSOCIATION

The word *scandal* is often coupled with the presidency of Ulysses S. Grant. The caveat usually added is that Grant himself was honest. How could a fundamentally decent man and clean politician oversee an administration that seemed corrupt?

There are two usual answers. The first is that Grant was too lax a president to notice the shady goings-on of the Gilded Age politicians of his era, including some of his friends. The second is that Grant was too kind and loyal, a virtue turned vice when associates revealed themselves as less than honest. A tougher man would have fired the wrongdoers, but Grant, for whom loyalty was a cardinal virtue and confrontation always difficult, looked away.

A third theory, however, is that Grant was tainted by scandals because he was president when they were perpetrated or revealed. In the Black Friday episode, speculators tried to corner the gold market, hoping that Grant's brother-in-law could convince the president not to sell government gold during their escapade. Grant avoided catastrophe by doing the opposite—selling the gold reserves—but he was implicated by family association.

The infamous Credit Mobilier was a phony Pennsylvania corporation used by directors of the Union Pacific Railroad to illegally funnel government funds to themselves. To prevent exposure of the scam, they passed stock (bribes by any other name) to congressmen. The scandal took place before Grant was in office, but because Republicans were implicated, so was Grant.

Was Grant completely innocent? Hardly. When it was discovered that civil servants had cost the U.S. government millions by taking bribes to reduce whiskey taxes, Grant demanded reform. When the investigation implicated his personal secretary, Grant defended him and was slow to let him go.

"He could see big things and big ideas," wrote one historian, "but he possessed little political cunning, he could not see the littleness of the little men who surrounded him."

WARREN G. HARDING'S REPUTATION—
KILLED BY CORRUPTION

Early in 1923, a visitor to the White House was directed into the Red Room to see President Warren G. Harding. There, he saw the president with his hands around the neck of a man he'd pinned against the wall. "You yellow rat!" Harding shouted. "You double-crossing bastard! If you ever—" The visitor made his presence known, the president whirled around, and Harding's victim escaped from the room.

Harding was wringing the neck of Charles Forbes, the director of the U.S. Veterans Bureau, who he'd just learned was taking kickbacks and selling veterans hospital supplies on the private market.

Rumors also circulated that Interior Secretary Albert Fall, a former senator from New Mexico and a poker buddy of Harding's, had taken $400,000 in bribes to lease oil fields, such as those in Wyoming's Teapot Dome, to two friends. Suicides by some of the accused and stories of orgies were scandalous subplots. When Fall resigned in March 1923, Harding told the press that he'd offered to appoint him to the Supreme Court, but that Fall declined, preferring to return to private life. Fall became the first cabinet member ever to spend time in prison.

Harding died in August 1923 and would never be implicated in any public wrongdoing. (Privately, Nan Britton wrote a tell-all that alleged she had trysts with Harding in the White House and had a child with him). Shortly before he died, Harding told an editor, "My God! This is a hell of a job! . . . I can take care of my enemies all right. But my . . . God-damn friends . . . they're the ones that keep me walking the floor nights!"

WATERGATE: NIXON DESTROYS HIS PRESIDENCY

President Nixon was vacationing in the Bahamas—just a few months from winning one of the biggest landslides in U.S. presidential history—when the event that would destroy his presidency unfolded. At 2:30 A.M., June 17, 1972, while the president slept, police arrested five burglars inside Democratic National Committee headquarters in the Watergate complex in Washington, D.C.

Investigating the break-in, *Washington Post* reporters discovered it was linked to extensive criminal activity by Nixon's White House. Using funds from Nixon's reelection campaign, a White House–directed group called the "plumbers" had for years engaged in countless other unconstitutional and criminal activities to discredit and destroy Nixon's political foes. Enlisting not only Nixon's top aides, but also the CIA, FBI, and IRS, Nixon's administration spied on and harassed those on his "enemies list."

As Watergate investigations began to uncover this wider conspiracy, the White House panicked, destroying evidence, committing perjury, and paying blackmailers. Eventually a public furor forced Nixon to release taped conversations between himself and his aides. Those tapes exposed not only the crimes and the cover-up, but also a thuglike atmosphere in the Oval Office that columnist Joseph Alsop described as that of "the back room of a second-rate advertising agency in a suburb of hell."

John Doar, special counsel to the House Judiciary Committee, stated at the committee's Watergate hearings: "[T]he facts are overwhelming . . . that the President . . . authorized a broad, general plan of illegal electronic surveillance. . . . Following that . . . he's been in charge of the cover-up from that day forward. . . . It required perjury, destruction of evidence, obstruction of justice. . . . But, most importantly, it required deliberate, contrived, continued, and continuing deception of the American people."

Impeached by the House and facing certain conviction by the Senate, Nixon resigned on August 9, 1974. "History will treat me fairly," he asserted in 1990. "Historians probably won't, because most historians are on the left." Yet most Americans, regardless of political party, understood that Watergate represented not just a crime and its cover-up, but the attempted shredding of the U.S. Constitution by those sworn to "preserve, protect, and defend" it.

BILL CLINTON: INFIDELITY ALMOST LEADS TO IMPEACHMENT

In his book *Presidential Scandals*, author Jeffrey D. Schultz points out that "voters have usually distinguished between private and public acts when it counted most—on election day. For example, not a single candidate has lost an election because of a marital infidelity." Bill Clinton almost became the exception.

Prior to running for president in 1992, Clinton had faced several allegations of marital indiscretion. One lawsuit had accused the then–Arkansas governor of using taxpayer money to entertain women and having state troopers transport him to trysts with various women, including Gennifer Flowers. Just before the crucial 1992 New Hampshire primary, a tabloid newspaper published Flowers's graphic account of what she alleged was her twelve-year affair with Clinton.

To salvage his suddenly reeling campaign, Clinton and his wife, Hillary, arranged to be interviewed on *60 Minutes*, where millions watched him deny the affair but admit "causing pain in my marriage." Hillary saved him, telling the nation, "You know, I'm not sitting here, some little woman standing by my man. . . . I'm sitting here because I love him. . . . [I]f that's not enough for people, then heck, don't vote for him." Clinton rebounded to win the primary, and eventually the White House. (He later admitted the affair under oath, though he denied that it lasted twelve years.)

Two years into his first term, another scandal broke when Paula Jones alleged he sexually harassed her while he was governor. Her suit was eventually dismissed. To avoid possible appeal, Clinton settled by paying $850,000, but he did not apologize or admit guilt. The Jones suit led directly to revelations that Clinton had an affair with Monica Lewinsky, a White House intern—revelations that, in turn, led to his impeachment.

The fallout from Clinton's extramarital affairs had left him with no political capital to pass his once-ambitious agenda through a Republican Congress. An even greater consequence was the possible impact of his behavior on the 2000 presidential election, in which Clinton's vice president, Al Gore, barely lost to George Bush. "Al Gore would have won had it not been for Lewinsky," declared Representative David McCurdy. "That's a bad legacy."

ABU GHRAIB AND A POLICY OF TORTURE

The infamous Abu Ghraib prison in Baghdad, Iraq, was long known under the reign of Saddam Hussein for its horrid conditions, torture, and weekly executions. But the prisoner abuses revealed on April 28, 2004, by CBS's *60 Minutes II* came after the facility had been converted into a U.S. military prison in 2003. The TV program aired explicit photos of Iraqi prisoners being humiliated and tortured by their American captors.

Two days later, a report in the *New Yorker* excerpted an army report of Abu Ghraib that concluded that "numerous incidents of sadistic, blatant and wanton criminal abuses were inflicted on several detainees," including the pouring of phosphoric liquid on detainees, beating them with broom handles, sodomizing them with objects, and using military dogs to intimidate them. All were clear violations of the Geneva Conventions, which forbade torture and "outrages on personal dignity, in particular humiliating and degrading treatment."

People couldn't forget the photos taken by American soldiers of themselves with their victims. Many depicted American soldiers smiling and giving a thumbs up, standing next to naked men who were often shackled in humiliating positions. One photo of a hooded prisoner, his arms outstretched, echoed the images of the tortured during the Inquisition. Digital photos circulated the world via computer. Hussein had once been derided for torture; now the Americans were. The scandal became a prime recruiting tool for the insurgents.

Neither the administration nor the military launched an independent investigation of who was responsible for the torture at Abu Ghraib. Secretary of Defense Donald Rumsfeld offered his resignation, but President George W. Bush refused it, insisting the acts were those of a few rogue soldiers. A dozen were prosecuted and given minor sentences. The administration's insistence that the torture at Abu Ghraib was an isolated incident, though, diverted attention from their policy that permitted and pursued "enhanced" or "coercive" interrogations of suspected terrorists, including waterboarding and extreme sleep deprivation, torture by another name under the Geneva Conventions.

"There was a before 9/11, and an after 9/11," said Cofer Black, the onetime director of the CIA's counterterrorist unit. "After 9/11, the gloves came off."

President Bill Clinton is shown embracing Monica Lewinsky as he greets well-wishers at the White House on November 6, 1996, the day after he was reelected. Clinton's affair with Lewinsky almost brought down his presidency, and he finally admitted under oath in 1998 that he had had an "improper physical relationship" with her.

Protecting—and Surrendering—
Civil Rights

WEEK 43

THE ALIEN AND SEDITION ACTS—A BLOT ON
THE ADAMS ADMINISTRATION

After his administration had fallen from power, John Adams tried to shift blame for the Alien and Sedition Acts onto the powerful Federalist Alexander Hamilton. It was a politic deflection of responsibility, but hardly an honest one. Adams might not have drafted the measures or pushed for them, but he fomented antiforeigner feelings and had tacitly approved the legislation.

"The acts were undertaken," concludes biographer John Ferling, "largely toward the goal of maintaining Federalist [power]," which at the time controlled the House, the Senate, the Supreme Court, and the executive branch. All of the acts trampled on the First Amendment. The Naturalization Act, which extended from five to fourteen years how long immigrants had to wait to become voters, was an effort to keep down the voter rolls of the Republican opposition. The Alien Act allowed the president to deport aliens deemed a risk to national security during wartime—in this case, Frenchmen and Irishmen. But it was mostly just a threat—only one person was deported under the act.

The Sedition Act called for fines up to $5,000 and sentences up to five years for anyone who made "false, scandalous and malicious" statements about federal officials. That the law was partisan became apparently clear when Federalists set the last day of Adams's term for its expiration. Vice President Thomas Jefferson was so appalled by these laws that he bolted from the capital for two months in protest.

The Sedition Law chilled opposition, and some Republican editors immediately cooled their attacks on President Adams. Before the law was even passed, the government jailed editors and journalists all over the country. The government prosecuted twenty-five cases, winning fourteen indictments under the Sedition Act, including ones against five of the six leading Republican newspapers. Most of the trials had suspicious timing—the eve of the 1800 elections.

The laws would expire when Jefferson was elected in 1800, but history would remember them as some of the most egregious violations of civil rights in American history.

THOMAS JEFFERSON FIGHTS FOR RELIGIOUS FREEDOM

Shortly before he died, Thomas Jefferson insisted that just three of his achievements be listed on his gravestone, "because by these, as testimonials that I have lived, I wish most to be remembered." The first was "Author of the Declaration of Independence" and the third was "Father of the University of Virginia." But less known is the second, which might have had the greatest influence on American history: "Author of . . . the Statute of Virginia for religious freedom."

Before the bill passed all Virginians were forced to pay taxes to support the Anglican Church and all officeholders had to be Anglican. Jefferson wanted individuals to be free to believe what they wished, and he also, along with Virginian James Madison and others, wanted to keep the state from getting in bed with religion—a coupling they believed had led to the religious wars that had racked Europe for centuries. He sought what he would later call "a wall of separation between Church and State." That meant forbidding the government from raising taxes that would support any particular religion. "[N]o man shall be compelled to frequent or support any religious worship . . . ," the law read, "nor shall be enforced, restrained, molested, or burthened . . . , or shall otherwise suffer, on account of his religious opinions or belief; but that all men shall be free to profess, and by argument to maintain, their opinions in matters of religion. . . ."

Jefferson, serving in Paris as a diplomat at the time, was thrilled at the news of the bill's passage in 1786, and wrote Madison that it was accepted "with infinite approbation in Europe and propagated with enthusiasm." Madison would embed the principle behind the Virginia law in a key clause of the First Amendment of the Bill of Rights in 1791. "Congress shall make no law respecting an establishment of religion," it said, "or prohibiting the free exercise thereof."

JAMES MADISON PROTECTS CIVIL LIBERTIES
IN WARTIME

Almost as soon as the War of 1812 broke out with England, President James Madison faced dissent at home. He wrote his friend and predecessor, Thomas Jefferson, that "the Federalists in Congress are to put all the strength of their talents into a pretext against the war." Richard Rush, one of Madison's closest friends, wrote, "Massachusetts and half New England, I fear, is rotten."

One Boston clergyman said that opposition was so strong in Massachusetts that "if at the present moment no symptoms of civil war appear, they certainly will soon" and another clergyman said, "[A]s Mr. Madison has declared war, let Mr. Madison carry it on." The governors of Massachusetts and Connecticut refused to furnish their quotas of men—moves upheld by the courts. In mid-August, Madison wrote Jefferson again, arguing that "the seditious opposition in Massachusetts and Connecticut" have "so clogged the wheels of the war that I fear the campaign will not accomplish the object of it."

Historian Ralph Ketcham has written, "Of all the burdens of his public career, none was more galling or in his sight more grievously and unforgivably imposed than this cancer of discord." What should he do? Other presidents—including Abraham Lincoln, Woodrow Wilson, Franklin Roosevelt, and George W. Bush—faced wartime dissent by clamping down on civil liberties, including the right to free speech.

But James Madison held true to his principles. Since the 1790s, Madison believed that one of the most serious threats to a republican government was the power of the executive, which often swelled in wartime. He was willing to sacrifice a more effective war effort to constitutional principles he held dear. One scholar of the early American Republic, Gordon S. Wood, argues that Madison defended the country and his administration "without one trial for treason, or even one prosecution for libel." It was an achievement few other war presidents could claim.

ANDREW JACKSON'S INDIAN POLICY—
THE TRAIL OF TEARS

Encouraged by the election to the presidency of Indian fighter Andrew Jackson in 1828, the Georgia legislature passed a bill that nullified all agreements with the Cherokee nation and gave itself power to take their land. Alabama and Tennessee quickly followed suit.

In 1829, Jackson followed up by urging Congress to treat Indians not as sovereign nations, a policy many previous presidents had pursued, but as subjects of the United States. Jackson saw Indians as dangerous impediments to white farmers settling the Southeast and Midwest, and wanted them removed. His solution was the Indian Removal Act, which forced Indians to trade their ancestral lands for reservations in what is now Oklahoma. Jackson said that the relocation was necessary because "humanity and national honor demand [it]." Politicians such as Henry Clay, Daniel Webster, and Davy Crockett saw the measure for what it was—a land grab—and denounced it, but Congress passed it in 1830.

In 1832, the Cherokee challenged the Georgia law in the Supreme Court, and Chief Justice John Marshall ruled it "repugnant to the Constitution, laws, and treaties of the United States." Jackson's response was, "Well, John Marshall has made his decision. Now let him enforce it."

The Jackson administration imposed ninety treaties during his two terms that forcibly removed some one hundred thousand Indians from the southeastern states. Twenty-five million acres were opened to white settlement and to slavery. When some Cherokees refused to leave their land in Georgia in May 1838, the U.S. Army removed them at bayonet point. So began the Cherokee "Trail of Tears."

Between June and December 1838, more than sixteen thousand Cherokee were marched from the southern Appalachians a thousand miles to Oklahoma. About four thousand Cherokee, or one in four, died from exposure, disease, and starvation. The U.S. government subtracted the estimated $6 million cost of removal from the $9 million it had agreed to pay for the Cherokee's eastern lands.

"I fought through the Civil War and have seen men shot to pieces and slaughtered by thousands," said one Georgia volunteer, "but the Cherokee removal was the cruelest work I ever knew."

LINCOLN'S CRACKDOWN ON CIVIL LIBERTIES
DURING THE CIVIL WAR

Lincoln understood that the Civil War was a battle for the survival of the Union and he was willing to do almost anything—even dismiss the Constitution—to preserve it. During the war, the Lincoln administration closed more than twenty newspapers, and between 1861 and 1863, had more than thirteen thousand people arrested, many for simply criticizing Lincoln and the war. He censored newspapers, and more than once suspended habeas corpus rights, which protect people from being imprisoned unlawfully.

Democratic Congressman Clement L. Vallandigham, of Dayton, Ohio, an eloquent minister's son, resisted Lincoln's crackdown, and even introduced a measure in 1862 to imprison the president for his reckless disregard of the Constitution.

Early in 1863, General Ambrose Burnside, charged with keeping the West loyal to the Union, issued General Order No. 38, subjecting to arrest anyone committing "treason, expressed or implied." Vallandigham responded by railing against the failed war and arguing that the conflict would end only if soldiers deserted and the people decided to "hurl King Lincoln from his throne." Burnside had Vallandigham arrested and he was sentenced to prison for the rest of the war.

Lincoln had to decide: Should he support his general or commute the sentence of the popular Ohio politician? He found a third option, publicly supporting the arrest, but swapping Vallandigham's prison sentence with exile to the Confederacy.

On June 12, Lincoln sent a public letter to a group of New York Democrats who had protested the arrest. He said that he was "pained that there should have seemed to be a necessity for arresting" Vallandigham, and said he would free him "as soon as . . . the public safety will not suffer by it." In the letter's most lasting passage, he wrote, "Must I shoot a simple-minded soldier boy who deserts while I must not touch a hair of a wily agitator who induces him to desert? I think that in such a case to silence the agitator and save the boy is not only constitutional but withal a great mercy."

WOODROW WILSON ALLOWS THE PALMER RAIDS

Following World War I, President Woodrow Wilson warned that "the poison of disorder, the poison of revolt, the poison of chaos" had been injected into the American bloodstream. Widespread labor strife in the country, a handful of anarchist bombings, and the recent Russian Revolution sparked fears of subversion and revolution at home. Wilson's attorney general, a Quaker named A. Mitchell Palmer, saw the danger as "a prairie-fire, [a] blaze of revolution . . . eating its way into the homes of the American workman . . . licking the altars of the churches, leaping into the belfry of the school bell, . . . seeking to replace marriage vows with libertine laws, burning up the foundations of society. . . ."

Palmer appointed an equally zealous twenty-four-year-old named J. Edgar Hoover to lead the Justice Department's newly created Radical Division. On January 2, 1920, they launched the now-infamous Palmer raids in thirty-three cities, smashing union offices and arresting over four thousand labor leaders, leftists, and immigrants deemed "subversive." Many were held incommunicado, beaten, and denied habeas corpus rights. Even legal residents were summarily deported.

While many Americans felt Palmer was a hero, others were outraged. Palmer's actions "have struck at the foundations of American free institutions," declared twelve prominent jurists of the day. Columnist Walter Lippmann wrote that he found it "forever incredible that an administration announcing the most spacious ideals in our history should have done more to endanger fundamental American liberties than any other group of men for a hundred years."

The president, having suffered a stroke, had not ordered the raids. When he learned of them in April 1920, Wilson admonished Palmer "not to let the country see red," but did not condemn Palmer's actions. Fairly or not, Wilson's reputation has been indelibly stained by the Palmer raids, one of the ugliest chapters in U.S. history.

JAPANESE AMERICANS ARE INTERNED DURING WORLD WAR II

This photograph, taken by Ansel Adams in 1943, shows the mess line at the Manzanar Relocation Center, a Japanese internment camp in California. During World War II, nearly 120,000 Japanese Americans were imprisoned at camps like these.

The Peacemakers

WEEK 44

WASHINGTON AVOIDS THE EUROPEAN WARS

After the French Revolution exploded in 1789 and war erupted between France and England, the United States had to decide whether to take sides or remain neutral.

President George Washington's secretary of state, Thomas Jefferson, welcomed France's revolution, with its cry of "liberty, equality, fraternity," as a cousin to America's revolution. But the revolution turned increasingly violent as the new leaders killed aristocrats and clerics. On January 1, 1792, the revolutionaries beheaded King Louis XVI, who had supported the American Revolution; some in the crowd dipped souvenirs into the slain king's blood.

After getting word of the beheadings, Jefferson admitted that "[m]y own affections have been deeply wounded by some of the martyrs to this cause, but rather than it should have failed, I would have seen half the earth desolated."

When England and France went to war in April 1793, Jefferson advised the president to see how England and France might curry American favor before deciding whether to take sides. But Washington called immediately for neutrality. "My primary objects . . . have been to preserve the country in peace, if I can, and to be prepared for war, if I cannot." Washington issued the Proclamation of Neutrality, which called on Americans to "pursue a conduct friendly and impartial toward the belligerent powers."

Washington hadn't conferred with the Senate on the decision, although Jefferson and others believed the Constitution required it. In this, Washington's action set a precedent: Except for ratifying treaties, the executive branch would conduct foreign affairs on its own. Popular opinion favored the country's former ally, France, over its former enemy, England, and Washington was pilloried for his decision, so much so that Jefferson believed it made him sick. "He is extremely affected by the attacks made . . . on him in the public papers. I think he feels these things more than any person I have ever met with." Nevertheless, Washington stuck with a decision that kept the United States out of war.

JOHN ADAMS MANEUVERS TO AVOID WAR

John Adams's administration, elected in 1796, was consumed by one issue—whether, in the war between France and England, the United States should side with France, its ally in the American Revolution, or England, their cultural forefather. Or should the U.S. stay out of the conflict altogether and sail a path of neutrality?

The French pushed for American support, trying to force acquiescence by seizing American ships and sailors. U.S. diplomats sailed to France to reconcile their differences, and French officials asked for a bribe; the incident became known as the XYZ Affair. This boiled the blood of many Americans, who began pushing for war.

At first, Adams's blood seemed to boil with the masses. He had asked for a navy to deter the French, and Congress approved it. In the spring of 1798, Congress allocated $1 million to militarize the harbors, authorized U.S. warships to seize any French merchant ships in American waters, and established a provisional army of ten thousand men, more than Adams had asked for. Adams, never a military man, began to wear a sword. Many expected him to cave in to popular pressure and declare war against France.

But Adams delayed, and on February 18, 1799, he informed the Senate in writing that he would send a minister to France to "discuss and conclude all controversies between the two Republics by a new treaty." Republicans who dreaded a war with France were stunned; Federalists who sought one met the statement with "surprise, indignation, grief, and disgust."

In avoiding war, Adams bucked public opinion and probably hurt his chances for reelection. But he was proud of his stand, and in retirement, he wrote to a friend, "I desire no other inscription over my gravestone: 'Here lies John Adams, who took upon himself the responsibility of peace with France in the year 1800.'"

GENERAL ULYSSES S. GRANT
PURSUES PEACE AS PRESIDENT

U.S. General Ulysses S. Grant was called a "butcher" in drawing rooms around the country after the brutal Civil War assaults in the spring of 1864, which led to sixty-five thousand Union casualties. Later, Grant told a friend, "They call me a butcher, but do you know I sometimes could hardly bring myself to give an order of battle. When I contemplated the death and misery that were sure to follow, I stood appalled."

Knowing firsthand what war wrought, Grant resisted the popular push toward war more than once during his presidency. When he came into office in 1868, Cuban rebels were struggling to overthrow Spanish colonialists. In April 1869, Congress passed a resolution supporting the president should he decide to intervene on the side of the rebels, and the Grand Army of the Republic, the veterans organization, offered to take up arms.

The *New York Sun* said that it was America's duty "at once to interfere in Cuba," and Grant's Secretary of War, John Rawlins, lobbied to send in U.S. gunships. (In 1898, President William McKinley would give in to similar pressure.) In the spring of 1870, newspapers and politicians pushed for a congressional resolution to recognize the rebels, but Grant spoke out against it, the resolution failed to pass, and the war cries grew fainter.

When Grant entered office, Americans were also clamoring for Britain to pay reparations for building and harboring Confederate raiding ships during the Civil War. War hawks were eager to do battle, and some suggested taking Canada in lieu of reparations. Grant instead pursued international negotiations, which led England to accept responsibility for building the raider *Alabama* and to pay $16 million in reparations. The Washington Treaty of 1871 was a landmark of international cooperation.

In his message to Congress in December 1871, Grant hailed the "peaceful arbitration" that had avoided a "bloody and costly conflict" and allowed the return "to productive industry millions of men now maintained to settle the disputes of nations by the bayonet and the broadside." The man they had called a butcher now spoke like a peacemaker.

WOODROW WILSON—FAILED PEACEMAKER

Before the United States entered the inferno called World War I, Wilson believed he knew the way out of it and toward everlasting peace. In 1917, calling for self-determination for all nations, mercy for the defeated, and a League of Nations, Wilson laid out Fourteen Points to "end all war."

Allied leaders weren't enthusiastic about the "points." Complained French President Clemenceau, "God Almighty gave us only ten, and we broke those." But when Wilson came to Europe for the peace negotiations—the first sitting president to cross the Atlantic—tremendous crowds of war-weary Europeans hailed him as a hero.

Germany and its allies surrendered in November 1918. In peace negotiations, France and England demanded "war guilt" compensation—monetary and territorial revenge. Though Wilson feared such humiliating demands would trigger another war, he believed the League of Nations could prevent that tragedy. He agreed to major compromises to save the League and therefore, he felt, the world. The Treaty of Versailles was signed June 1919.

The U.S. Senate now had to ratify the treaty. Wilson took the issue to the public, giving well-received speeches across the nation. Strained, perhaps, by the tremendous burdens of the past year, he had a severe stroke in October 1919. Subsequently, although he knew the treaty would pass only if the U.S. role in the League were modified, Wilson refused to compromise. The Senate predictably rejected the treaty. "[The League] is dead," grieved Wilson. "Every morning I put flowers on its grave."

Who killed the League? The consensus is that Wilson, in his disdain for any concession, "strangled his own child," as one senator grimly put it. "As a politician he had earned his defeat," said Arthur Willert, a journalist. "As an idealist he had deserved better things."

After Wilson left office, the Senate ratified a modified treaty, keeping the United States out of the League. The League, weakened without U.S. participation, was irrelevant by the 1930s, when Nazi Germany withdrew from it and Italy attacked Ethiopia, setting the stage for World War II.

KENNEDY FIGHTS FOR A NUCLEAR TEST BAN TREATY

At a White House meeting after the Cuban Missile Crisis, John F. Kennedy remarked, "It is insane that two men, sitting on opposite sides of the world, should be able to decide to bring an end to civilization." Premier Nikita Khrushchev felt similarly, and on June 20, 1963, U.S. and Soviet leaders signed an agreement to establish a hotline between the two leaders to avoid "the dangerous delays, misunderstandings, and misreadings . . . at a time of crisis." That agreement gave Kennedy some hope that a treaty that would slow down the proliferation of nuclear weapons, inspire other arms-control agreements, and reduce the spread of radioactive fallout was possible.

Kennedy raised the fallout issue with Jerome Wiesner, a science advisor, during a White House meeting that followed one nuclear test. Kennedy asked: How does the radiation from an explosion come back to earth?

"It comes down as rain," Wiesner answered.

Kennedy looked out the window over his beloved Rose Garden. "You mean there might be radioactive contamination in that rain out there right now?"

"Possibly," said Wiesner.

After Wiesner left, Kennedy sat looking at the falling rain. "I never saw him more depressed," recalled an aide.

"If I get an agreement I think is right, we are going to do our best to push it through . . . ," Kennedy said privately. "[O]ur world doesn't matter much. But I think Caroline's world does matter. . . ."

After eleven days of negotiations, the two countries signed a nuclear test ban treaty on July 26. It was modest, but it was the world's first. China and France refused to sign it, and the treaty didn't prevent underground testing or the stockpiling of nuclear bombs. But by forbidding nuclear tests in the air, in space, and in water, the treaty prevented the contamination of the environment. Kennedy's Secretary of State Dean Rusk said the treaty "opened the door to future agreements, a broadening of trade and exchanges, increases in American and Russian tourism, and a general lessening of Cold War tensions." Kennedy believed the treaty was his greatest achievement, calling it a "shaft of light in the darkness."

WAGING PEACE AT CAMP DAVID

In 2002, Jimmy Carter received the Nobel Peace Prize "for his decades of untiring effort to find peaceful solutions to international conflicts. . . ." Nowhere was the effort more "untiring" or the peace more elusive than in the Middle East, where Israel had been in conflict with its Arab neighbors since 1948.

Carter devoted an inordinate amount of his presidential time and attention trying to coax Egyptian President Anwar Sadat and Israeli Prime Minister Menachem Begin into a peace agreement. Finally, he brought them to meet with him in the isolation of the Camp David presidential retreat.

Carter kept the Camp David negotiations going through sheer determination. On the third day, he physically prevented the mutually antagonistic leaders from going home. "They were moving toward the door, but I got in front of them to partially block the way. I urged them not to break off their talks, to give me another chance. . . ." Over another eight days, he talked, bullied, and cajoled them into signing the Camp David Accords. Carter was "flushed with pride," believing that he had brokered not only an Egypt-Israel peace treaty but also a "framework for peace in the Middle East" premised on an end to the Israeli occupation of the Palestinian West Bank.

When Sadat and Begin implausibly shook hands on the White House steps after signing the accords, Carter's bold initiative was almost universally acclaimed as a "brilliant success." The luster of Carter's achievement would tarnish over the years: While the accords did produce a peace treaty, they failed to end the Israeli occupation of the West Bank, leaving in place the primary impediment to Middle East peace.

Carter later charged that Israel had "finessed or deliberately violated" its "solemn promises regarding the West Bank." Reflecting on what might have been, Carter lamented the ultimate failure of his efforts: "Israel must have a comprehensive and lasting peace, and this dream could have been realized if Israel had complied with the Camp David Accords and refrained from colonizing the West Bank, with Arabs accepting Israel within its legal borders."

In 1979, President Jimmy Carter brokered the Egyptian-Israeli peace treaty, following thirteen days of negotiations at Camp David. Here, Carter, Egyptian President Anwar Sadat, and Israeli Prime Minister Menachem Begin shake hands on the grounds of the White House, celebrating the signing of the accords.

Most Controversial
Foreign Policy Decisions

WEEK 45

THE "SPLENDID LITTLE WAR" THAT WASN'T

President William McKinley's secretary of state would call the adventure against the crumbling Spanish empire in the Caribbean and the Pacific a "splendid little war." The taking of Cuba would take just six weeks, and cost 250 American lives, but the war against Filipino independence fighters would be neither splendid nor little. By the time it ground to a halt a long two years later, it would be the costliest and bloodiest war Americans would fight between the Civil War and World War I.

Filipinos had expected that the Americans would free them from Spanish colonial rule, an assumption that was held by Emilio Aguinaldo, a charismatic Filipino exile who had been inspired by his study of American democracy. But that wasn't to be. Aguinaldo, knowing his forces lacked the firepower of the Americans, launched a guerilla war. American soldiers had a hard time distinguishing between soldiers and civilians, and in order to disrupt the support the *insurrectos* were getting from people in the countryside, American soldiers burned villages, killed livestock, and destroyed farms.

U.S. General Jacob S. Smith told his men to turn the island of Samar into a "howlin' wilderness." "I want no prisoners. I want you to kill and burn! Kill and burn! Kill all persons capable of bearing arms against the United States." When asked how old such a "capable" person would be, he replied, "Over the age of ten." After reading that eight thousand Filipinos had been killed in the first year of the war, Andrew Carnegie, one of the war's opponents, wrote a letter congratulating McKinley for "civilizing the Filipinos. . . . About 8,000 of them have been completely civilized and sent to Heaven."

It would take 270,000 American soldiers three years to put down the rebellion, at the cost of 4,234 Americans lives, with 2,800 more wounded. The cost to the U.S. taxpayer was $400 million, over $10 billion in today's dollars. The total number of Filipinos who died is unknown, but estimates put the figure somewhere between two hundred thousand and six hundred thousand, most of it coming from starvation and disease caused by war's disruptions.

TRUMAN DECIDES TO DROP THE ATOMIC BOMB

On August 6, 1945, Harry S Truman was sailing home on the USS *Augusta* after meeting in Potsdam, Germany, with Winston Churchill and Joseph Stalin. During lunch below deck, a soldier handed Truman a terse, urgent message from U.S. Secretary of War Henry Stimson. "Results clear-cut successful in all respects," he read. "Visible effects greater than in any test." On the map of Japan given to the president, circled in red, was the name of the city: Hiroshima. Truman responded excitedly, "This is the greatest thing in history."

Nearly everything within a one-mile radius of the detonation at Hiroshima was obliterated. Approximately eighty thousand people were killed instantly; as many as sixty thousand would die over the next few months. About ten thousand of the dead were Japanese soldiers. When the Japanese did not surrender, the military dropped another atomic bomb on Nagasaki three days later, causing about half as many casualties as at Hiroshima.

The decision to drop the atomic bombs would be one of the most controversial made by any president. Many have wondered: Was it wrong to use a weapon so much more destructive than any that came before? Or was it, as Truman would say, just a "bigger gun than the other fellow had"? And was it morally and ethically justifiable to destroy two entire cities, including civilians, without warning?

Looking back, Lieutenant Paul Fussell, a twenty-one-year-old lieutenant in France, remembered that American soldiers believed the atomic bombs prevented an invasion of Japan. "[W]e were going to grow up to adulthood after all." After the war, Truman said an invasion would have cost five hundred thousand American and Japanese casualties, and Stimson put the figure at a million.

Critics maintain the expected casualty figures were exaggerated. One wrote that Truman and his circle had a "compulsion to persuade themselves and the American public that, horrible as the atomic bombs were, their use was actually humane. . . ." They maintain that Japan was already close to broken, and that if the United States had waited a few weeks or months, the Japanese might well have surrendered.

THE KOREAN WAR—TRUMAN'S
BEST OR WORST DECISION?

Historians have argued—was Harry Truman's decision to go to war to stop North Korea's invasion of South Korea one of his best decisions or one of his worst? When Truman found out about the invasion in June 1950, his response was instinctual: "By God," he said, "I'm going to let them have it." Truman and his aides all agreed that the Communist assault must be stopped—not to fight the Communists, they believed, would be to repeat the appeasement of Hitler's Germany in the leadup into World War II. Truman went to the United Nations, and American forces, South Koreans, and some other forces repelled the invasion.

Then President Truman would make one of the most fateful decisions of his presidency. Despite warnings from the Chinese that they would enter the war if U.N. forces pushed beyond the dividing line between north and south, Truman authorized General Douglas MacArthur to launch a full-scale invasion across the thirty-eighth parallel in early October. In late November, three hundred thousand Communist Chinese troops, moving at night, attacked to blasts of bugles. The U.N. forces reeled back.

The war would drag on for three years, ending in the summer of 1953, and in the end South Korean independence was preserved, and Communists saw that the Americans were willing to fight off aggression. Many foreign policy analysts called that a victory.

But the war had consequences. Thirty-three thousand Americans were killed, and estimates of Koreans and Chinese killed, including civilians, ran to half a million, with the wounded numbering a million or more. And early in his first term, Truman had slashed funds to the army, navy, and air force, holding them down to historic lows. But the Korean War would turn the cold war into a hot one and launch a military buildup that would continue largely unabated until this day.

"The Korean War affected almost everything Truman did during his second term in office," writes Truman biographer Robert H. Ferrell, "causing almost as much confusion in American domestic politics as in foreign relations, and preventing the President from realizing more than a token of the domestic legislation he had hoped to see passed."

THE BAY OF PIGS

At a meeting on April 4, 1961, after less than three months as president, John F. Kennedy polled top officials whether to pull the trigger on an invasion by 1,400 exiles into Cuba to incite a popular uprising against Fidel Castro's government. When one of the men, Adolf A. Berle, an old hand in the State Department, began to prevaricate, Kennedy cut him off, insisting on an up-or-down vote. Berle's retort: "I say let 'er rip!"

With CIA experts pushing the plan, hatched under Eisenhower, and tepid support from the military, Kennedy gave the go-ahead. On the morning of April 17, the Cuban exiles landed at the Bay of Pigs on the island's southwest coast. What ensued, historian Theodore Draper later said, was "one of those rare events in history—a perfect failure." Landing craft hit coral reefs they didn't know existed. Portable radios got wet and went dead. Soldiers were deposited miles from each other without supplies.

After a black-tie White House reception on April 18, Kennedy met with his top advisors to decide what to do as the assault disintegrated. Some pushed for air support of the invasion; Kennedy refused. Advisors turned to Richard Bissell, the plan's CIA point person, to see if the invaders should dissolve into the mountains and begin a guerilla war, the fallback position that had been discussed. Bissell said the exiles couldn't get to the mountains from the new landing site, picked just weeks earlier, because of a swamp.

After three days, 1,189 invading Cubans were taken prisoner; 140 had been killed. Afterward, Kennedy would interrupt conversations with "How could I be so stupid?" He later told his aide Arthur Schlesinger that he'd assumed that "the military and intelligence people have some secret skill not available to ordinary mortals." Now he knew better. The lesson would serve him well in the Cuban Missile Crisis.

He admitted publicly that "victory has a hundred fathers and defeat is an orphan," and took sole responsibility for the failure. A Gallup poll conducted two weeks later found his approval rating had lifted to 83 percent. Sixty-one percent of the public supported Kennedy's "handling [of] the situation in Cuba." Kennedy dismissed the polls, saying, "It's just like Eisenhower. The worse I do, the more popular I get."

THE COST OF VIETNAM—MEN, MONEY, AND THE LIBERAL AGENDA

The Vietnam War cost Americans $150 billion of its treasure. About 58,000 American soldiers were killed, and many more maimed. Two million, perhaps more, Vietnamese soldiers and civilians were killed, and untold more injured. All the American involvement in the war achieved was to delay the Communist takeover from 1965 to 1975.

Johnson had inherited a commitment to fight Vietnamese Communists from Presidents Dwight Eisenhower and John Kennedy. Yet Johnson, taking what was near-unanimous advice from his advisors, was responsible for the war's escalation, often repeating that he didn't want to be the first American president to lose a war.

"I think President Johnson had a unique opportunity to get us out of Vietnam after the election of 1964," said James Thomson, an advisor to Johnson on East Asian affairs. "Johnson won overwhelmingly. He had promised not to send American boys to die there. He had the mandate and he had four years to do it, but he didn't have the courage and he didn't have the confidence and he didn't have the advice."

The war cost the United States what Johnson called his "first mistress"—the Great Society. He had raised the profile of poverty in America higher on the agenda than any president before or since. Only two days after he committed American soldiers to a ground war in Vietnam, he went to Independence, Missouri, to join with Harry Truman and to sign his Medicare bill. "I was determined to be a leader of war and a leader of peace . . . ," he explained after he left the presidency. "I wanted both, I believed in both, and I believed America had the resources to provide for both."

But it wasn't possible. "The war against poverty was killed by the war in Vietnam," stated Sargent Shriver, Johnson's point person in the war against poverty, years after Johnson left. "First of all, because of the lack of money. Secondly, it stopped because of preoccupation with the shooting war and the killing fields of that war. Death and destruction and bombing and all that captures the public imagination much more than creating something that's good. Birth is never dramatized like death."

NIXON TRIES TO END THE VIETNAM WAR
BY EXPANDING IT

President Richard Nixon vowed during his 1968 election campaign to end the Vietnam War. He believed the best way to do so was to expand the war and bomb Cambodia, a country that was nominally "neutral," although it had become a sanctuary for the North Vietnamese army and the Vietcong, who launched attacks against American and South Vietnamese troops near the Cambodian border.

Despite Nixon's conviction that bombing Cambodia was a way to end the Vietnam War, he was afraid of the backlash from the growing antiwar movement in the United States. As a result, he worked with his advisors to keep the bombings a secret, telling only a select group of officers. He told others they were bombing the enemy in South Vietnam near Cambodia. He told the press nothing.

From March 18, 1969, to May 26, 1970, the United States launched the top-secret bombing campaign known as Operation Menu, consisting of missions named after meals of the day, including breakfast, lunch, and supper. Over those two months, 3,800 B-52 carpet-running raids were launched. Eventually, the bombings were leaked to the *New York Times*.

The revelation of the covert bombings prompted a new wave of strong antiwar protests, including a demonstration at Kent State University in Ohio in May 1970 in which Ohio National Guardsmen shot and killed four students. Hundreds of American schools closed and millions of students protested the killings. During the time that the bombings continued on and off, an estimated six hundred thousand Cambodians were killed, since many of the targets were ill defined and covered civilian areas.

The U.S. bombings in Cambodia pushed the communists away from the South Vietnamese border, moving them deeper into Cambodia, whose government was already under attack from Marxist forces known as the Khmer Rouge. *New York Times* reporter Sydney Schanberg said that Khmer Rouge recruits "would . . . point . . . at the bombs falling from B-52s. . . . And it became a recruiting tool until they grew to a fierce, indefatigable guerrilla army." Kissinger has denied the connection between the bombings and the Khmer Rouge's rise. Whatever the case, the Khmer Rouge and infamous dictator Pol Pot came to power in 1975. They terrorized the country for four long years, and are estimated to have killed between 850,000 and 2 million Cambodians.

This photo shows the devastation at Hiroshima, Japan, in the aftermath of the dropping of the atomic bomb on August 6, 1945. Most of the city was leveled in the blast, with approximately eighty thousand killed instantly.

Most Memorable
Postpresidential Careers

WEEK 46

A SECOND CAREER FIGHTING SLAVERY— JOHN QUINCY ADAMS

John Quincy Adams called the crushing defeat by Andrew Jackson in the presidential election of 1828 the "close . . . of my public life." Four of the first six American presidents were reelected, three in landslides. The two one-term presidents had the last name Adams. Red Jacket, the Seneca Indian chief, visiting Adams just a week before he left office, told him both of them "were of the past age, and should soon be called for the Great Spirit."

At age fifty-three, John Quincy struggled over his next step and finally decided on a path that separated him from all the other presidents: He went back into electoral politics, representing his Massachusetts district in the House of Representatives. He held the position from 1831 until his death nineteen years later, and the issue he took on was emancipation.

The issue "transformed him into a debater so impassioned, so mischievous, so stubborn, and so radical that his foes and even some friends wondered at times if he had lost his sanity," writes Paul C. Nagel in *John Quincy Adams.* He opposed slavery's expanse westward and scrapped for years to overturn the gag rule that snuffed all antislavery petitions brought before Congress.

But his most memorable stand came when the Spanish slave ship *Amistad,* sailed by kidnapped Africans who had killed their Spanish shippers, turned up on Long Island in 1839. President Martin Van Buren wanted to return the Africans to the Spanish; Adams defended them before the Supreme Court. Instead of arguing maritime law or property rights, Adams argued human liberty he believed guaranteed by natural law.

"The moment you come" to the idea "that every man has a right to life and liberty, as an inalienable right, this case is decided," Adams told the judges. "I ask nothing more on behalf of these unfortunate men, than this Declaration." The court ordered the Africans freed, and they were sent to Sierra Leone, a British colony for free Negroes in West Africa. It was a redeeming victory by a former president committed to banishing slavery "from the face of the earth."

THOMAS JEFFERSON—FATHER . . . OF THE
UNIVERSITY OF VIRGINIA

Thomas Jefferson sent his grandson Francis Eppes to Columbia University, but in his older years he came to think that the northeastern colleges such as Harvard, Princeton, and Pennsylvania poorly served southern students. He estimated that there must be "five hundred of our own sons, imbibing opinions and principles in discord with their own country," adding that "the signs of the times admonish us to call them" back to the South.

Jefferson, an intellectual devotee of the Enlightenment, also wanted to counter the influences of religion. Until this time, most American universities, such as Harvard, William and Mary, and Yale, had been founded by religious groups. In his revolutionary days, Jefferson had hoped to institute a program of public education in Virginia, but he had failed. Now he tried again. The Virginia legislature turned him down but considered his plans for a university. Jefferson was thrilled, and he asked all for advice: What should the curriculum include? Who would make the best faculty? Jefferson also had to dance past conservative fears that the university would be a nursery of radicalism and atheism. In addition, those aligned with the state's dominant College of William and Mary worried that the university would supplant theirs.

The legislature's eventual approval of a university in Charlottesville was Jefferson's last great public endeavor, undertaken in his late seventies and early eighties. He laid out the campus, designed many buildings, and established what he called an "academical village." The heart of the campus would be a rotunda, half as wide as the one on the Roman Pantheon, and it would be visible from Monticello. On March 7, 1825, a little more than a year before his death, Jefferson was on hand to greet the first students of the university, flanked by James Madison, James Monroe, and other lesser dignitaries. On his tombstone, soon planted, Jefferson mentioned the Declaration of Independence and the Virginia Statute for Religious Freedom. But he also wanted to be remembered as the "father of the University of Virginia."

WILLIAM HOWARD TAFT—ASPIRING TO MORE THAN THE PRESIDENCY

All the twenty-five lawyers who were elected to the White House considered it the culmination of their careers. Not so for William H. Taft, whose aspirations were not in politics but in the law. "Politics make me sick," he once wrote.

"I love judges," said the son of a lawyer, "and I love courts."

He spent most of his professional life in the courts as a law reporter, government lawyer, jurist, law professor, and law school dean. He was a conservative judge, and for most of his career he ruled against labor unions. "The idea that a man who issued injunctions against labor unions, almost by the bushel, who has sent at least ten or a dozen violent labor agitators to jail," he wrote his brother, ". . . could ever be a successful candidate on a Presidential ticket, strikes me as intensely ludicrous."

But with a push from his ambitious wife, Nellie, and the blessing of Theodore Roosevelt, Taft was elected president in 1908. He made it a point of principle not to wield any more power than was explicitly outlined in the Constitution.

"The Supreme Court . . . has often stood between us and errors that might have been committed," he said in 1911, "and to turn on that court and . . . to attack it seems to me to lay the axe at the root tree of our civilization."

During his term, Taft appointed six Supreme Court justices. One judicial scholar suggested Taft appoint the elderly E. Douglass White as chief justice because he wouldn't live long, opening up a position for Taft after he left the presidency. Taft did so.

A year after Taft lost the reelection bid in 1912, he served as president of the American Bar Association, and Yale, his alma mater, offered him a professorship at the law school. In 1921, President Warren Harding, perhaps recognizing a man of similar mediocrity, appointed Taft chief justice. Upon the appointment, Supreme Court Justice Oliver Wendell Holmes, commenting on Taft's decisions, said, "I never saw anything that struck me as more than first-rate second rate."

STAYING TRUE TO HIS TRUCULENCE—HERBERT HOOVER

Herbert Hoover had been a progressive Republican during most of his career. Only fifty-eight when he lost his reelection campaign in 1932, he immediately sputtered at his successor, Franklin D. Roosevelt, and his New Deal policies. He called the National Recovery Administration "fascistic" and the Civilian Conservation Corps was like a "camp of potential mercenaries . . . under sinister military leadership." FDR's farm program was "goosestepping the people under this pinkish banner of Planned Economy." He asserted the entire Roosevelt administration had "a pronounced odor of totalitarian government." Once, when Roosevelt's voice rose from a radio during one chicken dinner with journalists, Hoover booed.

What Hoover cheered was unfettered capitalism, individualism, and self-reliance. Hoover hoped that GOP stalwarts who shared his values would select him as their 1936 standard-bearer, but Republicans were not about to put up the unpopular ex-president for office again. Spurned in his own country and his own party, he went to Europe in 1938, and met with Adolf Hitler and dined with Hermann Göring at his hunting lodge. He wasn't upset that Germany had devoured Austria, and while he spoke of the "heartbreaking persecution of the helpless Jews," he thought that they had too much influence in the Roosevelt administration.

When Bernard Baruch, leading the U.S. mobilization effort during World War II, suggested that Roosevelt tap Hoover's administrative skills honed during World War I to raise food, Roosevelt replied, "I'm not Jesus Christ. I'm not going to raise him from the dead." Hoover had become irrelevant.

After the war, the archconservative celebrated the rise of Wisconsin's Joe McCarthy and Arizona's Barry Goldwater. In a surprise gesture, President Harry Truman called on Hoover to investigate how to reduce the risk of famine and then to lead a commission to streamline the federal bureaucracy, and both bore fruit. In 1958, Hoover published a surprise best seller, *The Ordeal of Woodrow Wilson*, and was working on another on Roosevelt that was so unbalanced it has never been made public. During his thirty-one-year postpresidency, the longest of any president, historian Richard Norton Smith has written that Hoover "stayed young by working" and "nurturing the animosities of a lifetime."

THE HUMANISTIC POSTPRESIDENCY OF JIMMY CARTER

Jimmy Carter waited only six days after his failed reelection bid in 1980 to formulate his plan for a winning postpresidency. "I decided . . . to continue using my influence, perhaps with greater freedom now, to promote the same ideals I had espoused during my Presidency . . . , alleviating tension in the troubled areas of the world, promoting human rights . . . ." Thus began the most active, accomplished, and acclaimed postpresidency in U.S. history.

Though domestically he regularly built houses for Habitat for Humanity, global peacemaking topped his list. He energetically mediated disputes and attempted to negotiate peace agreements in the Middle East, the Horn of Africa, the Balkans, Central America, and the Korean peninsula. His diplomacy helped avert renewed civil war in Nicaragua in 1990, an imminent U.S. invasion of Haiti in 1994, and a potential nuclear confrontation with North Korea the same year.

The former president forged a new career out of international election monitoring. By 2011, Carter had monitored eighty-three elections in thirty-four countries, his stamp of approval the gold standard in legitimizing voting results. His verdict of fraud in the 1989 Panamanian election led directly to the U.S. invasion of that country (an invasion that Carter opposed). In Guyana in 1992, Carter confronted an angry mob of government supporters as he persuaded the incumbent to accept electoral defeat.

Carter also fought endemic diseases, particularly in sub-Saharan Africa. Traveling frequently to remote villages to investigate and educate, and using his status to raise money and awareness, he oversaw the virtual eradication of the devastating guinea worm disease and a significant reduction in the incidence of five other tropical diseases. One world health expert said that "the blow [Carter] dealt to guinea worm . . . resulted in the prevention of more suffering than anything he had done as president."

Because of such unstinting work around the globe, Jimmy Carter rebounded from the unpopularity of his term in office to become one of the most admired presidents. Respondents in a 1997 poll ranked his "moral character" above that of any other White House occupant.

GEORGE H. W. BUSH AND BILL CLINTON
BRIDGE THE DIVIDE TO DO GOOD

The day after Christmas, 2004, a tsunami swept through the Indian Ocean, devastating coastlands around the region. President George W. Bush asked an aide whether his father and Bill Clinton might work together to raise awareness and money for relief groups such as the Red Cross. Many would have said no. The ex-presidents were from different regions, different classes, different generations, and hadn't exactly had a friendly go of it in their 1992 presidential election—Bush at one point called Clinton a "bozo." But within ten minutes of being asked, both men accepted.

So began what Bush's wife, Barbara, called "the odd couple." The thaw had actually begun a year earlier, when Bush attended the opening of the Clinton Library in Little Rock. The two men delayed lunch one day when they got lost in conversation, prompting George W. Bush to send a note saying, "Tell 41 and 42 that 43 is hungry."

"Onetime political adversaries have a tendency to become friends," Bush, Sr., said when he spoke. "There is an inescapable bond that binds together all who live in the White House."

The bond between the two men grew stronger as they traveled through Thailand, Sumatra, and Sri Lanka. During a stop in Phuket, an island off Thailand, Bush mused to a reporter, "Maybe I'm the father he never had."

Ray Offenheiser, president of Oxfam, credited the bipartisan pairing with inspiring "unprecedented levels of philanthropy . . . on the scale of which most of us have never seen before. . . . Many of the private humanitarian organizations . . . broke every conceivable record for contributions." Americans gave $1.2 billion to organizations providing tsunami relief.

When the men came back to the United States they took part in a golf game sponsored by Greg Norman that raised almost $2 million for relief, and when Clinton had surgery on his left lung, Bush kept tabs on him. Afterward, Bush said, "The great thing about me and 42 is I say hello and that's all I have to say, and 42 will carry the conversation from there on. At my age, that's good."

In 2002, the Norwegian Nobel Committee awarded the Nobel Peace Prize to Jimmy Carter for his decades of "untiring effort to find peaceful solutions to international conflicts, to advance democracy and human rights, and to promote economic and social development."

The Best and the Worst

WEEK 47

THE BEST PRESIDENTS

In 1962, John F. Kennedy told a group of historians visiting the White House that he didn't like glib presidential rankings that graded some "Below Average" or even "Failures." "No one has a right to grade a President—not even poor James Buchanan," Kennedy told the scholars, "who has not sat in his chair, examined the mail and information that came across his desk, and learned why he made his decision."

Kennedy's protests haven't stopped presidential assessments that date back to Arthur Schlesinger, Sr., a Harvard scholar who surveyed fifty-five historians in 1948 to come up with the first ranking of presidents. The historians selected Abraham Lincoln, George Washington, Franklin Roosevelt, Woodrow Wilson, Thomas Jefferson, and Andrew Jackson as "Great," in that order. Schlesinger repeated the survey in 1962 and the results were nearly the same. In almost all presidential surveys, Lincoln, Washington, Roosevelt, and Jefferson are named the top presidents. Schlesinger's list has inspired a handful of others. Some include more conservative scholars, some use different criteria, but nearly every one has roughly mirrored his rankings.

But the public's ranking differs greatly. In a 2011 Gallup poll, Americans didn't place Jefferson, Wilson, and Jackson in the top ten American presidents (Jefferson, in fact, tied with George W. Bush for ninth place). Washington came in fifth, just behind Kennedy. Bill Clinton came in third, a percentage point behind Abraham Lincoln, in second place.

At the top of the list was Ronald Reagan. In the eight times Gallup has asked the same "greatest president" question over the past dozen years, people have chosen Lincoln, Reagan, or Kennedy as the greatest. Four of the five most recent presidents—Obama, George W. Bush, Clinton, and Reagan—were in the top ten in each survey, showing Americans tend to vote for modern presidents they've lived through over those they might have read about in books.

THE WORST PRESIDENTS

What characterizes the worst presidents of all time? Historian Sean Wilentz says that "calamitous presidents, faced with enormous difficulties . . . have divided the nation, governed erratically and left the nation worse off." Their failures are a mix of "disastrous domestic policies, foreign policy blunders and military setbacks, executive misconduct, crises of credibility and public trust."

Presidential scholars, interviewed five times since 1982 as part of the Siena Research Institute poll, have each time named presidents Franklin Pierce, James Buchanan, Andrew Johnson, and Warren G. Harding as four of the worst five. Herbert Hoover hovers in and out of the category, and younger historians put Richard Nixon near the bottom as well for undertaking, and then trying to cover up, a campaign chest full of "dirty tricks" that undermined the Constitution and broke the law.

Pierce supported proslavery forces in their battle for territories in the West, contributing to the Civil War. Buchanan did nothing to prevent Southern states from seceding from the Union; Johnson's stubbornness got him impeached for supporting the defeated white supremacists after the Civil War. Harding is the only twentieth-century president in the bunch, lodged there for abandoning the League of Nations and his knack for appointing officials with both hands in the public till.

"If you knew of a great scandal in our administration," Harding asked Herbert Hoover, his honest secretary of commerce, "would you for the good of the country and the party expose it publicly or would you bury it?" Hoover recommended transparency; Harding disagreed.

A 2010 Siena poll of historians ranked George W. Bush the fifth worst president, and placed him in the bottom five in twelve of the twenty rated categories, including intelligence, foreign policy accomplishments, and his ability to communicate. His presidency was tainted by what many believe was an unnecessary war in Iraq, an unpopular domestic agenda, and economic policies that contributed to economic collapse. Bush's disapproval rating hit 69 percent in April 2008, the highest in Gallup history.

"Right now there's a lot of emotion about Bush," said the survey's codirector, Douglas Lonnstrom, when the poll was released. "Time passes and people become more objective, so we'll see."

JOHN F. KENNEDY—EVER POPULAR
AMONG THE PEOPLE

Ever since John F. Kennedy's death, the public has consistently ranked him among the five greatest presidents. At the end of 1962, Americans placed Kennedy at the top of a list of leaders they most admired above presidents Dwight Eisenhower and Harry Truman, the World War II British leader Winston Churchill, and even the saintly Albert Schweitzer. A 1983 poll revealed that Americans saw him as committed to the poor, to racial justice, to stopping the Soviets, and felt he injected the country with a new spirit. Public opinion polls in 1975, 1985, and 2000 ranked him as *the* greatest president.

But historians have been far less enthusiastic, relegating Kennedy to the middle of the pack, and in 1982, seventy-five historians and journalists declared him "the most overrated public figure in American history." They point out he served only one thousand days in office, the sixth shortest tenure among American presidents, and had a mixed record in foreign affairs and little to show domestically, especially when compared to the achievements of the greatest presidents, such as Abraham Lincoln, George Washington, and Franklin Roosevelt, or even his successor, Lyndon Johnson. Historian Thomas C. Reeves has speculated that his presidency might have been brought down in a second term by his reckless womanizing, including his affair with the girlfriend of mob boss Sam Giancana, which made him vulnerable to blackmail.

Yet the public has not held Kennedy's womanizing against him, focusing instead on his cool magnetism and his youthfulness, amplified by the great communicator he used so effectively: television. Journalist Mary McGrory called him the "most attractive man of his generation."

Some say he became heroic only after his assassination, as Lincoln did. But Kennedy's approval rating never dropped below 59 percent while he was president. His accomplishments might have been few, but the call of the "idealist without illusions," as he called himself, was heard, and along with his rhetoric inspired social change after his death. "A short life, unfulfilled in action," wrote historian Daniel Boorstin of Kennedy, "is commonly and disproportionally judged by the eloquent utterance." Perhaps this is why, when a 1996 *New York Times*/CBS News poll asked Americans which former president they'd like to lead them, they chose Kennedy.

THE TRUMAN/EISENHOWER SYNDROME—
REPUTATIONS THAT HAVE GROWN OVER TIME

In 1952, Democratic President Harry S Truman attacked Republican presidential hopeful Dwight Eisenhower, saying that Ike knew less about politics than a "pig knows about Sunday." And when Eisenhower said, "We shall cast away the incompetent, the unfit, the cronies and the chiselers," all knew the party leader he was referring to.

Despite their mutual dislike, the two presidents have reputations that have risen over time. When Truman assumed the presidency in the spring of 1945, Americans rallied around him, and his approval rating shot to 87 percent. By 1953, only 23 percent of Americans approved of his performance, a rating lower than Richard M. Nixon's before he resigned.

"I wonder how far Moses would have gone if he'd taken a poll in Egypt?" Truman wrote in a memo to himself. "What would Jesus Christ have preached if he'd taken a poll in Israel? . . . It isn't polls or public opinion of the moment that counts. It's right and wrong."

Eisenhower had been elected in two landslides, but by the time he left office many saw him as detached and lazy. Even Nikita Khrushchev mocked him: "The Americans themselves say their President has two jobs—golfing and being President. Which is the main one? *Playing golf!*"

Eisenhower's reputation would begin to rise in 1967, when journalist Murray Kempton wrote an *Esquire* piece that hailed him as the "great tortoise on whose back the world sat for eight years," a world that never appreciated the "cunning beneath the shell." Kempton found him "neither rash nor hesitant . . . as calm when he was demanding the wisdom of leaving a bad situation alone as when he was moving to meet it on those occasions when he absolutely had to."

Fred Greenstein's 1982 book, *The Hidden-Hand Presidency*, made the case that Eisenhower was in control behind the scenes. Author Stephen Ambrose described Eisenhower as a "great and good man" who had kept the peace, squashed inflation, and stayed popular. "No wonder that millions of Americans felt that the country was damned lucky to have him." Eisenhower is now a reliable top ten president. And Truman? In every presidential poll since he left office, he's been ranked in the top ten.

HOW DO AMERICANS JUDGE THEIR PRESIDENTS?

Arthur Schlesinger, Sr., the first academic to poll historians on presidential writings in 1948, made the case that the times, as much as the man, make a great president. George Washington was faced with a war of survival against Great Britain and a people struggling to forge a nation. Abraham Lincoln faced a country broken in two over slavery. Franklin Roosevelt came into office when Americans were crippled by the Great Depression and then faced threat from the Axis powers, particularly Japan and Germany.

Some presidents fail when tested: James Buchanan bumbled when the nation unraveled; Herbert Hoover was paralyzed by the enormity of the Great Depression; George W. Bush misdirected the country's goodwill after the World Trade Center attacks. Another sign of greatness, Schlesinger argued, is an ability to connect with the American people. "I do not believe," said Woodrow Wilson, "that any man can lead who does not act . . . under the impulse of a profound sympathy with those whom he leads—a sympathy which is insight—an insight which is of the heart rather than of the intellect."

How else do we judge? In his book *Presidential Character*, published in 1972, political scientist James David Barber argued that the American people think highly of presidents who are confident and energetic in office ("active-positive") rather than reserved and insecure ("passive-negative"). In his 1987 book *Why Presidents Succeed: A Political Psychology of Leadership*, psychologist Dean K. Simonton came up with his own laundry list of American preferences: two-termers over one-termers—think the Roosevelts; war leaders over peacetime presidents—think Woodrow Wilson. Smarter presidents, such as Obama, also tend to fare better, as do those who write well, such as Jefferson. Simonton also calculates that one scandal can offset the boost provided by two terms.

In 2000, the *Wall Street Journal*, citing liberal biases in many of the surveys, included more conservative scholars in theirs, but found its list "remarkably similar" to the Schlesinger ones. In fact, no matter who does the ranking and what criteria are used, they all produce similar lists—except for one.

A DIFFERENT MEASURE—RANKING PRESIDENTS BY HOW THEY PROTECTED PEACE, PROSPERITY, AND LIBERTY

What if we ranked presidents according to how well they promoted peace, prosperity, and liberty? That's what libertarian writer Ivan Eland did in his book *Recarving Rushmore*, in which the author "judges presidents not by who they were, how they led, or how they governed, but by what they did."

Eland rejects the usual preference presidential analysts have for powerful, activist, charismatic, articulate, big government presidents who served in times of crisis—think the Civil War or the Great Depression. He favors those who preserved the peace, defended civil liberties at home, and promoted economic policies that encouraged economic prosperity in the long term.

Eland's criteria turns the usual "Best and Worst" presidential lists on their head. Through Eland's eyes, Abraham Lincoln "helped to provoke a massive civil war . . . and then pursued it ineptly and brutally." Afterward, African-Americans had only "marginally more freedom from bitter white southerners than before their emancipation" (ranking: 29). Thomas Jefferson "set bad precedents for acquiring new territory by purchasing the Louisiana Territory in an unconstitutional manner and for ethnically cleansing Native Americans" (ranking: 26).

Woodrow Wilson (whom Eland ranks dead last) crushed civil liberties at home when he intervened in World War I, and led to an outcome— and a peace Wilson helped muck up—that spawned World War II. George Washington "grabbed more presidential power" than the framers of the Constitution intended, although he keeps his number seven ranking because he "shunned being a king . . . and set a most valuable precedent by leaving office after two terms." The New Deal of FDR (ranking: 31) "cemented the expectation of permanent big government." Harry Truman (ranking: 39) "continued FDR's bombing of civilians . . . stole the constitutional power to make war from Congress, took actions that led to the creation of the military-industrial complex." Ronald Reagan (ranking: 34) "did not 'win' the Cold War," his massive peacetime military buildup "wasted money," and "his tax cuts were fake because they weren't accompanied by cuts in spending."

Who are Eland's favorite five presidents? Up from number five, they are Chester Arthur, Rutherford B. Hayes, Martin Van Buren, Grover Cleveland, and then his number one president: John Tyler. All were presidents who "largely respected the Constitution's intention of limiting government and restraining executive power, especially in regard to making war."

"Boring," Eland concludes, "can be beautiful."

President Bush on the aircraft carrier USS *Abraham Lincoln* on May 1, 2003. In his speech from the deck of the carrier, Bush stated that "in the Battle of Iraq, the United States and our allies have prevailed." A MISSION ACCOMPLISHED banner hangs in the background. The vast majority of casualties in the Iraq conflict, especially among Iraqi civilians, occurred after the announcement.

NOTES

GENERAL BOOKS ON THE PRESIDENCY

This book relied on many general references to the Presidents, including: the *Encyclopedia of the American Presidency*, by Michael A. Genovese; the Great Courses lecture series, *Great Presidents*, taught by Allan J. Lichtman; *To the Best of My Ability*, by James McPherson; and presidential biographies in the American Presidents Series, edited by Arthur M. Schlesinger and Sean Wilentz; and *Presidents: Every Question Answered*, by Carter Smith.

Part I. Presidents, Common and Uncommon

THE FOUNDERS (1778–1808)

GEORGE WASHINGTON

These entries relied on: *Founding Father*, by Richard Brookhiser; *His Excellency* by Joseph J. Ellis; and *Washington: A Life*, by Ron Chernow. The entry **FOX HUNTER** relied on *George Washington's War*, by Bruce Chadwick. For more on Washington's ambivalence to power, see *Realistic Visionary*, by Peter R. Henriques.

John Adams—A Volatile, Principled President—These entries relied on: *America's First Dynasty*, by Richard Brookhiser; *John Adams*, by David McCullough; and *Descent from Glory—Four Generations of the John Adams Family*, by Paul C. Nagel.

THOMAS JEFFERSON

These entries relied on: *Thomas Jefferson*, by Joyce Appleby; *Thomas Jefferson*, by R. B. Bernstein; *In Pursuit of Reason*, by Noble E. Cunningham Jr.; *American Sphinx*, by Joseph J. Ellis; and the Jefferson books by Merrill D. Peterson. An exploration of Sally Hemings's relationship to Thomas Jefferson can be found at the Thomas Jefferson Foundation's website, www.monticello .org. For more on Jefferson's writing of the Declaration of Independence, see *American Scripture: Making the Declaration of Independence*, by Pauline Maier.

Thomas Jefferson's Followers—James Madison, James Monroe, John Quincy Adams—These entries relied on: *James Madison: A Biography*, by Ralph Ketcham; *James Monroe: the Quest for National Identity*, by Harry Ammon; *The Last Founding Father: James Monroe and a Nation's Call to Greatness*, by Harlow Giles Unger; and *John Quincy Adams: a Public Life, A Private Life*, by Paul C. Nagel.

PRESIDENTIAL MUSCLE: ANDREW JACKSON
AND THOSE WHO FOLLOWED (1829–1849)

ANDREW JACKSON

These entries relied on: *Andrew Jackson*, by H.W. Brands; *American Lion: Andrew Jackson in the White House*, by Jon Meacham; *Andrew Jackson*, by Robert V. Remini.

Struggling in Jackson's Shadow—Martin Van Buren, William H. Harrison, John Tyler, James K. Polk—See *Martin Van Buren: The Romantic Age of American Politics*, by John Niven; *Martin Van Buren*, by Ted Widmer; *William Henry Harrison*, by Gail Collins; *John Tyler, the Accidental President*, by Edward P. Crapol; *Polk, The Man Who Transformed the Presidency and America*, by Walter R. Borneman; and *Country of Vast Designs: James K. Polk, the Mexican War and the Conquest of the American Continent*, by Robert W. Merry.

CIVIL WAR AND RECONSTRUCTION (1849–1881)

Stumbling into Crisis—Zachary Taylor, Millard Fillmore, Franklin Pierce, and James Buchanan—For a pre–Civil War history, see: *The Fate of Their Country: Politicians, Slavery Extension, and the Coming of the Civil War*, by Michael Holt. These entries relied on: *Zachary Taylor*, by John Eisenhower; *The Presidencies of Zachary Taylor and Millard Fillmore*, by Elbert Smith; *Millard Fillmore*, by Paul Finkelman; *Franklin Pierce*, by Michael Holt; *The Presidency of Franklin Pierce*, by Larry Gara; *James Buchanan*, by Jean Baker. The entry **BUCHANAN SUPPRESSES REBELLION—IN UTAH** relied on *Blood of the Prophets: Brigham Young and the Massacre at Mountain Meadows*, by Will Bagley.

ABRAHAM LINCOLN

These entries relied on: *Lincoln*, by David Herbert Donald; *Team of Rivals*, by Doris Kearns Goodwin; *Abraham Lincoln*, by George McGovern. The entry **WAS LINCOLN MELANCHOLIC?** relied on *Lincoln's Melancholy*, by Joshua Shenk; the excerpt in **LINCOLN'S GREATNESS—A CAPACITY TO GROW** is from W.E.B. DuBois's essay, "Again Lincoln," in the September 1922 issue of *Crisis* magazine.

The Reconstruction Presidents—Andrew Johnson, Ulysses S. Grant, and Rutherford B. Hayes—For more on Reconstruction, see *Reconstruction*, by Paul H. Bergeron. The Johnson entries relied on *The Presidency of Andrew Johnson*, by Albert E. Castel; *Andrew Johnson*, by Hans Trefousse; *Andrew Johnson*, by Annette Gordon-Reed, and *Andrew Johnson's Civil War*, by Bergeron; *The Avenger Takes His Place: Andrew Johnson and the 45 Days That Changed the Nation*, by Howard B. Means; *Ulysses S. Grant*, by Josiah Bunting; *U.S. Grant*, by Joan Waugh; *Grant*, by Jean Edward Smith; *Rutherford B. Hayes*, by Hans Trefousse; and *Rutherford B. Hayes: Warrior & President*, by Ari Hoogenboom.

Gilded Age Presidents—James A. Garfield, Chester A. Arthur, Grover Cleveland, Benjamin Harrison—James A. Garfield, by Ira Rutkow; *Chester A. Arthur*, by Zachary Karabell and *Gentleman Boss*, by Thomas Reeves; *Grover Cleveland*, by Henry F. Graff; *Benjamin Harrison*, by Charles W. Calhoun.

TAKING ON THE WORLD AND REFORM (1897–1921)

William McKinley Sails into War, and Theodore Roosevelt Rides into Power—The entry MCKINLEY TAKES THE PHILIPPINES—AND INITIATES A WAR relies on *Failures of the Presidents*, by Thomas J. Craughwell; see also *William McKinley*, by Kevin Phillips; *The President and the Assassin: McKinley, Terror, and Empire at the Dawn of the American Century*, by Scott Miller; for Roosevelt's early life, see *Mornings on Horseback*, by David McCullough; the entry "TEEDIE" ROOSEVELT, CHILD NATURALIST relies on *Lion in the White House*, by Aida Donald; the entry FROM INVALID TO PUGILIST relies on *Theodore Roosevelt, a Strenuous Life*, by Kathleen Dalton.

Roosevelt—Reformer, Conservationist, Internationalist—and William Taft—For more on Theodore Roosevelt, See Edmund Morris's books on Roosevelt; ROOSEVELT IS SHOT IN THE CHEST—AND THEN DELIVERS A SPEECH relies on *The William Howard Taft Presidency*, by Lewis L. Gould.

Woodrow Wilson—More Reform and Then World War—These entries relied on: *Woodrow Wilson*, by H.W. Brands; *Woodrow Wilson, President*, by Sallie G. Randolph; and *Woodrow Wilson*, by John Milton Cooper, Jr.

BOOM AND BUST (1921–1941)

Big-Business Presidents—Warren G. Harding, Calvin Coolidge, and Herbert Hoover—See *The Harding Era*, by Robert K. Murray and *Warren G. Harding*, by John W. Dean; the Calvin Coolidge entry relied on *To the Best of My Ability*, edited by James McPherson and *Calvin Coolidge*, by David Greenberg; the entry CONSERVATIVE, VIRTUOUS, AND FRUGAL—CALVIN COOLIDGE relied on *To the Best of My Ability*, edited by James McPherson; and the entry HOW DID HERBERT HOOVER GET IT SO WRONG? relied on *Herbert Hoover*, by William E. Leuchtenburg; see also, *Herbert Hoover: A Public Life*, by David Burner.

Franklin D. Roosevelt Tries a New Deal—These entries relied on *FDR*, by Jean Edward Smith and *Freedom From Fear: The American People in Depression and War, 1929-1945*, by David M. Kennedy; for the wartime relationship between Franklin and Eleanor, see *No Ordinary Time*, by Doris Kearns Goodwin; for Roosevelt's pre-presidential life, see *Before the Trumpet* and *A First-Class Temperament*, by Geoffrey C. Ward. The entry ROOSEVELT

LAUNCHES THE WPA—INCLUDING WORK FOR ARTISTS relies on *American-Made—When FDR Put the Nation to Work*, by Nick Taylor. For more on the internment of Japanese, see *Only What We Could Carry: The Japanese American Internment Experience*, by Lawson Fusao Inada.

WORLD WAR AND THEN COLD WAR (1941–1960)

HARRY S TRUMAN
These entries relied on *Conflict & Crisis: The Presidency of Harry S Truman, 1945-1948*, Robert J. Donovan; *Harry S Truman, A Life* and *Truman, A Centenary Remembrance*, by Robert H. Ferrell; and *A Man of the People: A Life of Harry S. Truman*, by Alonzo L. Hamby.

Dwight D. Eisenhower—These entries relied on: *Dwight D. Eisenhower*, by Tom Wicker; *Eisenhower, a Centennial Life*, by Michael R. Beschloss; and *Eisenhower, the President*, by Stephen E. Ambrose. For more on Eisenhower and Civil Rights, see *A Matter of Justice*, by David A. Nichols.

THE 1960S (1960–1968)

JOHN F. KENNEDY
These entries relied on *An Unfinished Life*, by Robert Dallek; *The Presidency of John F. Kennedy* by James N. Giglio; and *John F. Kennedy: A Biography* by Michael O'Brien.

LYNDON B. JOHNSON
These entries relied on the multi-volume biography of Lyndon Johnson by Robert Caro; *Lyndon Johnson and the American Dream*, by Doris Kearns Goodwin; and Robert Dallek's books on Johnson.

THE CONSERVATIVE ERA (1968–2008)

Corruption and its Aftermath—Richard M. Nixon, Gerald Ford, and Jimmy Carter—These entries relied on: *The Memoirs of Richard Nixon*, by Richard Nixon; *Richard Nixon: Alone in the White House*, by Richard Reeves; *All the President's Men* and *The Final Days*, by Bob Woodward and Carl Bernstein; *Richard M. Nixon: The Complex President*, Martin S. Goldman; *Gerald R. Ford*, by Douglas G. Brinkley; *Time and Chance: Gerald Ford's Appointment with History*, by James Cannon. **Jimmy Carter**—*White House Diary*, by Jimmy Carter; for more on the "malaise" speech, see *"What the Heck Are You Up To, Mr. President?": Jimmy Carter*, by Julian E. Zelizer. *Jimmy Carter, America's "Malaise," and the Speech That Should Have Changed the Country*, by Kevin Mattson.

RONALD REAGAN
These entries relied on Lou Cannon's books, especially *President Reagan, The Role of a Lifetime*. See also, *Ronald Reagan: Fate, Freedom, and the Making of History*, by John Patrick Diggins; and the PBS documentary "Reagan" on

American Experience. For an anthology of different viewpoints about Reagan and the Cold War, Reaganomics, and the Great Communicator, see *Ronald Reagan*, edited by James D. Torr; for the argument that Reagan ended the Cold War, see *Reagan's War: The Epic Story of His Forty Year Struggle and Final Triumph Over Communism*, by Peter Schweizer; for books on the conservative era, see *The Age of Reagan*, by Steven F. Hayward, and *The Age of Reagan*, by Sean Wilentz.

George H. W. Bush Tempers the Reagan Revolution—These entries relied on *George H. W. Bush*, by Timothy Naftali; *The Presidency of George Bush*, by John Robert Greene; and *George Bush, the Life of a Lone Star Yankee*, by Herbert S. Parmet; for contrasting analyses on Bush's Presidency see *The Bush Presidency: First Appraisals*, Colin Campbell and Bert A. Rockman; for Bush's role in the dissolution of the Soviet Empire, see *Out of the Shadow*, by Christopher Maynard.

A Democrat Moves to the Center—Bill Clinton—*Dead Center: Clinton-Gore Leadership and the Perils of Moderation* by James MacGregor Burns and Georgia J. Sorenson; *My Life*, by Bill Clinton; *In Search of Bill Clinton: A Psychological Biography*, by John D. Gartner; *A Complicated Man: The Life of Bill Clinton As Told By Those Who Know Him*, by Michael Takiff; *The Choice*, by Bob Woodward.

A Republican Moves to the Right—George W. Bush—These entries relied on *A Man of Faith: The Spiritual Journey of George W. Bush*, by David Aikman; *A Charge to Keep: My Journey to the White House* and *Decision Points*, by George W. Bush; *Reagan's Disciple*, by Lou and Carl M. Cannon; *Fiasco: the American Military Adventure in Iraq*, by Thomas E. Ricks; *The Bushes: Portrait of a Dynasty*, by Peter Schweizer and Rochelle Schweizer.

A New Era?—Barack Obama—*The Promise: President Obama, Year One*, by Jonathan Alter; *The Power of Words: The Stories Behind Barack Obama's Speeches, From the State House to the White House*, by Mary Frances Berry and Josh Gottheimer; *Dreams from My Father: A Story of Race and Inheritance* and *The Audacity of Hope: Thoughts on Reclaiming the American Dream*, by Barack Obama; *The Bridge: The Life and Rise of Barack Obama*, by David Remnick; *Obama's Wars*, by Bob Woodward.

Part II. The Best, the Worst, and the Most Interesting Presidents

(For more on these entries, see the presidential biographies mentioned in Part I of this book.)

Most Influential—and Interesting—First Ladies—For more on the First Ladies, see *First Ladies*, by Betty Boyd Caroli and *Presidential Wives: An Anecdotal History*, by Paul F. Boller Jr.; Abigail Adams, see *Abigail Adams* by Woody Holton; *Abigail Adams*, by Phillis Lee Levin; for more on Dolley Madison, see the American Experience documentary, "Dolley Madison," and the show's website: http://www.pbs.org/wgbh/americanexperience/films/

dolley/; the Edith Wilson entry relied on *Edith and Woodrow: The Wilson White House*, by Phyllis Lee Levin; for Eleanor Roosevelt, see *The Autobiography of Eleanor Roosevelt*; see books on Eleanor Roosevelt by Joseph P. Lash; *The Eleanor Roosevelt Encyclopedia*, by Maurine Hoffman Beasley; the Betty Ford entry relied on *Betty Ford: Candor and Courage in the White House*, by John Robert Greene; the Hillary Clinton page relied on *Hillary's Choice*, by Gail Sheehy; see also *Living History*, by Hillary Rodham Clinton.

Best Writers—and Speakers—For Thomas Jefferson's writing skills, see *American Scripture: Making the Declaration of Independence*, by Pauline Maier; for Andrew Johnson's speaking abilities, see *Andrew Johnson*, by Annette Gordon-Reed; for Ted Sorensen's perspective on his writing role, see *Counselor: A Life at the Edge of History*, by Ted Sorensen.

Most Controversial Elections—These entries relied on *Presidential Campaigns: From George Washington to George W. Bush*, by Paul F. Boller; see also *Presidential Elections 1789–2008*, by CQ Press.

Scandals, Dressed and Undressed—These entries relied on *Inside the White House: The Hidden Lives of the Modern Presidents and the Secrets of the World's Most Powerful Institution*, by Ronald Kessler.

Protecting—And Surrendering—Civil Rights—For more on Abraham Lincoln and civil rights, see *The Fate of Liberty: Abraham Lincoln and Civil Liberties*, Mark E. Neely Jr.

The Peacemakers—The entry KENNEDY FIGHTS FOR A NUCLEAR TEST BAN TREATY relies on *John F. Kennedy: A Biography*, by Michael O'Brien; for Jimmy Carter's perspective on the Mideast peace talks and their aftermath, see *Palestine: Peace Not Apartheid*, by Jimmy Carter.

Most Controversial Foreign Policy Decisions—For more on the Filipino-American War, see *A War of Frontier and Empire: The Philippine-American War, 1899-1902*, by David Silbey; for various views on Harry Truman's decision to drop atomic bombs on Japan, see *Hiroshima in History and Memory*, by Michael J. Hogan; *The Myths of Revisionism*, by Robert James Maddox; and *Hiroshima: Why America Dropped the Atomic Bomb*, by Ronald Takaki; for more on the Korean War, see *The Korean War: A History*, by Bruce Cumings; for more on the Bay of Pigs, see *The Bay of Pigs (Pivotal Moments in American History)*, by Howard Jones; for more on the United States involvement in the Vietnam War, see *The Best and the Brightest*, by David Halberstam; the entry NIXON TRIES TO END THE VIETNAM WAR BY EXPANDING IT relied on *Failures of the Presidents: From the Whiskey Rebellion and War of 1812 to the Bay of Pigs and War in Iraq*, by Thomas J. Craughwell.

Most Memorable Postpresidential Careers—For more on the postpresidential lives of the Presidents, see *Citizen-in-Chief: The Second Lives of the American Presidents*, by Leonard Benardo; for more on William H. Taft's postpresidential career, see *America's Lawyer-Presidents: From Law Office to*

Oval Office, by Norman Gross; for more on Jimmy Carter's post-presidency, see *The Unfinished Presidency: Jimmy Carter's Journey Beyond the White House,* by Douglas G. Brinkley; *Keeping Faith: Memoirs of a President* and *Beyond the White House, Waging Peace, Fighting Disease, Building Hope,* by Jimmy Carter; for Bill Clinton's post-presidency, see *Clinton in Exile: A President Out of the White House,* by Carol Felsenthal.

The Best and the Worst—For different theories on presidential greatness, see: *Presidential Greatness: The Image and the Man from George Washington to the Present,* by Thomas A. Bailey; *Presidential Character,* by James David Barber; *Recarving Rushmore,* by Ivan Eland; *Why Presidents Succeed: A Political Psychology of Leadership,* by Dean K. Simonton; For more on the rise of Dwight Eisenhower's reputation, see *The Hidden-Hand Presidency,* by Fred Greenstein.

INDEX

Page numbers in *italics* refer to illustration captions.

daguerreotype of, *93*
death of, *93*
duel fought by, 74
Eaton affair and, 84, *85*
elected president, 80
in election of 1824, 79
in election of 1828, 344
in election of 1832, 90, 91
family of, 71
inauguration of, 81
Indians and, 76, 88, 362
Kitchen Cabinet of, 83
Nullification Crisis and, 89
Revolutionary War and, 71
spoils system of, 82
Van Buren and, 83, 84, 90, 96
veto power used by, 87
Washington and Jefferson rejected by, 73
youth of, 71, 72
Jackson, Henry, 251
Jacksonian Era, 92
Jackson, Rachel, 74, 80, 84, 344
Jacobson, Eddie, 212
Japan, 183
  atomic bomb dropped on, 376, *381*
  in World War II, 203, 205, 206, 218,
    222, 225, 376
Japanese Americans, 204, 330, *365*
Jay, John, 22
Jay Treaty, 22, 23, 73
Jefferson, Martha, 42
Jefferson, Thomas, 22, 25, 41, 61, 62, 63,
    82, 97, 99, 286, 328, 344, 361, 367,
    391, 396
  Adams and, 33, 34, 39, 41, 57
  Alien and Sedition Acts and, 45, 47, 359
  death of, 34, 57, *59*
  Declaration of Independence written by,
    14, 26, 31, 39, 40, 41, *43*, 57, 58
  education of, 37
  in election of 1800, 343
  Embargo Act of, 55, 56
  formality repudiated by, 46
  inauguration of, 33, 45, 50
  Indians and, 54
  Jackson and, 73
  last letter of, 57, *59*
  legacies of, 58
  Louisiana Purchase of, 48, 49, 50, *51*,
    53, 54, 55, 73, 75
  marriage of, 42
  Monticello home of, 38
  national debt reduced by, 50
  religious freedom and, 360
  slave children of, 351

slavery and, 49, 53
University of Virginia founded by, 38,
  384
Washington and, 23
whiskey tax and, 21, 23, 50
writing and speaking of, 335, *341*
Jenkins, Roy, 192
Johnson, Andrew, 137, 138, 140, 392
  drunken speech of, 337
Johnson, Lyndon B., 251, 252, 279, 314,
  393
  civil rights and, 252, 254, *257*, 259, 260
  Great Society of, 253, 254, 260, 261,
    262, 263, 281, 285, 379
  immigration reform and, 255
  "Treatment" of, 251
  Vietnam War and, 261, 262, 263, 264,
    286, 379
  Wallace and, 256, 259
Jones, Paula, 355
Jungle, The (Sinclair), 165

Kansas-Nebraska Act, 108, *111*, 115
Kempton, Murray, 394
Kendall, Amos, 83
Kennedy, David M., 191
Kennedy, Edward "Ted," 320
Kennedy, Jacqueline, *241*, 247, *249*
Kennedy, Joe, Jr., 235
Kennedy, John F., 235, 263, 379, 391
  assassination of, 247, 254, 329
  Bay of Pigs and, 248, 378
  Catholicism of, 237
  civil rights and, 245, 246, 248, 252
  Cuban Missile Crisis and, 64, 243, 244,
    248, 340, 371
  elected president, 238
  health problems of, 236, 238, *241*
  inaugural address of, 239, *249*, 340
  Johnson and, 252
  legacy of, 248
  peace speech of, 244
  popularity of, 393
  press conferences of, 240
  Soviet Union and, 244, 371
Kennedy, Joseph P., 235, 236
Kennedy, Robert, 236, 237, 238, 245, 263,
  264
Kennedy, Rose, 236
Kerrey, Bob, 306
Ketcham, Ralph, 361
Key, Francis Scott, 81
Khomeini, Ayatollah Ruhollah, 273
Khrushchev, Nikita, 230, 243, 244, 340,
  371, 394

HILLSBORO PUBLIC LIBRARIES
Hillsboro, OR
Member of Washington County
COOPERATIVE LIBRARY SERVICES